THE TWO KINGDOMS

Elizabeth Whitley

THE SCOTTISH REFORMATION SOCIETY
17 George IV Bridge, Edinburgh

1977

ACKNOWLEDGMENTS

to Professor G. N. M. Collins of the Free Church of Scotland College for vital help and advice; to the Rev. Sinclair Horne of the Scottish Reformation Society for continual encouragement and support; to Dr J. D. Douglas for his scholarly book, *Light in the North;* and above all to Harry Whitley's ministry in St Giles, 1954-1972.

Printed by Lindsay & Co. Ltd., Edinburgh

CONTENTS

FOREWORD

We bespeak for this new book by Elizabeth Whitley the same cordial reception as was given to her popular *Plain Mr Knox*. It is written in the same felicitous style, and is marked by the same lively presentation. In many respects, indeed, it is a continuation of the same story; for the Second Reformation, as the Covenanting movement in Scotland is sometimes described, was nothing other than a resumption of the struggle for the Church's spiritual independence in which Knox had played such a conspicuous part in the sixteenth century.

When Andrew Melville, in a famous encounter with James VI, reminded the king that there were "two Kings and two Kingdoms in Scotland" he was enunciating no new principle of Church and State relations, but merely reasserting one which had been basic to the Scottish Reformation, and which inhered in the concordat between Church and State relating to the establishment of the Reformed Church in Scotland.

If Mrs Whitley's book serves to remind us that in the Church, as in the State, the price of liberty is eternal vigilance, she will have alerted us to a danger that is ever present — the danger of letting things slip; of sacrificing vital principle on the altar of expediency; and of letting spiritual freedom degenerate into spiritual license, thus eventually making the Church "a proverb and a byword among all people".

The Reformation Society have let Mrs Whitley tell her story entirely in her own way, and consider it their privilege to send it into circulation.

G. N. M. COLLINS,
President of the Scottish Reformation Society.

BOOK I
CHRIST'S CROWN

CHAPTER ONE

THE BATTLE BEGINS

Sunday, 9th November, 1572: raw and bleak no doubt, as such Sundays often are in Edinburgh, the sea-mist swirling round the towering tenements, the castle floating loose on its crags. Faces would crowd every window in the Royal Mile, as they still do today for special occasions. As the great bell of St. Giles, the High Kirk, rang for service they would see a bent, spent little man being helped up the steps, "creeping on his club." Those thronging in behind him would have to press and crane to hear his weak shred of a voice: that voice that once, like "ten thousand trumpets", changed the face of history.

Those near enough hear him speak of "the duty of ane minister and also their duty to him likewise." And so, as his secretary wrote afterwards, he "made the marriage, in a manner, betwixt Mr. James Lowsone then made minister, and the folk: and so praised God . . . and with the common blessing ended."

So John Knox, dying a fortnight later, handed on the heavy cross of this ministry. He was helped back down the High Street to Mossman the Jeweller's house—called John Knox's House today—and as he lay on his death-bed folk of every kind and condition came to take leave of him.

He had a last word for the new minister of St. Giles: "You, Master Lowsone, fight the good fight! Do the work of the Lord with courage, and with a willing mind, and God from above bless you, and the church whereof you have charge. Against it, so long as it continueth in the doctrine of truth, the gates of Hell shall not prevail!"

He died as Rome counter-attacked the Reformed faith. News of the massacre of St. Bartholomew's Day in France saddened his last days. Spain, checked in the Netherlands by Dutch resolution, was building the Armada to fall upon England. Queen Elizabeth held prisoner Mary, Queen of Scots, devoutly Roman and her possible successor on the throne. The Church of Scotland had charge of educating her son James VI of Scotland, still a small boy.

In this lull the Church also had the chance to try out Knox's dream of a covenanted nation: of a free people walking as Kings and priests to God. Parish ministers with territorial ordination and their Kirk Sessions—courts composed of men of all sorts and conditions, carefully chosen and ordained—cared for Scotland body and soul: and for education next to worship. It was more than social revolution

1

or blue-print for democracy. It was staking the claim of another King, another kingdom.

As for James, they determined, with prayer, to make him the best-educated and most religious sovereign ever seen. And so he was.

"The sweetest sight in Europe that day." wrote the Rev. Andrew Melville when he and his nephew saw James aged 8 at Stirling: "We heard him discourse, walking up and down in the old Lady Mar's hand, of knowledge and ignorance, to my great marvel and astonishment."

That same year the English ambassador heard James translate any chapter of the Bible "out of Latin into French, and out of French after into English."

The danger of prayer, as Juvenal once pointed out, was its being answered. James grew up educated, and ever ready to preach: but also a cunning dictator, perverted and depraved. The day came when the "sweetest sight" the ministers admired destroyed them both, and their church too.

His nursery playmate was Jockie Mar, older and stronger, but always obliged to give way because James was King. No doubt the mind of this old-fashioned bairn took in the advantage.

Later, James found in the library so carefully collected for him a copy of Bodin's book on the *Law of Monarchy*, which not only advocated absolute power for the sovereign, but argued that this was the divine Will of God.

In this James found his life's creed. It wasn't enough to be absolute: one had to be sacred too. With God on his side, it was sin to be against him.

James' chief tutor was Geordie Buchanan, "The Scottish Johnston": or as the Great Doctor was himself to put it later on: "The only great Scot."

Buchanan, half-Highland, and all his life half-starved, was one of the most famous scholars in Europe. Much of his life had been spent in Paris: but as his ideas had self-ejected him from this Chair and that, he had taught almost everywhere. He was caught once by the most ghastly terror of his age, the Spanish Inquisition; and might well have ended with the hideous tortures and the burning alive they so freely practised.

But Buchanan persuaded them of his misguided innocence, and was sent for re-education to a monastery.

There he found the monks "verra ignorant men, but kindly:" and there, perhaps as thanksgiving, he made that translation of the Psalms into Latin verse that became an international favourite, loved by Cardinals and Covenanters, Kings and Commoners.

When Buchanan did get round to studying Reformation principles he was convinced of their validity, left Paris and came home. His orthodoxy was not too carefully examined—he was, they said, "of very gude religion for a poet." But his support meant much to the early Reformers, with their eagerness to free the mind. His scholarship and fame made him welcome at court, where he read Virgil with Mary, Queen of Scots. But he unhesitatingly believed her guilty, at least as having "art and part" in her husband's murder: and wrote his own legal account to prove it.

James feared Buchanan, and hated even his memory. He rejected utterly all Buchanan's beliefs, which ran counter to his own, fighting them wherever they rose, in the Kirk of Scotland or the Commons of England.

Buchanan's creed was not Religion but Law. To him, Law represented Truth and Justice above the brutality of power. His brilliant exposition of this, *de iure regni apud Scotos*, in the form of a Socratic dialogue with Maitland of Lethington, was condemned as revolutionary and burned repeatedly—in the next century with works of Milton and the *Lex Rex* of Samuel Rutherford. One authority calls the argument "the core of the American Declaration of Independence."

Kings, Buchanan claimed, ruled by Law, and were themselves subject to its principles. Anyone outside the Law, whether King or criminal, was "no less an enemy of the people than a foreign invader."

The Law, like Truth, was one and indivisible. The little lies of the Roman Church, such as the sale of Bishoprics, were part of the great debaucheries, such as when Pope Julius II made "the Keeper of his apes, a man more bestial than the beasts," to be his colleague in the priesthood. (Maitland: "Perhaps there was some other reason for choosing him." G. B. "Some are reported, but I have chosen the most respectable.")

In contrast, Buchanan saw true greatness as greatness of character garbed in simplicity. He compared that of the classical Ancients with "some King you have seen decked out like a child's doll, and paraded in great ceremony and with a prodigious hubbub in order to make an empty show." Yet this was 300 years before Abe Lincoln!

Buchanan may have been still working on this, and troubled with his usual gout, that time that small James twice disobeyed him and then deliberately defied him to his face. Buchanan turned him up and laid on so heartily that Lady Mar came running, horrified by the howls, to ask: "What dost thou do to the Lord's Anointed?"

"I have skelped his airse, you may kiss it if you like!" he is said to have answered.

James was to assume power when he was 17, but when he was only 12, in 1578, the Regent Douglas, Earl of Morton, found himself dangerously unpopular and proposed that he take over forthwith: and this was duly proclaimed at the Town Cross of Edinburgh and elsewhere. Buchanan retired, and published his work on Law, which cost him even a pension.

Regent Morton went back to Lochleven Castle, where he "seemed to do nothing but to make alleys and gardens, yet was he contriving

3

deeper matters . . . he could not suffer Christ to reign freely . . . and, no question, he would have stayed the work of policy in hand . . ."

The work of policy in hand was the creation of presbyterian government in the church. Morton threatened to take Andrew Melville, its' main architect, and hang him alive in chains. "The earth is the Lord's—what matter if I rot in the air or the ground?" retorted Melville.

The familiar authorities were sloughed off, and "the priesthood of all believers" became a practical as well as a mystical concept. People from every corner of the world today look to St. Giles in Edinburgh as the Mother Church of Presbyterianism. But every inch had to be fought and paid for: and often it seemed a forlorn dream.

Andrew Melville, an international scholar and great administrator, had returned to Scotland from the Continent: building up first Glasgow University, which had fallen on evil days, and then going on to St. Andrews. In that same year of 1578 he produced the *Second Book of Discipline* for the Kirk.

It speaks of "The Two Powers"—the Sword and the Keys—which "be both of God, and tend to one end, if they be rightly usit . . . the exercise of both . . . cannot stand in one person ordinarily."

He proposed four offices in the Kirk:

1)   Pastor, minister or bishop
2)   Doctor or teacher
3)   Elder or presbyter
4)   Deacon or manager

The first two were to sow the Word, the third to "seek the fruit": and those "lawfully callit" to that office . . . "may not leave it again."

There were to be four sorts of Assembly:

1)   Of particular kirks, "ane or mae."
2)   Of a province
3)   Of ane haill nation
4)   Of all and divers nations professing one Lord Jesus Christ

Further, "The haill rent and patrimony of the Kirk . . . may be dividit in four portions:"

1)   Ane . . . to the pastor
2)   Ane other to the elders, deacons, and other officers of the kirk; sic as Clerks of the Assembly, takers-up of the psalms, beadles and keepers of the Kirk . . . joining therewith the doctors of schules
3)   The third . . . upon the puir members of the faithful and on hospitals
4)   For reparation of the kirks

4

XI.13. states: "It agrees not with the word of God that bishops should be pastors of pastors . . . of many flocks, and yet without any certain flock . . ."

Morton emerged from his gardens and made a swoop on Stirling. The King woke to the yells of fighting men, the clash of steel which always terrified him, the scream of a companion trampled to death.

A Parliament was called in the Great Hall of Stirling Castle, and the King brought in in his robe-royal. The nobles began to quarrel. Morton whispered in his ear. "The King said, blushing and somewhat stooting, "Lest any man should judge this not to be a free Parliament I declare it to be free . . ." It also rejected the *Second Book of Discipline*.

But Morton's reign was unexpectedly short. A ship came into Leith that September, where Mary and her four Maries had landed twenty years before, bearing another beautiful half-Stewart from France. Esme Stewart, Sieur d'Aubigny, was an accomplished courtier of over 30, already married: and James fell deeply, desperately in love with him.

From the start, d'Aubigny was all. It was with him that James made his state entry into Edinburgh next month, riding in to be received "under a pompous pall of purple velvet."

There were wonderful pageants all down the Royal Mile, and at St. Giles "Dame Religion desired his presence; so he lighted at the Lady's Steps and went in . . . Mr. Lowsone . . . exhorted the King and subjects to do their duty, to enter in league and covenant with God, and concluded with thanksgiving. When he came to the Cross there Bacchus sat on a puncheon, with his painted garment and a flower garland. He welcomed the King to his own town, and drank many glasses . . . there were run three puncheons of wine." At the Nether Bow there were trumpets, more speeches, a set-piece of the planets: and "from the West Port to the Nether Bow, all the fore-stairs on the High Street were covered with tapestry, cards and brods."

d'Aubigny rode at James' stirrup, sat at his right hand, joined his Privy Council, to the English Ambassador's disgust. The Queen of England was deeply worried, the Kirk still more alarmed: for he represented the policy of the de Guises, the Holy Catholic League, the power and persecution of Rome. There was a secret "Association" including Mary to that end.

"The ministers of Edinburgh, like faithful watchdogs, made loud and timeous warning." d'Aubigny piously reminded the Assembly that he had made "open declaration of this my calling, first by my own mouth in the kirk of Edinburgh, secondly by my hand-writ in the Kings' kirk in Stirling, where I subscribed the Confession of Faith, yet I found it was my duty . . . to make you . . . free and humble offer of due obedience . . ." And his man-servant ostentatiously did so too.

Elizabeth wrote anxious letters: to James, urging him from elderly experience "rather to fear (for) his ambition than to comfort and delight his affection." To her ambassador Bowes, Knox's brother-in-law, she suggested almost everything but money. (Bowes had written that he could buy anyone in Scotland except Peter Young, James' under-tutor, and the ministers: but Elizabeth would try everything else first). The danger was very real. Armada ports were vital, and as her agents could already tell her, some Scots nobles were in touch with Spain.

Morton, who once "abode ever starkest about the King" now faded into the shadows. James acquired a body-guard under Captain James Stewart of Ochiltree, a lesser and coarser favourite. He spent the next summer on a Royal Progress, moving in a golden dream through Scotland, his adored d'Aubigny by his side. "At Dundee he rode for the ring on the pied horse, and ran right bravely."

The Progress was also an economy measure, since the vast Royal household were guests wherever they went. The Treasurer, Lord Ruthven, Earl of Gowrie, of that great historic house, had recommended it. He said James was £40,000 in debt to him.

On the last day of that December Captain Stewart knelt before the King in Council and accused Morton of treason: especially of having fore-knowledge of the murder of the King's father, Lord Darnley, which he had not disclosed. Morton in his trial admitted this, but asked to whom he could have disclosed it? To the Queen, whom all thought guilty? It did not matter, as he realised. "It is but my life they seek."

He was executed in June, the ministers of St. Giles, whose parish duty it was, going all through the last hours with him; Mr. Lowsone kneeling and crying to God with him as the blade fell.

A few weeks later d'Aubigny was solemnly proclaimed Duke of Lennox; Lord Darnley; Lord Tarbolton, Dalkeith and Tantallon: Captain of Dumbarton Castle: Great Chamberlain of Scotland: Commendator of Arbroath with the right of Sunday markets in Tranent. Captain Stewart was made Earl of Arran.

Now the court was filled with "wicked monsieurs" and Jesuits in attendance. French brothels opened in the Canongate. James was in touch with the Duc de Guise in France, who sent him presents of horses, and secret messages. d'Aubigny was in touch with Mary in her prison. French armies were rumoured, and Papal moves. Everyone knew the Spanish Armada was nearing completion. The crown in England, the kirk in Scotland were both in danger. The ministers of St. Giles warned the people from the pulpit: and the Rev. John Durie had a spell in the dungeons of Edinburgh Castle for it. He must have hated the close confinement, for Andrew Melville once said of him: "The gown was no sooner off and the Bible oot o'hand frae the kirk whan on gaed the corselet and fangit was the hackbut,—and to the fields!"

The Kirk tried bringing out a second Confession of Faith for the nation to sign. First after the King signed the obliging d'Aubigny,

Duke of Lennox, and then Captain Stewart, now Earl of Arran. Lennox even offered to get a Huguenot pastor, the better to be converted: and the ministers wasted time and effort writing to London for one.

But he did not carry a joke too far. When the King gave him the Archbishopric of Glasgow he hastened to find a "tulchan"—stuffed calf-skin—cleric called Montgomery to take his duties while he drew the rents: as a cow may be decieved by the dummy while she is hand-milked. The Assembly censured Montgomery, now appointed Archbishop, the King defended him. Montgomery with a royal guard entered Glasgow Cathedral and pulled the minister in the pulpit by the sleeve, ordering him: "Down, Sirrah!" The minister resisted, there was an uproar, and nearly a riot.

The Presbytery of Stirling suspended Montgomery, and the Synod of Lothian summoned him to hear sentence. The King summoned the Synod before the Privy Council: but agreed to hear Durie of St. Giles and John Davidson of Liberton in private instead. They got nowhere.

The next Assembly prepared to excommunicate Montgomery, but he appeared in tears, sustained by Davidson, and confessed his fault. Later, he fell back into error and drink "chasing the servants with a drawn whinger:" and the Presbytery of Glasgow met to depose him. He burst in with the Lord Provost and magistrates, and an armed band, and a free fight took place. The Moderator was dragged from his chair, had his face bashed, his beard pulled and a tooth knocked out, and was flung into the Tolbooth, where he sensibly said he would stay. Yet sentence was pronounced and repeated from pulpits throughout Scotland, though Galloway of St. John's kirk, Perth, was threatened by Lennox (d'Aubigny) himself for it: Davidson had to be guarded by armed friends: and Durie was ordered by the Privy Council to cease preaching and leave Scotland.

On his behalf, Davidson cried to the next Assembly: "What flesh may, or should, displace the Great King's ambassador, he keeping the bounds of his commission? Who gave Kings especially power to meddle in that matter?" But the Assembly lacked courage to support him.

Melville preached against "the bloody gullie of absolute authority, whereby men intended to pull the crown off Christ's head, and to wring the sceptre out of his hand." But, in this first head-on collision, power remained with the King. Durie, stopping only to see his latest-born baby, "took instruments" at the Town Cross and left for exile.

Meanwhile Archbishop Montgomery, rash enough to visit Edinburgh, was pelted for dear life with rotten eggs and fish, and glad to dodge down the darkness of the Kirk-wynd. "When the King heard of it, he laid himself down on the Inch of Perth, not able to contain himself for laughter." That was James all over.

The Kirk drew up a list of legitimate grievances, and tried to present them to the King. But the delegates were met by the favourites. Arran, with a thrawn face roared at them "Who dare subscrive these treasonable articles?"

"We dare and will subscrive them," answered Andrew Melville, snatching up the clerk's quill: "and will render our lives in the cause." So they all signed.

But it was all a futile gesture. The two favourites ruled Scotland, insolent and ruthless. James, feeling himself supreme in power as in affection, gloried in it. He could hardly bear Lennox out of his sight.

He grew secure, even careless. In August, 1582, he went hunting near Perth, for once without either Lennox or Arran. Again armed men made a swoop: and again James found himself a prisoner, this time in Gowrie Castle, home of the Earl of Gowrie. Lennox and Arran were cut off, and could do nothing.

At first James could not believe his position. He put on his riding-boots and tried to leave. Gowrie thrust out a leg, barring the way.

James burst into tears—of rage and frustration, like his mother years ago, when Knox uncovered her plans. He choked out threats with his sobs. The armed men laughed, and one used the schoolmasters' phrase: "Better bairns greet than bearded men!" Meaning, that boys should learn their lesson.

James did. A poem he wrote in these last years of boyhood is perhaps the best thing he ever wrote, and possibly the only time he showed a glimpse of his secret self.

> "Since thought is free, think what thou will,
> O troubled heart, to ease thy paine!
> Thought unrevealed can do no ill,
> But words passed out turn not again.
> Be careful aye for to invent
> The way to get thine own intent . . .
>
> Since fool-haste is not greatest speed,
> I would thou shouldest learn to know
> How to make virtue of a need,
> Sin' that necessity hath no law.
> With patience, then, see thou attend,
> And hope to vanquish at the end."

James was forced in the end to sign an order exiling Lennox from Scotland for ever: and he never saw him again. He never forgot and he never forgave.

CHAPTER TWO

THE OTHER KINGDOM

The darkness of Edinburgh was alive with the sound of men's feet on the cobbles. Up from Leith they came, swelling in number till they reached 2,000 strong: making for the great Kirk of St. Giles, with John Durie, back from exile, in their midst. As they came up the Royal Mile the men's deep voices suddenly burst into the Psalm of Deliverance "in four parts, known to most part of the people . . . they were much moved themselves, and so were all the beholders:"

> "Now Israel may say
> And that truly
> Had that the Lord
> Not been upon our side
> When cruel men
> Had risen up furiously . . .

The song swelled victoriously under the windows of the Duke of Lennox, under sentence of banishment in his turn. He was seen to look out and "rive his beard" in a French passion . . .

Lennox went back to France without seeing James again and shortly died. But within a year the King was free, and Arran recalled to greater supremacy.

Durie was back in exile, and Lowsone and Balquancal of St. Giles had to join him in England. The Earl of Gowrie was first ostentatiously pardoned and then, as opportunity offered, executed in May.

The King came in state to open Parliament in the Tolbooth, Edinburgh, the "Honours of Scotland"—crown, sceptre and sword—borne up the Royal Mile before him: and Lennox's son, brought over from France, carried the Crown.

It was a hurried Parliament. "It was almost ended before it was well heard of." The Lords of the Articles were sworn to secrecy: but one of them told a minister friend privately: "The whole force of this Parliament is bent against the Kirk."

When the Acts were made public, the second one made the King sole and absolute judge of matters temporal and spiritual: of "the Word of God itself . . . the power of binding and loosing." The fourth one made all assemblies and convocations illegal, unless specially sanctioned: and the 20th "ratifies, approves and re-establishes the state of Bishops."

B

The ministers of St. Giles preached against these, and then left for exile, pursued by Arran's threats. James Melville had shortly to follow his uncle Andrew over Tweed: Galloway of Perth hid while his Manse was searched and stripped, the mattresses "stogged through with swords." Archers of the Royal Bodyguard rounded up other ministers and put them in the Castle dungeons.

Andrew Melville had been first to stand his ground, defying the Court's "roarings of "Lyons", and messages of death." Summoned to the Palace, he "plainly told the King and Council that they presumed over-boldly in a constitute estate of a Christian King, the Kingdom of Jesus Christ passing by . . . to tak' upon them to judge the doctrine and control the ambassadors and messengers of a King and Council greater nor they."

"And that," says he, "ye may see your weakness, over-sight and rashness in taking upon you that which neither ye ought nor can do" (loosing a little Hebrew Bible from his belt and clacking it down on the board), "There is," says he, "my instructions and warrant. See which of you can judge thereon, or control me therein."

But James issued another warrant, to ward him in Blackness: "a foul hole." So on his last free evening he dined at St. Giles Manse.

Lowsone and the other guests were "exceeding heavy-hearted," but "Mr. Andrew eat, drank and cracked, as merrily and free-minded as at any time and more." According to his habit, when at table in his Universities, conversation was general and gay: he toasted his Captain and warders, who charged him to be in Blackness within 24 hours: then slipped away and out of the town's port, "hand for hand," and rode for England.

Lowsone packed up his books and set them aside. "It was a pity to see that new work begun in the College to be cutted off from all hope of harvest." But there was another and very worthy harvest, long years later. The books became the nucleus of Edinburgh University Library, and are so honoured today.

Lowsone and Balcanqual fled at the end of May, and Lowsone died in London in October. Some of his own people in St. Giles had signed an officially-issued letter which denounced the ministers as guilty of treason: and this disloyalty "wasted his vital spirits by piece-meal." It is a clinically accurate description of the effect of that kind of treachery—that breaking of the fellowship that is like breaking an electric current: no light, no warmth, no power runs through.

For the first time, elders of the kirk had to stand their share of the persecution. Eleven elders and deacons of St. Giles were summoned before the King and Chancellor (Arran) at Falkland, charged with treason because they had not signed that accusing letter. Peter Blackburn answered the King courageously, in spite of jeers: and was six days chained in irons for it. Others were imprisoned. It seems always the few who have to bear the burden for the rest.

Wives joined in. Mrs Lowsone and Mrs. Balcanqual wrote a reply to an Archbishop who had attacked their exiled husbands. It is a powerful document, in which for four glorious pages the down-trodden creatures give a glimpse of their mind. They used English, Latin, French, Greek and broad Scots: and some of it can only be rendered by asterisks even today. I hope the luxury of it was its own satisfaction: for the Archbishop then got an edict to have them evicted and they had to "redd up and void" their manses, and give up the keys. Mrs. Durie was only given enough money to transport all her small bairns and household gear, and that in deep snow. But when Lowsone's widow was in desperate want, the Town granted a pension to her and her children. Free speech is too dear for ministers wives. Young Durie was later an ecumenical and young Balcanqual episcopalian.

The pressure to make the ministers subscribe "The Black Acts", as they were called, increased hotly. Some thought it politic, to preserve the Kirk from total suppression, to sign "with mental reservations." The Presbytery of Ayr went a little further, all signing their names under the Declaration: "The 1st Act of Parliament . . . we approve. The 3rd and 4th we damn as devilish, and express against God's Word." Whereupon "their stipends were taken from them."

As the King processed to the next Parliament, the widowed Countess of Gowrie fell on her knees to him, trying to present a petition begging him, for the sake of her four small sons, to remit some of his enormous debt to her: but Arran, "his hand on the King's arm," bore him swiftly past, striking her down so savagely with his free hand that she was hurt, and had to be carried into a near-by close.

In 1582 old Geordie Buchanan, the King's tutor, died in the same poverty in which he had lived. Andrew and James Melville, with George's cousin, Thomas Buchanan, visiting him in his lodging in the High Street not long before, had found one of the greatest scholars of Europe teaching the A,B,C, to his illiterate servant. Possibly it was all he could give him.

"I see you are nocht idle!" said Melville.

"Better this nor stealing sheep—nor sitting idle, which is as ill!"

They had come, they told him, from seeing his *History of Scotland* in the Press: and feared that part of it "anent the burial of Davie" (Rizzio) would certainly anger the King.

"Tell me, man, if I have told the truth?"

"Yes, sir, I think so."

"Then I will 'bind his feud, and all his friends . . ."

He had but one more job to get through, he told them as they left: his dying. How he ordered it spiritually he alone knew. But financially he was destitute. When he, who for years had given his best to the King, was on his death-bed, he asked his man how much money was left. There was not enough for a funeral.

"Give it to the poor."

The man protested, horror-struck. Who would be at charges to bury him? Surely never the disgrace of a pauper burial?

"If they will not bury my corpse they can leave it here." said Buchanan, with a Johnsonian exit-line: "Or throw it where they please . . ."

The King was pushing steadily for that power which he saw as the solution of all his problems. He tried again to coerce the ministers, and when they held back:: "His face swelled, and he said: "I have made no laws but such as are agreeable with God's laws; and therefore if any of you find fault, tell me now." They kept silence . . ."

But once outside the presence, they were "discontented" at missing such a chance, and "minded on the morn" to speak their mind: but it was too late, as always.

The new favourite was the Master of Gray "beautiful exceedingly", and a kind of butterfly of treachery whom James sent South, 1584. He flirted with Rome, intrigued with Mary and then sold her secrets openly to Elizabeth to whom he also was alleged to have hinted, apparently on behalf of James, that the dead bite not—"quia mortui non mordent, yet it were no wise meet that the same were done openly, but rather by some quieter means." This year saw James' last letter to his mother.

Agitation to have Mary beheaded was again rising in England. Elizabeth, genuinely reluctant, could still plead the fear of a Scots rising: but James was as eager as any to reassure her. "I pray you, take me not to be a chameleon," he wrote to her. To Leicester on 15th December, 1586, from Holyroodhouse he was plainer. "But specially how fond and inconstant I were if I should prefer my mother to the title, let all men judge." (He used the word "Prefer" in the sense of "advance": but it adds up to the same). He suggested Mary should be shut up "in the Tower, or some other firm manse," and "all her auld knavish servants hangit".

That month he sent the Master of Gray South, as his own personal ambassador. Did he carry further, more explicit reassurances?

In January James ordered the ministers to pray for his mother in a form that cast any impending blame on Elizabeth. They refused. On Sunday in St. Giles James interrupted the minister's prayers, and ordered him to give place to the Bishop: which he did, declaring furiously that the King would one day answer "to the great Judge of the world for such dealing!" For this he went to the dungeons. Next Sunday after sermon the King made a soothing speech: "He said he was of that mind, that none of his subjects would blame him for his affection which he carried to his mother . . ."

Gray returned to Edinburgh on February 7th, and next day, February 8th, 1587, Mary was beheaded. There was an outburst of anger in Scotland.

The Borders armed, and many offers were made to James to attack England. He soothed these down also. Whether or not he sorrowed for a mother he had not seen since he was ten months old, her going took a shadow from his sovereignty. That year he celebrated his 21st birthday with a great love-feast in Holyrood, and a procession of (forcibly) reconciled nobles hand-in-hand to the Mercat Cross "where a long table was set, furnished with bread and wine and sweetmeats." The Cross was covered with tapestry and upon it "the trumpeters blowing and the musicians singing." The King drank to the nobles, who drank to each other. The glasses and left-overs were flung to the crowd.

Some discontent remained, so Gray was the scapegoat. He was accused of various treasons including "pushing the Queen of England to cut off the King's mother": and exiled. Arran had already gone, after a concerted move by both Gray and the Lords the year before. James had now two new young men about Court; Huntly, Cock o' the North, and Bothwell of the Borders, nephew of his mother's third husband—Mary's Bothwell. The Kirk called them the Candy Captains. (Was "candy" a French word, French pronounced? When I was a child the village sweetie-wife sold "gundy"—the same word?).

James had now only to wait, for that supremacy in both Scotland and England that would compensate for the insecurities of his childhood. And, as his unboyish boy's poem showed, he knew how to wait.

There was in any case a lull. The Spanish Armada, so long in building, was ready to sail. Elizabeth made approaches to James, James made soothing speeches to the General Assembly. All the land waited, the balefires ready on the hills that had warned of Viking raiders. It came, it passed. What possessed the Spanish Admiral to think he could take "floating castles" through the storms and skerries of the far North? A few survivors came ashore on Fair Isle, where half of them died. The rest went home via Arbroath where it was found—astonishment!- that the Bogey Men were "but halflin' laddies." So they were "courteously entreated," as their own records show to this day.

In the lull, more exiled ministers came home: but all who were not willing to "fold their feet and crave pardon and grace of the King" continued partly with their people, partly in prison or in England.

No wonder ministers were few. "There is in the Lennox twenty four kirks and not four ministers amongst them all." The nobles found "nocht need" of religion, the merchants thought it a poor return for the "bairns' part," or inheritance. The poor, though more willing, could not afford it. St. Giles called Davidson of Liberton, but still had vacant pulpits. It had been divided into several kirks because until the 1960's one man's voice could not be heard over the whole great building. And also because the Table Communion, the heart of the kirk, restricted each congregation to a manageable family group.

Today the church has scrapped it for an uncomfortable and meaningless rite in overcrowded pews.

At this low ebb a new and most unexpected champion appeared: Robert Bruce, a younger son of the Bruces of Airth Castle, descendant of King Robert the Bruce and nephew to "Lusty" Livingstone, one of the Queen's Four Maries. Brought up in the Roman Church, he graduated in Philosophy at St. Andrews, and Law at the Sorbonne. He guided his family's affairs at Court and in the Court of Session: seeing the conflict between the Two Kingdoms in close-up. And for years he "never leapt on horseback nor lighted" without his conscience accusing him for standing aside.

"The last night of August, 1581," he was sleeping "in the new loft chamber" of his family home, Airth Castle, when the devil, huge and terrible, summoned him to an Assize of Soul. One by one his sins were cited; and though half-forgotten were conjured up vividly alive. His conscience, called to witness, testified against him. One by one they added to the burden of the indictment till he felt himself dragged down to the depths of Hell by that "unsupportable weight." Till, with the maniacal strength of one bursting from a nightmare he cried out in confession: "restored God to his glory, and craved God's mercy for the merits of Christ."

The Bruce crest was: "Doe well: let them say,"—a shorter version of the better known: "They say: what say they? Let them say." On a wooden beam of an old upper room in Airth Castle there was carved: "1581 Let Them Say."

No doubt they said a good deal. Bruce's mother made him hand over all his small lands and properties: so he "cast my clothes from me, my vain and glorious apparel: sent my horse to the fair, and emptied my hands of all." Yet one guesses that pride of birth and intellect was not so easily jettisoned.

For Bruce, in spite of his dramatic calling, was passionately scrupulous about his faith: a lawyer still who cared about the truth. His sermons on the sacraments are still re-printing, still a preacher's treasury: but still best in the original homely Scots he was careful to use. He struggled above all, "by the grace of God," to be clear: and next to that to be brief. He said of the sacrament that it gave folk "a better grip of Christ:" he spoke of a "wonderful and miserable madness in the soul of man." Yet he could rise from his knees in the pulpit to cry only to the people, out of his own heart: "I think it a great matter to believe that there is a God!"

He had a horror of long prayers in public: his own were always short, but each sentence "like a strong bolt shot up to heaven," powered by the hours of private prayer behind it.

He hesitated long over ordination; till one sacrament Sunday as he sat with the congregation of St. Giles at the long table covered with white linen, he looked up from prayer to find the other ministers had slipped away, and the people were looking expectantly to him. The

14

elders brought him the elements: he accepted, and ministered with long-remembered grace: counting himself ordained, by the calling of God, from that hour.

"I had no will of the Court," he wrote, "and refused long the burden of Edinburgh." He had seen it too close, and too clearly. But St. Giles was determined to have him. His call was backed by the Provost and whole Town Council. "Laith was I to go." But their determination triumphed and he went, for twelve years known as familiarly to the poor in the High Street as to the King in his palace.

In 1590, James decided to marry. It was time, he explained in his usual pompous prose, "being King not only of this realm, but heir-apparent of another." Also his delay "had begot in many a suspicion of impotency." He set out methodically to disprove it. Princess Anne of Denmark having been selected and negotiated, he announced himself in love, and wrote endless poetry.

When Anne was storm-stayed in Norway on her way to Scotland—for which witches were burned in both Denmark and Scotland—James decided to sail over and bring home the bride. He charged Bruce of St. Giles principally to keep peace and order in his absence: and this he did better, it was said, than when the King was at home. The King himself wrote to Bruce, thanking him and saying he was worthy of "a quarter of my petite kingdom": "I have heard of your daily travail now during my absence and I think myself beholden while I live, never to forget the same."

He also begged him "for God's sake, take all the pains you can to tune our folks well against our home-coming, lest we be all shamed before strangers."

Again Bruce rose to the occasion. There were all sorts of splendid pageants, both for the State entry of the little 16 year old Queen, and for her coronation: and all her life she loved such shows. Andrew Melville's Latin oration was so admired that the King had it printed. Bruce preached at her coronation and, reluctantly, to please the King, anointed her with oil. Next Sunday King and Queen came to morning service in St. Giles, and after the sermon the King rose to tell them all he had come "to thank God with the people for his prosperous return and to thank them for good order keeped . . . to thank the ministers for their care . . . and peace of the town." He promised to prove "a loving, faithful and thankful King: to execute justice . . . and to see the kirks better provided."

Climax of all came at the General Assembly where the king, who had often attended to complain, now came to bless: to exhort them to be yet more reformed—"In no point was he so earnest as in this."

"He fell forth in praising God that he was born in such a time . . . in such a place as to be King in such a Kirk, the sincerest Kirk in the world." He scorned Geneva, still keeping Pasch and Yule. "As for our neighbour Kirk in England, it is an evil-said mass in English, wanting nothing but the liftings." He promised them his support and defence

"So long as I brook my life and crown," and "there was nothing but loud praising of God and praying for the King for a quarter of an hour."

CHAPTER THREE

PRINCIPALITIES AND POWERS

Honeymoons don't last, as Queen and Kirk discovered. The Candy Captains returned. Huntly was a Papist: Bothwell had yet darker sins.

There had been a witch-hunt after the storms that delayed first the Queen's arrival and then the King's return. One Agnes Sampson of North Berwick was strung up by the neck, shaved, and pricked all over the a large brass-headed pin to find the "witches mark." Grown insensible—one way or another—she confessed.

Close on a hundred, nearly all women, had met in North Berwick kirkyard, and gone dancing along behind John Fian, wearing a beast's muzzle, with Geilie Duncan playing on the trump. When they came to the Kirk, Fian "blew" open the door, and "blew" in the lights—"great black candles sticking roundabout the pulpit." They all whirled round widdershins and curtsied to the Master, who started up in the pulpit "like a muckle black man" and called the Roll, in false names (he got one wrong). When everyone had answered "Here!" he asked them if they had obeyed all his orders? Rifled the graves, stolen the fingers and toes? ("The said Agnes got for her part a winding-sheet and two joints.") The Master then gave them a blasphemous sermon and required them all to do him obscene reverence.

Later they danced reels on the sandy shores of the Forth, with a flagon of wine, to the jolly tune: "Cummer, go ye before, Cummer, go ye!" To raise the storms, they sailed out in sieves with a christened cat, which had joints of the dead tied to every part, and threw it over with suitable incantations.

The King "who took delight to be present" at these confessions, declared they "were all extreme liars." But one took him apart and "declared the very words that passed between the King's Majesty and the Queen at Upflo in Norway, the first night of marriage: after which he was convinced." (Was this an old wise-woman's chestnut?)

We are appalled at the tales of witch-hunts today. But these people lived in the double-dimensional world of Hieronymous Bosch, painter of these times, whose great landscapes are all thronging with powers of light and of darkness, winged and hoofed: and but one short step away from a tumultuous eternity.

The half-starved parish minister was still "the Great King's ambassador," not doubting the power of his commission: nor that the Devil also walked with him, and that his works were part of his parish duties. John Buchan's *Witchwood* gives an uncannily vivid picture of minister and people struggling with the powers of evil and their own ignorance.

The best Scots writing, at its most flat and factual, does not accept the sharp line of visual reality. Hogg's *Confessions of a Justified Sinner*, Barrie's *Farewell, Miss Julie Logan*, Stevenson's *Dr. Jekyll and Mr. Hyde* all have a plain, reporting style. Yet not more so than the account of the trial of Bessie Dunlop, an Ayrshire lassie of those times.

Bessie was driving her cows to the field one day, weeping sorely, when she met "ane honest, weel, elderly man, gray-beardit, and had ane gray coat with Lombard sleeves of the auld fashion: ane pair of gray breeks and white shanks, gartered abune the knee: ane black bonnet with silken laces drawn through . . . and ane white wand in his hand."

"Sancta Maria," said he, saluting her: for he knew nothing of the Reformation. Why did she greet? Her husband, her new baby and her best cow were all sick, she told him: and she, weak from child-birth, must take on all the work.

The baby and the cow would die, he told her, but her husband would recover, and things prosper. And he passed into the solid wall of Maybole Castle.

Bessie dried her tears. It all happened as he said, and they prospered well. This Tam Reid, killed at the battle of Pinkie thirty years before, helped her quietly with spells and charms, curing cattle and finding lost things: till her fame spread over the country. Though it is not stated, Tam appears to have fallen in love with her. She glimpsed him once walking in the Kirkyard of Dalry after service: once, he showed her the whole faerie rout riding in Middle-earth with a tremendous rushing noise. Once he laughed to her out of all the crowds in the busy High Street of Edinburgh. And once, jealous perhaps, he called her out from her husband and a gathering of friends by their fireside to show her his own coven—twelve persons sitting "seemly-like in plaids." Was he not, he asked her wistfully, "meat-worthy and claith-worthy"? But she would "in no wise" go with them. He did not press her: but led her back—to safety? "Convick and burnt" was her epitaph.

Witches did exist: they were serious practitioners. Covens did meet: they could be, and were, used as a political fifth column: a sort of Mafia. But they drew their real power from the old, dark gods who lingered in the lonely places. An Act of Assembly of 1592 ordered the ploughing-up of the "Goodman's piece"—the fallow corner—on all the farms in the Garioch. But witches in Orkney went on calling on the Norse gods "in the ancient tongue." It was a State crime, with State trial.

As late as the seventeenth century the parishioners of Applecross—an isolated mainland spot opposite Raasay—sacrificed a white bull at Midsummer "with sic-like abominations," as the report primly puts

18

it. When challenged, they said it was to "Sainct Mhairi"—that is, the Virgin Mary: which only showed they were 100 years behind in doctrine as well as 1,000 (or 2,000) in religious ritual. Belief in the Evil Eye has never wholly left the Isles to this day.

Does it sound so far away and out of date? How many of us have seen the same black, unreasoning horror, the same old leper-loathing conjured up by Hitler against Jews? By South Africans against Africans? White Americans against blacks? Irish Roman Catholics against Protestants? Satan is conservative: and eternal.

In these and other quite different witch-trials later on in James' reign the same name kept recurring: Bothwell.

Bothwell may well have been the witches' Master. It would give him unrivalled opportunity for intrigue, for influence, for information: and for cheap debauch. Whether true or not, the tale was widely believed: and added awe to the practical fear in which he was held.

James now was playing a waiting game, the hardest game of all, with the crown of England as stake. At Armada time he had pledged to Elizabeth the full support of "the whole Isle of Britain", and he aimed at nothing less for himself. Elizabeth in return had promised him a large pension, which she never paid. Nor did she name him heir. But all other alliances—with de Guises, his mother, Spain—had been checked in this game of chess. She "used him like a boy," he complained. But in the power game James and Elizabeth were well enough matched. Neither used gold or force where skill or cunning would do.

It was no private game. All the world was the stage, as their great contemporary wrote. What a keen topical edge the plays of Shakespeare must have lost with the years!

Critics have suggested that Bothwell, dashing and ambitious, was Shakespeare's model for *Macbeth*. Surely his reputation as Witch-master must have travelled. Moreover, anyone seeing the play *Much Ado About Nothing*, might easily think they had seen the Candy Captains, large as life. "Know ye not I am Richard II?" said Queen Elizabeth once at the time of Essex' rebellion. No one dared openly to mock the great ones of the day: you can only imagine the turn of speech, trick of movement, that would make a character instantly recognisable on the stage, and given instant zest to the play.

The Danish Queen, blonde and gentle, could have been a happy woman with a little love. But not only did James openly prefer his Candy Captains, but as soon as her first baby, Prince Henry, was born, he had him taken from her and handed over to the Mars, hereditary guardians of the heir to the throne. This had a colour of reason, of tradition: but also a streak of his twisted cruelty. Ann grieved bitterly for her baby.

Soon she gathered round her a circle of friends and sympathisers. Chief among them was the young Earl of Moray, outstandingly tall and handsome—"the Bonnie Earl." He was a nephew of Knox's friend and Mary Stewart's half-brother, the Good Regent Moray; and a man of character and courage. The King mistrusted him and his popularity.

In February Huntly picked a quarrel with him, followed him over the Forth and attacked his castle of Donnybristle. It held out, so he piled up all the remaining fodder—an added crime in such hungry days—and set fire to all. As the flames roared up the Earl tried to break out: but his blazing hair and helmet plumes betrayed him. He was chased into the sea, shot and stabbed. As Huntly slashed him down he jeered: "Ye have spoiled a better face that your own!"

His mother had his body embalmed and brought to Edinburgh to lie in state: and had his bloody shirt on a spear carried in funeral procession through the High Street of Edinburgh. He was eventually buried in the Good Regent's tomb in St. Giles. One or two of Huntly's servants were hanged.

So loud was the outcry, from both pulpit and people, that the King thought it better to leave Edinburgh for a while. In one sermon in St. Giles, on Cain and Abel, the preacher bluntly told him: "I assure you the Lord will ask you, Where is the Earl of Moray, your brother?"

"My chamber door was never steeked against you!" cried out the King from his pew: "ye might have told me anything you thought in secret!"

"Sire, the scandal was public!"

Once or twice, when the tumult was at its height, there was a public demonstration of Huntly going into ward; with affectionate farewells from the King. But whenever it died down, he was released again. The old ballad, so glorious when sung by a good bass, hints at a possible reason:

> "He was a braw gallant,
> He rode at the glove,
> The bonnie Earl o' Moray!
> He was a Queen's true love . . ."

The dead Earl's mother, giving up hope of justice, "left her malediction upon the King and died in displeasure."

> "Lang, lang may his ladie
> Look frae the Castle Doon
> Ere she see the Earl o' Moray
> Come soonding through the toon!"

Bothwell was already nominally under arrest: but no one dared execute the warrant. A short time before he had quarrelled with a courtier called Watson in the King's presence, each giving the other "the lie direct": to which Watson added a vulgar invitation. They met in the High Street "on the penult of July, and Bothwell invaded him." Watson killed one man, but his sword stuck in him and he fled unarmed. Bothwell wounded him, cornered him in a cellar, and he and his men "stabbed him with whingers till he was dispatched."

In another High Street brawl the King, terrified always by the clash of steel, fled up a close and hid in a skinners booth "filing his breeks for fear". Again, Bothwell abducted a key witness from a friend's trial while the Judges were actually sitting, and "threatened him with the gallows." At Christmas time Bothwell and his gang broke into Holyrood, in an attempt to seize the King. The fight raged along the Long Gallery, and a courtier wrote after of "that strange hurly-burly—beholding with torchlight their reeling, their rumbling with halberts, the clacking of their culverins and pistols, the dunting of mells and hammers and their crying for justice—"Justice! Justice! A Bothwell! A Bothwell!"

Word got to the Provost, who had the city roused by the Great Bell, and seven or eight of the lesser men were caught and afterwards hanged.

A year later Bothwell tried again, this time at Falkland Palace. Nine or ten of his Border ruffians "specially Armstrongs" were taken, and five hanged: the rest were let off, as not being "ordinary or usual riders." And Bothwell continued to swagger in the High Street.

The immunity of the Candy Captains encouraged lawlessness everywhere. Robbery, violence, abduction and continuous murders went on "as if there had been no King in Israel." Even John Craig, the Royal Chaplain, when the King came to St. Giles to give thanks for his escape from Bothwell, said it was a judgement "that made the noise of crying and fore-hammers to come to his own doors."

Queen Elizabeth wrote roundly: "Good Lord! Methinks I do but dream. No King a week would bear this."—and much more on the same lines. James had risked one comment on her father—Henry VIII's—anti-social habits "in the beheading of his bed-fellows", which had roused her to transports. Now he stayed calm.

At one point the Provost and Magistrates came to the King, who asked them whom they accused—"my Lord Home, the chief author of the riot committed the last Lord's Day standing by. They answered nothing, because they expected for no justice."

But the ministers spoke up courageously, especially in St. Giles: which was then—as now—"as a watch-tower to the rest." Having admonished the King in vain, they held a meeting "in Mr. Bruce's gallery", with leading nobles: who all pledged themselves to see justice done on Huntly and Bothwell, the King reminded of his promises to the Kirk and "order taken" with the latest influx of Jesuits. Bruce and Lindsay led a deputation to Holyrood "but little thanks for their labour." After waiting an hour and a half all were allowed in the great hall and "the King sitting in a chair covered with velvet made a long and confused harangue. First, he condemned them for meeting without his warrant, and said he knew not of it till all the wives of the Kail Market knew of it . . . His harangue was tedious and ungracious."

Another time the King attacked the ministers hotly for speaking so freely against him and his friends in the pulpit, and for defending Knox, the Good Regent and Geordie Buchanan—"who could not be defended but by traitorous and seditious theologues." They replied "soundly and coldly."

Captain Stewart, once Earl of Arran, and the Master of Gray were both back at Court. Bothwell continued to escape like a Wild West film—or witchcraft.

Twice the Town Bell was rung, to warn Edinburgh that Bothwell was in town: twice he escaped. The second time two or three of his favourite women were arrested for harbouring him. Once he was chased to Leith, and his famous horse, Valentine, captured: but he went free.

Recurring fear of intrigue with the Pope flared up with the finding of the Spanish Blanks. The minister of Paisley got certain information, and although it was mid-December he at once set sail with some students of Glasgow University for the Great Cumbrae, an island in the Clyde. There, in Bute, they searched the luggage of a suspicious character, and found papers revealing negotiations between Jesuits in Scotland and Spain, blank terms signed by sympathetic Lords: and an actual memorandum drawn up by the King weighing the pros and cons of Spanish aid and the use of Scottish ports, for an English invasion. It concluded against it, with James' usual caution: but showed how seriously he considered it.

After several false alarms, Bothwell made another raid on the King: getting into Holyrood through the Gowrie town house next door. "He rapped rudely on the King's chamber door" and forced his way in—"the King sitting in the mean time on the privy and William Murray with him." Bothwell and his men seized the doors, "the King rushed in, his breeks in his hand" and "seeing no other refuge, asked what they meant? Came they to seek his life? . . ."

Bothwell fell on his knees—mockingly?—and explained that this time he came only to secure pardon, for his former raids and other "offences": and he offered to thole an assize for witchcraft. The King agreed to everything and "pardoned him all by-gauns."

But it was a crisis: James had at last been pushed too far. The English ambassador noted of him shortly after: "Then began he to reign in severity like a King."

Bothwell did do public penance in St. Giles: but as his public performance fell short, the Kirk excommunicated him. The King's favour withdrawn, men grew bolder to claim his forfeited estates: poverty discredited him, and he faded away into exile.

The King then led a campaign in the North, and compelled Huntly to become publicly a Protestant. He took Andrew Melville with him, to see justice done, and incidentally used him to collect the money for the soldiers' pay.

Only a fool would still think James a fool, when the last trick was played: for James always won. His image as an educated idiot, a pedantic buffoon, suited him very well: and he acted up to it increasingly as he aged. But behind the antics he was true to one thing only: his boyhood creed:

> "Be careful aye for to invent
> The way to get thine own intent."

So now, order restored, he turned on the Kirk. To break it, as James had always clearly understood, it was necessary to break its backbone—its "imagined democracy." His whole power was concentrated on this.

The General Assembly was his first target. Originally any business that concerned Scotland could come before this free-spoken gathering. Now James created "Permanent Commissioners", of whom he approved, to sift the business beforehand: and also arranged conferences in Holyrood before the Assembly, so that any troublesome matters likely to arise "might be quietly reasoned." This stifled free speech. (In our own day, Standing Committees and Presbytery Clubs have the same effect). Still more, it created a class of men with superior powers over their brethren. "They were as a wedge taken out of the Kirk," it was sorrowfully said, " . . . the very needle to draw in the episcopal thread."

So, in exactly the same way, are all "permanent members" of the Assembly today—ex-Moderators, officials, and other episcopal aspirants.

Davidson of St. Giles led the protest, demanding to see the King in person.

"Have ye Commission?" demanded James.

"Yes, from my Master!"

"That is witch-like spoken! Are ye a Commissioner or messenger from Christ?"

"Yes, and that ye shall find, by the Grace of God!" "At which words the King shrunk."

They then fought mainly in Latin, "going from scripture to Titus Livius." But as usual James had the last word: he refused to sanction the next Assembly unless Davidson and Andrew Melville left it: and he got the Town to put Davidson out of St. Giles. His farewell words might stand for others who have had to choose between their calling and the favour of the Establishment.

"I came not hither by haphazard, but sent of God more than seven years since. So long as I had place to teach I dealt faithfully . . . I was counted rude and rough by many: but I thank God I wist what I spake. So that I have uttered nothing against preacher or people

23

which I have not my warrant for, and by the help of God will stand to the defence of in the face of man or angel.

So that my first preaching and my last are one, without differing . . . The mighty hand of God sent me hither for causes known to Him. And so, having cleared my ministry hitherto, I take my leave of you in Christ."

James then rode to St. Andrews, to suppress a young minister called James Black. Andrew Melville came to his defence, and "breaks out in free speeches, letting the King understand plainly, as he did before, that there were two Kings in Scotland, two Kingdoms and two Jurisdictions, Christ and his." For this, James got him deposed as Rector of the University; but he was made Dean of the Faculty of Theology "to content strangers, Polonians, Danes, Low-Countrymen, Frenchmen, who had come drawn with the fame of his learning." So James got the local Presbytery to expel all Professors and so keep him muzzled.

The Assembly was, and is, the only effective Parliament Scotland ever knew. The Three Estates had always been an ineffective body: but now James declared his dismay that the Church was no longer represented on it.

"Our Sovereign Lord", began the declaration, " . . . having special consideration and regard of the privileges granted by His Highness' predecessors, of worthy memory, to the Holy Kirk within this realm and to the special persons exercising the offices, titles and dignities of prelacies within the same . . . His Majesty, of the great and singular affection he always has to the advancement of the true religion, presently professed within this realm . . ." duly decreed in short that representatives of the church should take their seat in the Three Estates. They would of course be called "my Lord," and need a due allowance to maintain their station . . . Like today's, "life peers!"

"A Trojan horse!" was the description of old Fergusson of St. Michael's, Linlithgow: and his cry, "Equo ne credite, Teucri!" "Aye!" said Davidson, "Busk him as bonnily as ye can, bring him in as fairly as ye will, we see him well enough—we see the horns of his mitre!"

But the church was at a low ebb. Its new government was not strong enough to resist the Royal pressure: the first inspiration of the Reformation was spent; it was a divided and wavering body. James might well have finished it, there and then.

The next Assembly—the 60th—was in the spring of 1596. It was encumbered with complaints, worries, directives from the King. But before it got down to business Davidson, who had gone to a little village between Edinburgh and Haddington, presented an Overture from the Presbytery of Haddington, asking them to put first things first, by calling the fathers and brethren to "universal repentance and earnest turning to God" . . . and then "maintenance of the liberty of religion and country."

The Assembly after debate accepted the Overture, and, beginning soberly with themselves, appointed "a day of humiliation before the Majesty of God", and "to make new Covenant with Him". They sifted the people: and at 9 a.m. on that March morning 400 men, ministers and "choice professors" entered the East Kirk of St. Giles, with its mud floor and white-washed walls. Many came fasting. They sang psalms, and Black preached on Joshua and the new Covenant: then Melville on Ezekiel 34, on the false shepherds, and was "very moving." He called for private prayer and repentance: and as silence deepened and grew, a sighing and then a sobbing filled the building. "They were moved as one heart." Davidson rose to preach, from Luke xii, on thanksgiving and return to God: and in climax called for all those ready to enter into a "new league with God" to raise their right hands.

This "renewal of the Covenant" brought fresh life-force into the Kirk. Men went out to carry it to the furthest corners of Scotland, to their Synods, Presbyteries, Kirk Sessions: they responded, some with communions, some fasting, all "for the getting of grace." The Kirk had re-armed: till all Scotland, like Judah of old, "rejoiced at the oath."

James retaliated at once. Davidson was sent for, and the King called him to his face "a verie stark fool, an heretic, an Anabaptist, a traitor to him, to the commonwealth, to Christ and his Kirk." He was sent to the dungeons of Edinburgh Castle, then, ill with fever, sent to answer before Haddington Presbytery: and banished from Edinburgh.

The King then summoned Black, of St. Andrews, to answer for his sermons before the Council: Black "declined their judicature" in spiritual matters as going beyond their powers. The ministers met in St. Giles, the King and his Councillors in the Tolbooth just outside. Messengers went back and forth. The crowd began to gather. They scented that this was a critical point, they grew more and more excited. Finally they broke into uncontrolled cheering and jostling— possibly on the Kirk's side.

One can imagine the wifies from the Luckenbooths that clustered round the Cathedral adding fuel to the fire! Something like a riot threatened, though the ministers tried to calm it down.

Then James played a trump card. He prorogued the Council, withdrew down the High Street to Holyrood, and next morning early sent a Herald to the Town Cross to declare a complete boycott of Edinburgh. The Court would immediately be removed: and all nobles and all strangers were ordered to withdraw at once. Edinburgh was ruined!

The ministers knew they were beaten. They had to leave Edinburgh for the city's own good. The magistrates then sought out James, went down on their knees and promised to pay 20,000 merks if he would lift the ban. It was his complete victory.

C

The money would be useful too. As his mother's French secretary had once noted, James lived entirely on debt. His servants, unpaid, could not afford to leave him. At this very time one of his goldsmiths had fallen down in a seizure through worry over the King's debts. His problem was met by absolving him from paying his creditors, who were ordered not to trouble him. Only "Jinglin' Geordie" Heriot, the High Street goldsmith, was always able and willing to finance the King.

Andrew Melville also went after the King, on what was meant to be a peace mission and a plea for the Kirk and its absent ministers. It began that way, but "The King interrupted and crabbitly quarrelled their meeting, alleging it was without warrant and seditious . . . Mr. Andrew could not abide it, but brake off upon the King in so zealous, powerful and unresistable a manner, that howbeit the King used his authority in a maist crabbit and choleric manner, yet Mr. Andrew bore him down, and uttered the commission as from the Almighty God, calling the King but God's sillie vassal, and taking him by the sleeve, saying this in effect . . . "Sir, as divers times before so now again I must tell you, there are two Kings and two Kingdoms in Scotland: there is Christ Jesus, and his Kingdom the Kirk, whose subject King James VI is, and of His Kingdom not a King nor a Head nor a Lord, but a member."

Melville was lucky to be merely exiled: but James bided his time.

Having cowed the Kirk, James had the next Assembly called to Dundee: to suit the Aberdeenshire members, who had, traditionally, episcopal leanings. There at last it was passed that the Kirk should have a vote in the Estates:- that is, that it should have special commissioners thereto, with special rank and privileges, though they were not officially called Bishops. The rest of the Assembly was "drifted and wearied at the King's pleasure." But the main point had been gained: the democracy of the Kirk was destroyed.

James celebrated his victory by two publications; pedantic in style, possibly, but revealing in the depth of their conviction. The first was the *Trew Law of Free Monarchies*, and the second, fuller book, designed to be a manual of Kingcraft for his infant son, Henry, Duke of Rothesay, was called the Golden Book, *Basilicon Doron*. Both are impassioned expositions of the Divine Right of Kings. "The free and absolute monarch," wrote James, was the sole natural father to all his people: and even among "brute beasts and unreasonable creatures . . . we never read or hear of any resistance to their parents, *except among the vipers*." He sums it all up with three lines of Virgil: "that sublime and heroicall Poet wherein also my diction is included" (and the last line he had printed in italics: "To spare the humble, and to cast down the proud"): *"Parcere subjectis, et debellare superbos"*.

Against the confidence of this faith in naked power, the Kirk's belief in another system, another Kingdom, seems pathetic, even ludicrous.

Seldom more so than in the interview—one of many such—between the King and a minister. This was one Gibson, who with his wife and family lived and died on the very edge of want. The King heard treasonable reports of his preaching, sent for him and, eventually, interrogated him.

"What was your text?"

"Out of the 16th of Matthew, sir, these words: "If any man will come after me, let him deny himself, and take up his cross, and follow me.""

That was unexceptional: but the sermon had somehow preceded to the 2nd Chronicles, chapter xxiv, with its story of the infant prince, Joash, preserved and brought up by the High Priest, and presented by him to the people to be their King: who, after the death of the High Priest, forsook the ways of the Lord and when the prophets reproved him, killed them: so that judgement came upon him, his country was ravaged with war, his sons deserted him, and his servants slew him; and eventually his whole House fell: "and so should the King, if he continued in that cursed course . . ."

"Said ye that?"

"Yes, sir."

Surely the King looked at the starveling, scarecrow figure in front of him, and burst out into roar of laughter as he cried:

"I give not a turd for thy preaching!"

Yet so fell the House of Stewart.

CHAPTER FOUR

MURDER MYSTERY I: THE POT OF GOLD

Having lived nineteen years in the Manse of St. Giles, and known at first hand the continuous pressure put on its minister to conform and keep his mouth shut, it is a grim comfort to look back at the minister's wife whose least fear was destitution: and whose husband risked public hanging, or the living death of the dungeon.

James had always been friendly with Robert Bruce, who was at least his equal in descent, and so much his superior in gifts. Bruce seems to have been genuinely fond of him, perhaps sorry for his loneliness. But after the tumult in Edinburgh over Black, the King took a different line. Bruce must be brought to heel, St. Giles curbed. The ministers were allowed back to Edinburgh, the King kept their manses and held parties in them. There seems to have been no fixed manse since.

His first step was to appoint "colleagues"—accursed word!—to the ministers of St. Giles. They were two dim creatures, chosen by the King for their subservience. The Kirk thought it better to give way and accept. After all, it needn't make much difference! But Bruce held out. He refused to accept them, refused to give the Moderator a brotherly hand when out-voted, refused to attend the Session when they had been voted into it. He was threatened with being put out: and had immediately to face the dilemma of every minister under pressure, in every age: how far to give way, in order not to give up. In a letter to a friend he sums it up in words that do for all.

"I am lost in verie great doubt. On the one hand I am sorry to leave the children of God in the city: I am sorry to want my exercise, that presence of God that sanctified me: and fear to incur the bruit that I left my station, that I have given over the battle, and put up my sword.

"On the other side again, I see this manner of entry is not sanctified, but very corrupt . . . and if we shall accept of them at this time I see a dangerous preparative established in this city, to be a precedent for all the Kirks of Scotland . . .

"If I hold out, and accept not, my removing may be a ground another time to reform the corruption. If I accept, I cannot see how it can be reformed in any time hereafter . . . rending of action followeth rending of hearts.

"What is most expedient I am uncertain. But I am instant with His Majesty that in the light of his Spirit it may be given me to see which of the two will please him best."

The next move was more subtle. The King suggested that Bruce take "a particular flock," along with some new-appointed ministers: and the Moderator then said, at the King's direction: "Ye must have ordination besides" (i.e. more than) "the rest." For Bruce had never been formally ordained.

Bruce realised that to accept this, to "be made a spectacle more than the rest," would mean that he had "run unsent to this people eleven years bygone," and that his minstry there was invalid, his sacraments a mockery.

"As to the ceremony, I take it to be indifferent, and may serve as well for confirmation" (in his ministry) "as ordination; I will not refuse it, if that may please you," he said in St. Giles, addressing the King's Commissioner who occupied the pulpit: "Only subscribe this ticket, that I may be sure ye mean no other thing." He read the "ticket" to the congregation, then asked the commissioner to sign it, offering a quill: but the latter threw it over the pulpit instead. The Session stood by Bruce. "The Elders sitting on the forms, cried all with a loud voice, "We acknowledge him to be our pastor!" and in token thereof took him by the hand."

So the Kirk Session of St. Giles showed their courage and their loyalty.

But the argument dragged on, with Bruce's ministry at a complete standstill while he was badgered and bullied, back and forth, from this body to that. If only he would agree to this, or see that one, or accept the following! He wrote things down, they were re-written, argued over, delayed. Preaching the word of God, shepherding the people, giving of himself in any fruitful manner, must have been at a standstill.

His Moderator was anxious to keep peace with the great ones, and gave way to them completely. His friends too deserted, and condemned him for "standing on trifles." ("Do the Christian thing, old boy, and give way! . . ."). When he held out, he was called a very familiar word: "Trouble-maker!" Always and everywhere it is one man's burden.

One morning he was found to be missing, and discovered walking several miles out of Edinburgh—"to get some air." Again, he turned on his tormentors and "bursting forth in the grief of his heart, said they had persecuted him extremely . . . that he could never remember that he ever abused any of them." Then "there passed not a Saturday for fifteen weeks whereon the King did not send one messenger or other to trouble his meditation."

Bruce was outed in May. But Edinburgh presbytery, remarkably, stood by him and "gave their resolute answer, without contradiction, that they acknowledged, and acknowledge him to be a lawful pastor of the said Kirk."

Possibly because of this a compromise was reached. A hand was laid on his head during the service: but only after a signed declaration had been read from the pulpit that this was not an ordination! (All Churches threatened with unity take note!)

At this time a blind minister had been ordained: another break with Roman tradition, which accepted no one physically imperfect.

James had decreed that ministers should be "snybbed sharply" if they preached politics: but "godly, learned and modest men . . . whom-of, God be praised, there lacketh not a reasonable number," should be "entertained and advanced" to Bishoprics, which would "banish their Parity which cannot agree with Monarchy . . ." He proudly claimed "my aphorism—Nae Bishop, Nae King!"

"Yes, Sire, ye may have Bishops here," said old Fergusson of St. Michael's Kirk, Linlithgow," but remember, you must make us all Bishops . . . we are Paul's Bishops, Sire, Christ's Bishops . . ."

The King next sent for the four ministers of Edinburgh, and gave them a sharp talk on keeping within the Law: which they assured him they were humbly willing to do, if only he would "save our religion as we have it already established by our own laws and the Word of God."

"Will ye suspect me?" sayeth the King.

"We suspect an angel, if an angel bring another gospel," say they.

"Well," says the King, "upon your own peril be it. I assure you ye shall be punished, to the example of others." And this he repeated oftener than ten times.

He grew more detailed. "If ye speak against me, my crown or estate, hanging shall be the pain for the first fault . . ."

"In whose hands is the pain, Sire?"

"It is in my hands, given to my arbitrement . . ."

The result of the King making himself the law was soon seen. When Bruce married, his father had given him back the little family property of Kinnaird, and this he had settled on his wife and family. The King now seized it, on a pretext. Bruce took the matter to law: the judge happened to be something of an enemy to the Reformed Church, but with a courage and integrity rare in any day he found for Bruce. The King seized the property none the less.

"Brother, my heart:" wrote Bruce to a young man entering the ministry: "I write thee to prepare thee in good earnest and with a good heart, lifted up and poured out upon God in Christ. Take pains, my heart, great pains, inward and secret pains: nothing is won without great diligence. My enemies, the worst that they can do, the Lord has turned into the best. I never got such access in my time as I have gotten since I went from you. The treasures of his riches have been opened unto me. Howsoever Edinburgh has cast me off, rejected and banished me out of their parts, I leapt no sooner on my horse but the gates of heaven were cast open to me. And so, my heart, although man has left me, and namely your ministry; yet my sweet Lord has not left me. I never

30

foregathered with a better Master: I never got a sweeter fee and better wages: and I look for a very rich reward."

In this last year of the 16th century James was master in Scotland: almost that absolute ruler which was his dream and his people's dread. He might complain in a letter to Cecil that "he was daily dauntoned in trying to bursten in a wild unrewly colt," but only Bruce remained unbroken. Then a last hope arrived to cheer his discouraged people.

Since the execution of that Lord Ruthven, Earl of Gowrie, who had been one of James' captors in the days of his first love, (d'Aubigny) the young Earl his son had lived abroad. He had studied at Padua University, and had been so popular that he was made Rector. If you go to the University there, and into the old quadrangle, you will find painted on the roof of the cloister the arms of these medieval rectors—many more "Scotus" than "Anglicus," (including the suspiciously elaborate crest of one, "Sandius Scotus!") There too you will still see the proud arms of young Ruthven, Earl of Gowrie: all these centuries after they were stamped out in Scotland.

When Gowrie set off to return to Scotland he went first to Geneva, where he stayed a while, meeting Beza, who had so admired Knox. Beza was greatly impressed with him, both with his qualities of character and leadership, and with his great sincerity in the Reformed faith. From there he went on to England, where he was well received at Court. Queen Elizabeth praised him, and may have wondered what use she could make of him: for like many of the Scots nobles, he was partly Royal, and that part was said to be descended from Margaret Tudor, sister to Henry VII, (grandfather of Queen Elizabeth) and wife of James IV. A contemporary called Gowrie:

"Queen Margaret's grandson, nigher in degree
Was Gowrie's ruin, and King James' plea . . ."

If that could be proved, he might have a better claim to the throne of England than James himself: and Elizabeth, who had taken James's measure through letters and her spies, might well prefer him. He was described to her, by her Ambassador in Paris, as "one of whom there may be exceeding good use made".

By the time he landed at Leith in February he received an almost Royal welcome. A great concourse of nobles and commons met him, and escorted him tumultuously up Leith Walk to the High Street. When James heard what the crowd was for, he made one remark: "There were more to see his feyther, when he went to the scaffold."

Gowrie was in time to attend the Convention of the Three Estates: where he courageously opposed the King's request for more money. The thought of the huge sums still owing to his house must have been in men's minds. Later that week he breakfasted at Holyrood, and as he leaned on the King's chair, while they discussed dogs and horses, the King asked what seemed most likely to cause miscarriage, in hound or woman? A sudden fright, said Gowrie: and the King turned on him: "If that had been true, my Lord, I had not been sitting here."

And men knew this was a reference not only to the stabbing of Rizzio as he clung to his mother's skirts three months before he was born, but also to the prominent part played by Gowrie's grandfather, old Lord Ruthven, on that occasion.

Gowrie went home to his Castle at Perth, welcomed surely by his mother and young brother, and most royally by the city of Perth, which had kept the Provostship vacant for him for the six years of his exile. He was adored by the townsfolk, and throughout his broad heritage of "lands, baronies, castles and fortalices: mills, fisheries—salt and fresh water—manors, farms, "touns" and chapels." He must have enjoyed himself riding round them again, that spring and summer of 1600: but such possessions bred covetousness, and he had his enemies.

On the 5th of August the King and his court were about to start hunting in Falkland Great Park, when young Ruthven, the Earl's brother, advanced to speak to him. The King said afterwards, in his official narrative, that he told him a tale of a mysterious stranger with a pot of gold who had been discovered at Gowrie Castle, and that he had asked the King to come and see it without telling anyone. (It was, as Bruce pointed out afterwards, an odd tale).

The King and court then rode for Gowrie House, arriving quite obviously unexpectedly. The Earl was attending a wedding in Perth, and had to be fetched. One tradition says he borrowed the wedding breakfast to feed his unlooked-for guests: and certainly they all had to stand about and wait while dinner was got ready, with frantic confusion all around.

(If all this was a plot, argued Robert Bruce afterwards, "why was there not better cheer prepared, if it had been but to colour the enterprise?" Also, while they all stood about and waited, why did the King not go at once to see this pot of gold?)

Dinner of a sort was scraped together: and after it the King pledged Gowrie in a loving-cup and asked him to take it throughout and share it with his other guests: while he siezed the chance to slip away with young Ruthven secretly—the official narrative says, at Ruthven's request. They went up to one of the high turrets where, in a top room, said the King, they found no prisoner with a pot of gold but an armed man. Ruthven snatched a dagger from this man and held it at the King's breast, "swearing many bloody oaths, that if the King cried one word, or opened the window to look out, that dagger should presently go to his heart; affirming that he was sure that now the King's conscience was burdened, for the murdering of his father."

The narrative then forsakes circumstantial evidence for poetic effect; and James is discovered, calm and unmoved, using such

32

persuasive and effective arguments, both on religious and human grounds (and they are given fully) that Ruthven is quite abashed, and says that he will fetch the Earl his brother: and while he is away the King uses the same argument on the armed man, who was masked, until "God so turned his heart at that time, as he became a slave to his prisoner." Yet James was always faint over naked steel!

Meanwhile the Earl, having missed the King, was told by one of his royal servants that he had ridden off to Falkland: and vexed by this unceremonious departure, called for horses at top speed. The court flung themselves again into the saddle, and were passing beneath that very turret—which overlooked the road to Falkland—when the topmost window was flung open, and the King appeared shouting: "Help! Murder! Treason!" and struggling with Ruthven whose hand was at his mouth—to kill him, as the King said? Or merely to stifle these dreadful cries?

One of the Murrays—enemies of the Gowries—cried out that the Earl was to blame, and knocked him down: he jumped up and ran for arms. The King's page, Ramsay, meantime led other nobles at top speed up the turret stairs—having no trouble with the locked doors James mentions in such detail in the account—and rushed in where the King and Ruthven were grappling, Ramsay striking at him with his sword, and the King calling out to strike low, as he wore a padded doublet: so he stabbed him twice, and threw him down the stairs, where the two nobles following finished him off: though it was said he still had strength to roll over and cry out: "Alas! I had not the wyte of it!" (i.e. guilt).

Gowrie then ran in—the account says, with seven servants, all with drawn swords, and crying with a great oath they should all die as traitors. Yet it was after proved that only Thomas Cranston of Cranston was with him. He seems to have brought two swords—one for his brother?—but when he saw a bloody corpse lying covered with some cloth, and someone said it was the King, he lowered the points in horror: and at that moment Ramsay stabbed him to the heart from behind. Was there silence then, but for the flapping of Ramsay's hooded hawk through the blood?

The King fell on his knees, calling on all those present to do likewise, and "His Majesty out of his own mouth thanked God of that miraculous deliverance and victory, assuring himself that God had preserved him from so desperate a peril, for the perfecting of some greater work behind, to His glory" . . .

The whole town of Perth came crying to the gates, "Give us our Provost!" but according to the narrative the King quieted them with soothing speeches and gestures from the turret. (At one point the old cry of "Come down, thou son of Signor Davie!" was raised—but this is *not* mentioned in the official account).

The court rode off, leaving behind a building to be known henceforth as "Huntingtower"; for the very name, and arms, of

Gowrie were to be stamped out for ever. They left desolation behind. The very corpses of the young men might not be buried, but kept, decomposing, for trial. This did not take place till November, when they were naturally found guilty, dismembered, and quarters sent to be hung above the gates of Perth, their own city. But the men sent to take the two younger brothers were just too late: they had been warned, and had slipped over the Border. There they managed to live, penniless and friendless, until James' accession in England, when he put both in the Tower.

One eventually disappeared abroad, the other was released after nearly twenty years, married the only daughter of Vandyke, the court painter, and left one lovely, penniless daughter, Justiniana, whose face was her fortune, for she married a knight. So, in one afternoon, fell the whole House of Gowrie: eighteen years to the very month after the King had been held prisoner within its walls: "With patience then see thou attend, And hope to vanquish at the end."

Meanwhile James sent Heralds posting through the country to declare at each Town Cross the King's wonderful deliverance, and to call on the people to rejoice and give thanks. The narrative, printed a month after the event, mentions specifically the grateful throngs coming forward to cheer him as he rode back. But it is undeniable that the estates would only accept the directive with the added phrase: "if it be true:" and the Kirk would only give thanks for his escape "from whatever danger it had been." When the King summoned them to answer for that, they said they "could not descend into particulars . . . in respect they had no certainty." Yet the King's Chaplain, becoming literally a propaganda minister, had already given long detailed accounts at Edinburgh Town Cross, with passionate invective against the Gowries, and exhortations to rejoice.

Much of "the matter of Gowrie" remains mystery. Books have been written by royalist supporters—presumably episcopalians—to prove James completely innocent. But they over-strain credulity. As the people noted at the time, there were inexplicable gaps. The character of Gowrie himself, so praised by Reformer Beza, who wept for his death. How could such a man turn traitor and murderer without warning? Or at the least, without preparation? Indeed, why should he, with the ball at his feet? Above all, why in his own house, where he could not but be held accountable? Then, though no one could expect to see the pot of gold, what happened to the armed man in the turret, or to his dagger which young Ruthven was supposed to have taken? Ruthven had neither dagger nor whinger on him when found dead, only an old dress rapier rusted into its scabbard. The Earl himself had only the swords he had fetched, and his cloak was still fastened up for riding. Also, why would Ruthven hold a dagger to the King's breast and then "stay for parley?" How could the King drag young Ruthven, who was twice as as strong, to the window and back to the door?

("Mr. Patrick Galloway, the Chaplain, in his harangue, calleth this a miracle.")

Unfortunately Mr. Patrick Galloway got so excited in his harangues to the crowd that he deviated quite palpably both from his previous accounts and from the King's "History."

Had this been all, it could still have been some unexpected incident.

The King might have made some amorous attack on young Ruthven, who had already applied to be a Gentleman of the Bedchamber and then fiding himself repulsed, taken revenge. But there were other unexplained oddities: the cry that the King had gone off to Falkland, for instance, which ensured that the rout was clattering by beneath the turret window at exactly the right moment . . . Most of all there is the tale of rewards and punishments afterwards, which adds up to a damning total.

First, Ramsay the page who did the deeds was created Viscount Haddington, given Melrose Abbey, a pension of £1,000 a year and the right to ask a favour at the anniversary banquet James gave in celebration each 8th of August. Like his mother, James was strongly addicted to anniversaries. Of course, if Ramsay had to be kept silent, an annual sum was the best way to do it. As a footnote: it was recently proved it was Ramsays' (lucky?) dagger that was used later to assassinate Henri IV, King of France.

Of the Lords who rushed to attack the Gowries at the King's first cries, Erskine got Dirleton, Sir Hugh Herries got Coupar, and Sir David Murray, Gowrie's chief rival, was made Lord Scone and Provost of Perth and was very much the King's creature from then on.

Perth itself, lest it murmur, was granted a special charter on the very day of Gowrie's forfeiture, which gave it supremacy and special rights, long coveted, over its age-old rival, Dundee. And as a mark of special favour, the King consented to be made a Freeman of the City. When signing his name as "the youngest Burgess" he added—was it a particularly nasty joke?—that line of Virgil:

"Parcere subjectis et debellare superbos."

Two loyal servants were hanged, for no apparent reason other than that they had run, unarmed, to aid Gowrie at the first outcry. One, McGregor, had actually risen from his bed, being ill: the other, Craigengelt, had been first to take up the new-killed bodies (at this point in evidence he "interrupted long, when remembering on my Lord.") Cranstoun of that Ilk was also hanged, for running behind Gowrie with a sword drawn, though he had thought it was for the King's protection. He made a rather witty speech on the scaffold, saying his death should be a warning against swearing: for his besetting sin was to use three oaths: "God, nor a sword go through me!" "May I be ta'en for a traitor!" and "God, nor I be hanged!" and though he thanked God he had deserved none of these things, yet they had all come to pass . . ."

Rhind, Gowrie's young tutor and companion, was tortured savagely to make him incriminate the Earl: but since he could not or would not do so, he too was hanged.

On the other hand Henderson, Gowrie's chamberlain, was at once taken on in the service of the new Lord Scone, Gowrie's enemy. As if in penance, he tried to confess that he was the man in the turret: but the King would have none of it: he said he "knew yon wee smeek well eneuch!" The missing man was decided to be a servant of Gowrie's called Younger who had disappeared—presumed fled. However, he turned up in Dundee, having been sent on an errand previously. Horrified to hear the tale against him, he set off in haste to clear his name: but a guard of the King's set off to intercept him. They met him at a cornfield, and the poor wretch took refuge among the stooks. A nightmare game of hare-and-hounds followed: the hallooing and running, the spent breath choking the exhausted quarry: the forseen end, the squealing, the stabbing: the silence.

Why was he not taken alive? people asked: and asked the same of Gowries and others. But no material witness was.

Younger's corpse was taken to the Cross, where Galloway made another harangue, glorying in so suitable an end to such a traitor. Galloway's pension was now doubled by the King, and he was later made a Bishop.

Meanwhile the King, feeling in spite of a public declaration that he was not making headway with public opinion, blamed it on the Kirk. Davidson, who had refused to preach thanksgiving, was told he would not preach at all, unless he confessed his fault and craved pardon. He was ordered into close house-arrest for the rest of his life: "Were he not an auld man, he should be hangit!" said the King. Melville, who made neat references to Caligula, was punished: and Cornwall the Town Officer who was auctioning a debtor's effects when he found a portrait of the King and nailed it to the gibbet— presumably with suitable comment—was hanged for it.

The King then summoned the minsters of Edinburgh and demanded of them, one by one, if they were "fully persuaded" of the truth of his narrative. Two accepted, and promised to preach on his behalf. Others refused: were sent out: brought back: forbidden to preach, and ordered to leave Edinburgh within forty eight hours. Next day they offered to thank God for the King's delivery, repeat his own "history touching that treason," and speak nothing "to the contrary." But now the King's terms had stiffened: they must also humbly confess their fault and crave pardon. So they went.

Robert Bruce, trained lawyer, said he "must have further light, before I preached it—if I were but a private subject, not a pastor, I could rest upon your Majesty's report, as others do."

Then began a fantastic campaign. The King knew that unless Bruce confessed himself fully convinced, the doubt would remain. So the whole force of possible pressure—threat and exile, bribe, persuasion and tantalising promise—was brought to bear on this one man standing quite alone, confused by his own doubts, baffled by his own loneliness. (Across the centuries I catch the echo: "They can't *all* be wrong!")

In the first interview with the King—the first of so many—the chancellor made Bruce hold up his right hand and solemnly swear to tell the truth. He was asked where he had been? Who had been in company with him? And if he was "resolved touching the last treason or not?" He answered: "I am in the way of resolution, but not fully resolved." "What moveth you," said the King, "more than the rest of your brethren?" . . .

"Well, Sir, let them live in their own faith," said Bruce, "I must live in mine: so far as I know, I shall preach, and further I will not promise" . . .

"I see, Mr. Robert, that ye would make me a murderer," said the King at the end.

Finally, Bruce was told to confine himself to the family home at Airth. There he heard that one by one the other ministers had given in and were "resolved" of the King's innocence.

"If we had spoken all one thing, I had not been in this case", wrote Bruce to his wife: "And yet I would not be in their case for all the benefit they have gotten: for the court giveth it out, that they are sent to make their repentance, each of them in so many Kirks . . . So, he maketh a triumph and spectacle of their ministry".

Bruce's agony was as much the conflict within as that without. He surely longed to believe James innocent, for his King and country's sake as well as his own. Eagerly he pursued every thread of evidence; only to run, each time, into a dead end.

"The Lord help my unbelief!" he wrote, "I will trust the report of my Prince: I will trust the report of noble men . . . but I can trust no report of man as a very undoubted truth, but the report of Him who is God also . . . I crave to be led by the Spirit of Truth in this particular, and have been instant, after my manner, with my God: and I am in that hope, that as yet he has not deserted me . . . communicate your light with me, any of you that has farther than I . . ."

But the darkness deepened. He was beginning a journey into the desert that would take him the last thirty-odd years of his life: where no fruitful thing could grow, and the devils of mist and mirage continually assaulted him. The very worst of his agony was not so much its uselessness as its needlessness: for James had already determined that he would never get back to St. Giles. Yet the promise of it, temptingly nea was dangled before him all that time!

He was banished to France: he was banished to England: he was interviewed by Scots nobles passing through, with that mixture of half-promise and vague flattery that, as an ex-courtier himself, he recognised for what it was worth: and this he wrote to his wife— "Dear Heart"—as frankly as to another man. (But the servants had gone out of their way to show him kindness: he was grateful for it).

He was brought back to Edinburgh, and had a long interview with the King at Craigmillar. He was now asked not only to believe the official narrative, but to crave pardon and "purge the King" in various places. Bruce spoke of St. Giles "where I behoved to stand, while I got very good light . . . I had never a calling of God, as yet, to any place in this land, save to Edinburgh. There I found His Majesty's blessing in some measure. Place me there where God placed me . . . but as to go through the country and make proclamations here and there, it will be counted either a beastly fear or a beastly flattery in me."

One noble tried to persuade him that the word "fully" was unnecessary, and meant nothing. "Not so, my Lord," said Bruce, "for if you and I were *fully* persuaded there was a Hell, we should act other than we do!"

Three months later the King sent for Bruce again, trying every wile of friendly persuasion. Bruce kept up a silent prayer: "O Lord, keep my heart unto Thee, and save me from the danger that this traitorous and false heart would cast me into." To the King he pleaded: "I have a body and some goods, let his Majesty use these as God shall direct him: but as to my inward peace . . . suffer me to keep it as God of His mercy enable me." Not only was he badgered about the country, interviewed by this one and that, but the nightmare of endless papers, altered here and there, twisted this way and that, occupied his life continuously. To win free, he at last gave in and agreed to sign a paper accepting what the Parliament had already accepted legally. But he then found it was not enough, unless he thoroughly discredited the Kirk and "stained the glory of my ministry." He gave up hope.

"I have wracked certainly a piece of my heart to pleasure your Majesty. Now, seeing your Majesty cannot be satisfied except I make shipwreck of all, let me go in God's name."

His brethren now came to Bruce, set on no doubt, by the King, with what is always the bitterest blow of all: "The whole number said, he stood upon trifles."

But his own way was growing clearer to him, and he was able to answer: "There is a better cause nor I wracked, and in greater danger nor I am in. Ye know yourself in what estate the discipline of the Kirk stands in: what encroaching, what usurpation is daily increased on the spiritual Kingdom."

Against the wasted years and wasted gifts was the achievement of standing steadfast in the gate. As he faced exile in Inverness—further and more heathen, in these roadless days, than France—a friend heard him crying out of the desolation of his isolation that "if it be the Lord's good pleasure to exercise him with a new temptation, to pull the people and the ministry both from him, that it would please the Lord instead of the King, priest and people's favour to triple his Spirit upon him, and let him see in his heart His face brighter and brighter . . ."

CHAPTER FIVE

MURDER MUSTERY II:
THE KEGS OF GUNPOWDER

March, 1603, and the Warden of the Marches knelt, bruised, bloodied, mud-soaked, by James' bed: handing him a ring which he had once given to Queen Elizabeth, and hailing him as King of England. The Marches between the two countries no longer existed.

James could hardly wait to set off. He polished off some minor details—hung Black Pate of the Orkneys, which was welcome, and outlawed all clan MacGregor and clan MacNab, which was very severe (the pibroch runs, "We are landless! landless! Gregalach!"): and he made a farewell speech in St. Giles after the sermon. "There is no more difference betwixt London and Edinburgh," he said, with horrid prophetic accuracy: and then with much less accuracy: " . . . I shall visit you every three year at least, or ofter, as I shall have occasion." He returned in fact only once. He thanked God he had settled both Kirk and Kingdom; and "left them in that estate which he intended not to hurt or alter any wise, his subjects living in peace."

"Tuesday, ye 5th Aprile: the King riding by to England," noted John Davidson in the diary which surely helped him through the weary days. All along James' triumphal festal route the gaols were opened and prisoners freed—except for murderers and ministers! Having seen his last hope pass by, Davidson died next year. He had one interesting visitor first: John Knox's widow, who had married Kerr of Fawdonside and now came, a laird's wife, with one of her grown sons—a lad new-come from France in the latest fashion of short scarlet cloak and long rapier. Seeing gifts in the lad, Davidson suggested he lay cloak and sword aside and tackle the harder battles of the Kirk: which he afterwards did.

After James had gone, the Queen made a pathetic and very vigorous effort to get back her little son, Prince Henry: and was in the end successful. She took him back to Holyrood with her: and on Tuesday the last of May she rode up to the Great Kirk of St. Giles with him in a coach—"accompanied with many English ladies in coaches, and some riding on fair horses. Great was the confluence of people flocking to see the Prince." They travelled South together next month.

England gave James a royal welcome, and he gave it his whole heart. Everything delighted him—the riches, the Bishops, the soft speeches, the soft air: it is summed up for ever in his speech at the Hampton Court Conference the following year, where he could not restrain "a gratulation to Almighty God . . . for bringing him to the Promised Land."

Only for a moment did a caterpillar show among the bed of roses, when on the second day of the conference, some Puritans spoke: James was swift to squelch. "I will have one doctrine, one discipline, one Religion, in substance, in ceremony." The suggestion of clergymen meeting every three weeks roused him to fury. "If you aim at a Scottish Presbytery, it agreeth as well with monarchy as God and the Devil. Then Jack, and Tom and Will and Dick shall meet the censure me and my council."

He stormed on. Theology he revelled in, using the longest and occasionally the foulest words: but the faintest whiff of "imagined Democracy" touched what Williamson called "the throbbing nerve of sovereignty" in him.

To the English he was a joke, and a bad joke at that: a pompous, hypocritical buffoon. Judging by the history-books, he still is! But James as usual bided his time: and, as usual, got the last word.

His manners certainly startled them. He had a habit, at the mort of the stag, of slitting up its belly and paddling his weak legs in the hot blood. "The manners," wrote one courtier, "made me devise the beasts were pursuing the sober creation."

He had installed his wife and children—whom he had always disliked about the house—to begin with in Denmark House, later in St. James'. His Candy Captains he had brought with him: of whom a courtier wrote: "The King's kissing them after so lascivious a mode in public . . . prompted many to imagine some things done in the (re)tiring-house that exceed my expressions no less than they do my experience." They found his steady, continual tippling, even when all day in the saddle, more disconcerting than debauch. He never washed, he gobbled his food, he was a perfect pig over strawberries: he talked braid Scots, made bad jokes and gave comic and often insulting nicknames. In short, he acted fully up to his part as a clown.

But it was James who invented the name Great Britain: James who imposed it on a reluctant England: James who invented that Government of Scotland "by the pen"—so damnably effective still. He tried hard also to get a joint Parliament, and parity in trading privileges: but these the alarmed English would not grant to "the beggarly Scots." He could, when he chose, sift true from false evidence, and eventually discredited witch-hunts. And he published an extensive treatise on the evils of tobacco-smoking, and the harm that must follow from drawing dirty flue-smoke down into the lungs, besides blowing it "athwart the dishes," which it has taken the medical profession nearly 400 years to appreciate. If you go to the tiny library of Innerpeffray, near Crieff in Perthshire, you can see a lovely copy of this work.

"So is an Ant an animal as well as an Elephant: a wren is Avis as well as a Swan: and so is a small dint of the Toothache a disease as well as the fearful Plagues. And surely in my opinion "—(hear hear)?—" there cannot be a more base and yet hurtful corruption in a country than the vile use, or abuse, of Tobacco."

He writes of "This filthy smoke being sucked up by the Nose is cast forth again in watery distillations." And he cites that courtier to Alexander Severus who was choked to death by smoke for selling his master's favours: "What of those who spend £300 or £400 a year on this precious Stink?"

"Is it not shameful imbecility that you are not able to ride or walk the journey of a Jew's Sabbath but you must have a reekie coal brought to you from the next poor house to kindle your Tobacco?"

Smokers, he maintained, had "an oily kind of soot inside" when opened after death. The habit was "a custom loathsome to the eye, hateful to the Nose, harmful to the brain, dangerous to the lungs and the black stinking fume thereof nearest resembling the horrible Stygian smoke of the Pit that is bottomless."

He deserves reprinting.

James began his reign with an act of mercy: James' kind of mercy. Three plotters had been caught, in one of Cecil's endless webs of information. They were sentenced to death, and brought out one by one to the public scaffold. The slow ghastly ritual was gone through: the last prayers, the farewells: then, at the last minute, the first man was given a postponement, two hours more to prepare. The second man was then brought, and again the ritual mounted slowly till he turned to the block: where he was halted because he was told, the third man was to die first. So he too was taken back. The third man was brought out—the most timid: the over-wrought crowd can hardly have helped him as he struggled for composure: but he had in fact achieved it, and was facing his end with some courage when he too was halted: to wait for the other two. They were then brought back, and so they met once more in life—"gazing at one another strangely, like men met between heaven and earth." The sheriff once more read over their crimes, their sentences: waited for their assent to its justice: and then announced the King's mercy—a pardon, but to ruin and imprisonment. So the grisly farce closed in great cheering.

Another of James' interests was the Ecumenical Movement: the dream of a World Church, with all its possibilities of power and its suppression of minorities and dissenting voices, appealed to him most strongly. He planned a General Council with the Pope, and was in correspondence about it for some time. He had begun his reign by suspending the Recusancy Laws against the Roman Catholics, and letting them live in peace. The size of the Catholic congregations which now re-appeared in public and began to grow was indeed alarming. But the legislation proposed against them, for the sake of the peace of the country, would have been unpopular at this point. It was only when the Gunpowder Plot apparently forced his hand that it went through, and they were crushed: like the Gowries . . .

41

D

So like the Gowries that to read one plot on top of the other takes one's breath away.

This one also began with a mysterious message. It was in the shape of a letter which had come to Chief Minister, Cecil's hands, and which he presented to the King in a public place: explaining at the same time that it was really of no significance. James was immediately guided to believe that it was: and quite a duologue took place between them on those lines.

The man who produced the letter for Cecil in the first place was one Monteagle: a shadowy figure, who was clearly in the confidence of the Catholics of the day. But unlike them, he did well out of the revelations. As with Gowrie, the rewards and punishments were extravagant.

The letter begged the recipient not to attend Parliament, because of some great and dreadful danger, which was not detailed; but it would be "over so soon as this is read." Cecil drew the King's attention to this in particular, as being nonsensical: and the King was not only guided to see it of the deepest significance but somehow inspired further to solve the riddle with the word: Gunpowder!

From then on, all was discovery: and London rocked and reeled under the ever-growing revelations, the out-size evil. This wholesale crime,—and it grew like the quantity of powder with every telling—gave wholesale horror. Yet again, there are curious blanks. "From the moment of the discovery," notes Father Gerard, "the discovered gunpowder disappears from history." So oddly like the pot of gold! The more remarkable, in fact, in that gunpowder was at that date a State monopoly, and it was never explained how the conspirators had got all that amount in the first place.

Guy Fawkes, a known Roman Catholic and possibly an agent, was caught and consigned straight to the Tower. James himself sent word, in Latin, that he was to be tortured gently at first and then by slow degrees to the very uttermost. By the 7th he had said nothing—yet the Government then issued a Proclamation for the arrest of all other conspirators by name. By November 17th, Fawkes "confessed" anything and everything they wished: but he could no longer sign more than a few letters of his name. Without Guy Fawkes, the Attorney General Coke noted with satisfaction, "the proceedings would not have been so orderly or justifiable."

For the men named as the main conspirators—Catesby, Percy and two brothers Wright—were all killed at Holbeach, where they had been pursued. How were they all killed? Sir Thomas Lawley reported to Cecil that due to "the extreme disorder of the baser sort" they had all died of wounds. But it is a fact that John Streete, sheriff's officer, was awarded 2s. a day for life "for that extraordinary service by him performed in killing those two traitors, Percy and Catesby, with two bullets at one shot out of his musket." Is there not an echo of Gowrie here, of the insistent question why not one was saved alive for trial?

"The oddest thing about the Gunpowder Plot," wrote Donald Carswell in his book on it: "is the mortality of those who could have told most about it."

He is referring to the very sudden death, on November 5th itself, of a man Whyneard, who could have been a key witness. Those who were caught seem lesser men, whom it is hard to imagine criminals. They include Sir Edward Digby, a gay and charming young man, father of the famous courtier Sir Kenelm: and a rather disreputable priest called Father Garnet. Digby met capture gracefully, tried to caracole his horse through the ranks, but surrendered cheerfully when he could not. The fact that they were all practising Roman Catholics made them in a sense conspirators already. But did they in fact have any knowledge of a Gunpowder Plot? Who now could tell?

They were kept apart, tortured apart, each being told that the other had confessed. A document later discovered at Hatfield, it is claimed, shows how a blend of clever editing and slight forgery makes the "confessions" obtained under torture so complete. There was in any case nothing ahead of them but death: but Digby spoke up with great courage for his faith at his trial: and for this suffered first, and most brutally. But the crowd had become so worked up over the Plot that over-night they found that all the conspirators "had the mark of evil on their foreheads," and some were afraid even to look on "any so horrible."

"The success of the Plot, from Cecil's point of view, was complete," wrote Williamson, "the proposed anti-Roman Catholic legislation could now be put into effect not merely without a protest, but with enthusiasm." As with the Gowries, a danger had been removed.

But no parallel is so striking as that of "the official narrative." As with Gowrie, there was a short account first, then a full, pompous, literary effort—openly and unmistakeably by James—in the next year. It is indeed revealing.

"Kings are in the Word of God itself called gods, as being his lieutenants and Vice-regents on earth, and so adorned and furnished with some sparkles of Divinity," James modestly explains: and so he thought it would be instructive to compare "some of the works of God the great King toward the whole and general world to some of his works towards me and this little world of my dominions." There was Noah's Ark, for instance: and of course the Last Judgement to come. "In the like sort I may justly compare these two great and fearful Doomsdays wherewith God has threatened me"—that is, the Gowrie Conspiracy, and the Gunpowder Plot. "Both occurred upon one day of the week, which was Tuesday, and likewise one day of the month, which was the fifth: thereby to teach me, that as it was the same Devil that still persecuted me, so it was the one and the same God that still mightily delivered me."

James' narrative, as with the Gowrie account, is full of circumstantial detail which no one left alive, except those drawing their life pensions, could refute. And it is haunted by other echoes. By the echo of that other gunpowder explosion, that lit the sky of Edinburgh in January forty years before, when his father was killed, a year after Rizzio's murder. And by that passion for anniversaries, which recalls his mother, turning at the door to say her last, terrible words to her husband: "It was just this night twelve months since Davie died."

All the conspirators were executed, and those whose loyalty might have made martyrs of them. So too a faithful old servitor of Digby's, who wrote to him that one morning instead of the torturer one came to measure him as for a new suit of clothes, assuring him that it would all pass like a nightmare and he would find himself walking out a free man. But he was not deceived, but wrote that he answered, his clothes would serve long enough. The torture of hope was the most subtle of all.

The prisoners were left in utter isolation for forty eight hours before their death. Digby spent it in cutting his name deep into the walls of his cell, where it is said you can still see it: and in writing poetry:

> "Who's that which knocks? O stay, my Lord, I come:
> I know that call, since first it made me know
> My self, which makes me now with joy to run,
> Lest He be gone that can my duty show.
> Jesus, my Lord, I know Thee by the Cross
> Thou offer'st me, but not unto my loss."

He had need of his faith. He mounted the ladder, praying: "Lord Jesus, save me and help me." He took the full drop: was instantly cut down and dragged fully conscious to the chopping-block where his genitals were chopped off and burned, he was disembowelled and as the executioner groped for his heart to tear it out, with the traditional phrase: "Here is the heart of a traitor!" Bacon, who had a good front seat, thought his lips uttered: "Thou liest!"

Father Garnet (said to be "the Equivocator" in MacBeth) produced a note verging on comedy on the scaffold by his apology for Anne Vaux, the lady who had accompanied him on all his travels. She was, he declared, "an honourable gentlewoman who hath been much wronged in report, for it is suspected or said that I should be married to her, or worse." (The last two words are surely worthy of a celibate). "But I protest to the contrary: she is a virtuous gentlewoman, and for me a perfect pure virgin." As she ended her life the Headmistress of a girls' school, comment seems dangerous.

James of course called for thanksgivings—nationwide thanksgiving. Bonfires were lit, "Guys" were burnt, public rejoicings were everywhere.

44

"Remember, remember the Fifth of November
Gunpowder Treason and Plot!
There seems no reason why Gunpowder Treason
Ever should be forgot!"

So every year the celebration grows greater and greater. Money and effort are poured into it, property and life endangered. It became and remains the English people's one great national Festival Day.

Was it a hoax?

Almost certainly there was some Catholic plot—there always was. And certainly Cecil would know of it. But did anyone know of the gunpowder? So clearly do we all see the rows of little kegs, and the men in their steeple hats and pointed beards, familiar in so many pictures, it comes as a shock to find how vague is the evidence of the gunpowder's existence at all. Yet, if barrels of it had failed to kill Darnley, who was apparently strangled, what huge quantities must in fact have been hoarded if it was intended to blow up effectively a whole Parliament! Where did it all come from? More important still, where did it all go to? Like the crock of gold, none of it was ever found: nor even certainly seen. As with Gowrie, the mystery remains.

As nothing is left of the firework but the stick, so nothing was left after the Plot but James, secure and smiling: but not unmindful of mercies, nor of what Rome was about to call in a new word "Propaganda."

Next November that great cleric and scholar Lancelot Andrewes was consecrated Bishop of Chichester and appointed Lord High Almoner. One of his chief duties was to preach a Thanksgiving Sermon to James and his court on each anniversary of "Guy Fawkes Day." He came to call it "the abomination of desolation," and to dread it more and more. A critic says of him: "With his elevation to the Bench of Bishops that sad drop and deterioration of Andrews' character begins which cannot be kept hid . . . and which stands written out in tears . . . in every page of his Penitential Devotions."

On one of those sermons to James, preaching on Fear God and Fear the King, he said, "There are not two fears but one . . ."

This was Jacobean religion at its purest.

CHAPTER SIX

"PEACE! PEACE!"

For the last twenty years of his life James had that absolute power for which he had craved in his insecure childhood. The Roman Catholics were quelled by the Gunpowder Plot, the Scots Kirk crushed by episcopacy. James had peace for his endless hunting, drinking, love-making with his pretty boys. He had a sort of policy, to appease Spain, to make a balance of power in Europe: but, as the French ambassador observed: "The end of all is the bottle." Only for his own sovereignty he remained clear and cunning.

The dangerous greatness of Raleigh was shut up in the Tower: but even that could not rot him. He cut leisure, even sleeping time, and worked harder than ever at reading, writing, map-making. Pretty Arbella Stewart, the King's full cousin on his father's side, who had played Pig-in-the-middle with his children and attended his Queen, ventured to marry in her thirties, and went to the Tower. She contrived eventually to escape in boy's clothes, got to France, missed her husband there by accident, came back to seek him and was caught. She died, mad, in the Tower.

Andrew Melville was summoned to London in 1607, and lived for a while as free as a mouse under the eyes of a cat: for Scots ministers were billetted on English Bishops, thus embarrassing both. (When one tried to harangue Bishop Bancroft on theology, his very English answer was always: "Tush, man! Take here a cup of good sack!") Then one Sunday, at the end of April, Melville got an urgent summons to Whitehall. He set off on his landlord's horse, his nephew following on foot. He hung about, waiting, till afternoon: then went to dine in an inn at Westminster with his nephew and friends. They had the usual fascinating table-talk at which Melville was such an expert: and he also quoted his latest Latin verses on St. Georges' Day. "They will keep you for that," said his nephew: "If God has anything to do with me in Scotland more, He will bring me home to Scotland again . . . if not, let me glorify Him whither or wherever I be."

They had not half-dined when three urgent messengers arrived, one after the other, to summon him away. His sentence was the Tower: and there for over a year he had solitary confinement, without books, paper, letters. He kept his sanity by covering every inch of his cell walls with Latin verses, scratched out with the sharpened prong of his shoe-buckle. Then a friend finally procured some terms of ease for him. At length he was allowed to go to Sedan, where he died. Again, James had had the last word.

As another step towards forcing Bishops on Scotland, the King proposed life-Moderators. Originally the office was only that of Chairman—*primus inter pares*—and only lasted as long as the Assembly sat. But the temptation to inflation is always with us: infinite damage has been done to the Kirk in every generation by old men who simply cannot give up! At least in 1607 the Kirk put up a fight. But preachers were warned that anyone speaking against the new office risked their living. Lord Scone (ennobled after the Gowrie affair) came fully armed to St. John's Kirk in Perth, to terrorise the minister, John Row, who had sworn to preach against the Perpetual Moderators. But Row contented himself with a vigorous tirade against *"praeses ad vitam"*—a phrase that passed over Scone's unlettered head.

The King having taken to himself the right to call the General Assemblies, called no more. But some determined ministers tried to carry on by meeting in Aberdeen. Six of them were singled out, and charged with treason: and had to journey through the bitter depth of winter to trial in Edinburgh. They were sent first to the dungeons of Blackness, then to exile. One of them was John Welsh of Ayr, a wild lad in his youth, who had run off to join the Border reivers.

He was a passionate preacher now, and married to Lizzie Knox, youngest daughter of the Reformer. From his dungeon he sent out, defiantly, 2 basic principles:

1) Christ is Head of the Kirk
2) She is free in her government of all other jurisdictions.

He went to France, quickly learnt to preach in French, and was called to the congregation of St. Jean d'Angely. Later on this Huguenot town rebelled, and was besieged by royal forces. Welsh's Border blood rose to the occasion, he preached resistance, he fought on the ramparts. When the King, young Louis VIII, entered the town on treaty terms, he sent the Duc d'Esperon and a guard to arrest Welsh in the pulpit. But seeing them enter, the preacher called on the congregation to make room for a Marshal of France, and invited him to sit down and hear the Word of God. The Duc courteously accepted: and later brought Welsh to the King, who asked how he dare defy him and preach? "Sir, if you know what I preached, you would make all France come to hear," said Welsh: for he preached first salvation through Christ alone: and second, freedom from the Pope of Rome. (As it happened, the second coincided with Richelieu's policy for a time).

"Eh bien, vous serez mon ministre!" said the King: and when next the town was besieged Welsh and his family were sent under safe conduct to La Rochelle. Collections were made in Scotland for the Huguenots for years, and a French agent came for them. There are still Protestant Kirks in La Rochelle.

But in Scotland the continuous eviction of all independent-minded men, the drive to starve them out through their wives and children, wore the heart out of the Kirk. There were many like Dunbar, also of Ayr who, on his second eviction, said only to his wife, "Margaret, prepare the creels again!" Creels——deep panniers—being used on shelties to transport goods and little children: and this brought 'he sorrowful cry from one small daughter: "What! And is Pharaoh's heart hardened still?'

Then there was Duncan of Crail, in Fife, banished all the way over the Border to Berwick with his wife and small children, and another baby due. They reached a point of starvation when the children cried sleeplessly for hunger, and he divided his time between comforting them, cheering his wife and praying to God. As dawn broke, a horseman galloped up to the door, dropped a sack of provisions and rode off again at full speed. "See what a good Master I serve!" said the minister. Later, a masked lady rode up with a servant, helped his wife through the birth, left linen and money, and disappeared as she had come.

Duncan's last will and testament is worthy of his service: "Having received sundry advertisements and summonses from my Master to flit out of this uncouth country, home to my native land" . . . he thanks God for His gifts of children, and leaves them to Him alone to be "their tutor, curator and agent in all their adoes . . ." He left the youngest daughter to the eldest son: and appointed the sons to be executors to the daughters. "Concerning my temporal goods, the baggage and blathrie of the earth, as I have gotten them from God's liberal hand, in this world, so I leave them . . . giving humble and hearty thanks for so long and comfortable a loan of the same."

One by one the lights of the Kirk were put out, and the people left leaderless. By 1610, Scotland had eleven Bishops, two Archibishops, and two Courts of High Commission to enforce the King's authority.

One Archbishop was Spottiswoode, weak but well-meaning son of one of the Reformers: and the other was Gladstanes, a glutton and a groveller. It became the habit of the Archbishops to claim the chair as Moderator of presbyteries and synods: and there was some protest at this, as having no "warrant of the word." But Gladstanes was always ready to explain that it was "an indifferent matter. What matter who be a Moderator, provided nothing be done but to all your contentment?"

Gladstanes' rank was anything but an indifferent matter to himself. He wrote to James: " . . . may it please your most excellent Majesty, as of all vices ingratitude is most detestable, I, finding myself not only as first of that dead estate which your Majesty has re-created, but also in my private condition so overwhelmed with your Majesty's princely and magnifique benignity, could not but repair to your Majesty's most gracious face that so unworthy a creature might both see, bless and thank *my earthly creator*. As no estate may say that they are your

Majesty's creatures as we may say, so there is none whose standing is so slippery when your Majesty shall frown as we: for at your Majesty's nod we must either stand or fall." There indeed he spoke truth.

With such a spirit gaining place, it is little wonder that 1610 saw a Glasgow Assembly, full of picked men and many of them bribed, who officially accepted episcopacy. James had achieved his end in Scotland.

He celebrated it by ordering the ministers to give up their old Geneva cloaks, and wear instead black clothes and black pulpit gowns. In London he had a portrait of himself painted going down a staircase which had "Peace! "Peace!" on every step!

He had a new Candy Captain, a golden lad called Carr or Kerr, a Border Kerr probably, who had fallen from his horse at the King's feet during a joust. The King visited him as he lay recovering from a broken leg, and undertook to teach him Latin. James adored instructing!

"Beauty vanishes, beaty passes, however rare, rare it be"—nothing is so incomprehensible as the effect of physical beauty, when it is no longer visible. Carr was beautiful: and there came to the court one of the loveliest girls, who fell in love with him. She was already married.

Frances Howard was married as a child to the Earl of Essex: he had gone abroad, the marriage yet unconsummated, and she came to court. She even made a conquest of Prince Henry, who was famous for his austere life, in contrast to the Court. He loved study, sport and jousting: and for a while wore Frances' glove in his helm: till she fell passionately in love with the King's favourite, Carr. Then he tossed her glove away, saying, "It hath been stretched by another!"

In his very short life, Prince Henry made more memorable remarks than many a long-lived sovereign. "None but my fader would keep such a bird in such a cage," he said of Raleigh, whom he greatly loved, shut in the Tower. "Two religions should never lie in one bed," he said of the Spanish match proposed for him. He and his sister Elizabeth were dear friends—baby Charles was too young and weakly to count, though he too adored his elder brother, and wrote him hero-worshipping letters. When there were jousts and masques in honour of the King of Denmark, baby Charles was allowed to step through a certain window in Whitehall on an improvised scaffold to watch, along with his big brother. Many years after he stepped through the same window on to a scaffold modelled on that same one: alone, and never to return.

But Henry died of typhoid in 1612. Would Raleigh's Indian powder (quinine?) have helped him? James forbade it till he was in any case past hope: then he did rally, to cry out for his dearest sister Elizabeth. But she was kept out for fear of infection. His mother by this time had taken to drink and excessive eating: his father, who had a horror of illness and death—things outwith the control of power—

was absent. He died lonely: but the whole new British people mourned him as a loss. "And did not good Prince Henry die?" bereaved mothers would say, for long after.

The next year Frances Howard, Countess of Essex, brought a nullity suit against her husband, alleging his impotence. The Earl, who had been home for some time, and apparently in love with his wife, maintained a dignified silence throughout: but James threw himself into the trial with all the enthusiasm of a voyeur. Two chief obstacles—apart from the evidence—were the Archbishop, Lancelot Andrewes, whom James over-bore eventually, and Carr's friend and patron, the poet Thomas Overbury, who opposed the Countess. Overbury, who had first met Carr on the cobbles of Edinburgh High Street, went to the Tower on some charge from the King: and there, by slow poisoning, he died. There was then a spectacular wedding when Frances, the loveliest woman at court married Carr, now Earl of Somerset and still its handsomest man. She wore virginal white but cut rather below her breasts, which were pushed up in the fashionable pigeon shape, as seen in her portrait, and her wonderful golden hair was loose and streaming to her ankles. No doubt the crowd had their comments.

But less than two years later an apothecary's prentice died in France: and purged his soul at the last of the confession that he had been the means of carrying all the poisoned dishes—junkets and possets and wine—to Overbury in the Tower: and all at the Countess' instigation. A scandal burst, involving a Mrs. Turner, whose yellow-starched ruffles had been famous in society, and her Master who had practised witch-craft with rites and images—and significant potions—for clients who could afford it. Frances went to the Tower, and the warrant came also from Coke for Carr.

"Ye maun go," said the King, who had grown tired of him anyhow: "for if Coke send for *me* I maun go." But still the king saw him off with a typical piece of Jacobean play-acting. He hung round his neck, sighing and slobbering: "For God's sake, when shall I see thee again?" "On Monday." "For God's sake let me," said the King: "Shall I? Shall I? Then for God's sake give thy lady this kiss for me." In the same manner at the stair's head, at the middle of the stairs, and at the stair's foot." Carr got into the coach and drove off. James watching him go, said, "Deil tak' him, I'll never see his face more."

It was partly the Bishops who had found the new favourite George Villiers, soon made Duke of Buckingham and had the Queen introduce him at court: which was the procedure the King liked; and she presumably had got beyond caring. From now on, Buckingham was James' grand passion: and he lived only to exalt him and all his family, as he frankly explained. For Carr and Frances, the King devised an act of characteristic "mercy". They were banished to perpetual seclusion in each other's company for ever: the memory of what they had done living constantly with them. James was happy in the arms of his "Steenie"—short for Stephen, for he had seen him, like the first martyr, "as it were, the face of an angel." James' theology never left him, for good or ill. "Jesus had his John," was his classic defence: "and I must have my Steenie."

When Buckingham wanted Coke's daughter for his younger brother, who had fits of violent insanity, Coke was only too willing to oblige. The girl fought desperately, pleaded another—mythical engagement, ran away: but was caught, and Coke had her roped to the bedpost and flogged into submission. The wedding and bedding of the happy pair was celebrated by the whole court: and James was first to leap playfully through their bed-curtains next day.

Coke himself contrived to be a considerable architect of the English law, and yet completely a creature of the King's. He suited James admirably.

The Princess Elizabeth had gone from a court she could never have liked, shortly after Prince Henry's death, to be wife of the Elector Palatine. He succeeded to the throne of Bohemia, that Protestant Kingdom, with its table communion, set between Latin Europe and Slavonic East: the heritage of Jan Hus, the first great Protestant teacher and martyr. There they reigned for six months: and Elizabeth, once nicknamed the Queen of Hearts, became to the Czechs their "Winter Queen." Turned out in spring by a coalition of Roman Catholic powers they appealed to James: but appealed in vain. With a growing tribe of children and a great deal of charm she remained homeless: and the Czech Protestants were crushed and their leaders very horribly put to death. Their church lives still, but was never again nationally established.

She was not the only one betrayed to preserve James' peace. Raleigh was released to sail to El Dorado to bring back gold for James' debts. Even as his ships fitted out the reports went to Spain, and went officially. His every move was charted, the Spaniards were alert and ready when he came: and he found the evidence of the treachery in their hands. His beloved son—the touching image of him in every detail, in the portrait where they stand side by side—was killed: and his letters home to his wife are almost unbearable to read.

He came home to trial and to certain condemnation. Great to the last, he mounted the scaffold like a throne, chaffing the crowd, taking all their hearts with him. To the slow-moving English people, his death was another—eleventh—wave in the rising tide of their resentment.

In 1617 James paid his only visit to Scotland. He had, he said, "a natural and saumon-like affection" to see the land of his birth again. He installed symbols of his own ideal religion in Holyrood Chapel: two unlit candles in candlesticks: two large unopened Bibles: an empty chalice and basin: and kneelers, one suspects unused. He also defined his ideal Church government. Things would not go on as they had in General Assemblies, he told them: but "Bishops should rule the Kirk, and the King rule both." He also pressed for the Five Articles of Perth—all fairly small matters, such as kneeling for communion: but all designed to chip away the doctrine of the Kirk in some way. Next year an Assembly where the ministers were mere hangers-on of the dignitaries accepted them all. It was the last Assembly for twenty years.

There were still those ready to fight. A Scottish book-seller was arrested in London for circulating Calderwood's tract against the Articles, and had to withstand James' personal wrath against "thir people of Edinburgh."

A deacon called John Mein—still an Edinburgh name—also refused to accept them. It was a point of papistry, he told Galloway, the King's preacher, "to believe as the Kirk believes." "The Kirk has concluded it," he was told, "and the King and council has confirmed it. Would ye set yourself above both Kirk and King?"

"Sir," says John, "ye were wont to say to us langsyne, thus saith the Lord," but, now ye change your tune, and say, "Thus saith the Kirk and the King!"

Calderwood himself, whose painstaking History of these times I have used so often, was arrested and brought before the King on his Northern visit. The King told him all that the General Assembly might do: preserve doctrine in purity, keep the Kirk from schism, make confessions of faith and put up petitions to the King: "But in matters of order, rites and things indifferent, that belongs to the King, with the advice of his Bishops." In spite of a terrifying march to the Tolbooth, and being told he would be hanged, the good minister survived, and died in a quiet parish, long after.

James knew precisely how far to push the Scots at one time without making them desperate. During his last years the future Archbishop Laud first came to his court as a bishop: and began immediately that steady drive for preferment which meant all to him.

But James would not promote him. Laud had met a mind as cunning as his own, and James put him down as "a troubler of the waters." Presumably it was with James' acceptance that Archie Armstrong, his Fool, gave his famous grace of "Great Praise to God and Little Laud to the Devil!" The little man who dreamt of power, "the pastor who wore the purple", as Coffin calls him, developed a pathological hatred of Scots.

One more echo came to James out of the past in these last years. John Welsh developed consumption, and was advised by the French doctors that his last hope was to win home to the clean air of his own moors. So he came with his wife and children to London, and Lizzie Welsh contrived to have an interview with James: the daughter of John Knox before the son of Mary Queen of Scots!

"Knox and Welsh!" said James, "The deil himsel' never made such a match!"

"Its likely so, Sir, for he wasna speired!"

By all accounts, she gave James back a good answer for every jeering remark: but when he told her her husband could only go back to his native air if he would submit to the Bishops, she snatched up the corners of her apron with the cry: "I had rather kep his head in this!"

So he died in London, and she went back to Scotland with her three small sons. One was killed in an accident, one lost at sea, and the third became minister of Temple Durham in Ireland. It was this one's son who was the famous Scarlet Pimpernel of the Covenanters, the preacher of the mists who was never caught.

Shakespeare, the essentially Elizabethan genius, died in 1618. In 1620 the *Mayflower* landed in America some of the first of the many. Unlike the Scots, the English found their voice for freedom not through their State church but through their unique form of Parliament—their House of Commons. Already James had had some stormy passages with them: and in one famous scene sent for their record book and tore out the pages. The disastrous Spanish trip, organised by Buckingham to bring home a Spanish bride for Charles, heir to the throne, increased the people's anger. It was an extraordinary trip, involving both Sir Edmund Verney, the King's Standard Bearer, and Archie Armstrong the Fool. Charles's wooing of the Spanish princess was fortunately ineffective, for the promises made had compromised England in every direction. The two adventurers—James' "sweet boys, worthy to be put in a new romanzo" at last came back, to the relief of England and especially of their "sweet dad and gossip", the King: "I care for match nor nothing, so I may once have you in my arms again. God grant it, God grant it! Amen, amen, amen!"

Yet James was not too senile to see the danger when Charles and Buckingham insisted on calling a Parliament to push through an impeachment. "You are a fool," he told Buckingham bluntly: and to "Baby Charles": "You will live to have your bellyful of Parliaments."

James died in 1625, in that Latin with the odd accent that Geordie Buchanan had taught him in his childhood "ere I could speak Scots." He died in peace, Parliament not yet roused and the Kirk that had troubled him so long crushed to silence at last.

CHAPTER SEVEN

A COVENANTED NATION

The year that Charles I was crowned King of England a minister in
Scotland, David Dickson, who had opposed episcopacy, was allowed
to return from exile in the North to his own parish of Stewarton in
Ayrshire. There he began to preach with the power and authority that
had come out of the long prayer and meditation of his exile. The Kirk
had grown a quiescent and indifferent body, without leaders, and
largely unregarded by the people: but here a flicker of its old
inspiration awoke. People gathered, word spread, they came from
farther afield. On Mondays, which was the market-day in Stewarton,
hundreds would flock to hear Dickson preach, to beg his advice. So
swiftly did the interest spread that it was called, half-jeeringly, "the
Stewarton sickness." "It is not the abuse of power which our Lord
forbiddeth his ministers," said Dickson: "but simply and absolutely
he dischargeth all majority of power, all greatness of jurisdiction of
one over the rest." He struck to the root.

Two years later, owing to some unexplained rebellion, the brilliant
young Professor of Latin at the new University of Edinburgh left his
chair and retired to the tiny Kirk of Anwoth, in a nook of the
Solway. He did not bury himself in vain, for he became one of the
best-loved of all parish ministers.

His days were so full he had to rise at 3 a.m. to pray in quietness.
"For such a piece of clay as Mr. Rutherford, I never knew one in
Scotland like him," wrote the minister of Kinloss: "He seems to be
always praying, always preaching, always visiting the sick, always
teaching in the Sabbath schools, always writing treatises, always
reading and studying." He knew all his parish from the laird,
Kenmure, in his castle, to the smallest herd-lad, and was beloved of
all. His name will always be associated with the hymn which uses his
own words and expresses so much of his own radiant faith, "Glory,
glory dwelleth in Emmanuel's land."

"The sands of time are sinking,
The dawn of Heaven breaks . . .

As if in exile, remembering his own people, there was added a verse
not given in the hymn-books (which now exclude him totally):

54

"And if one soul from Anwoth
Meet me at God's right hand
My Heaven will be two Heavens
In Emmanuel's land!"

Kenmure had manned the ramparts of St. Jean d'Angely with
Welsh, and had been deeply influenced by his preaching. After his
death Rutherford wrote to his widow some of those famous letters of
consolation which are almost a ministry in themselves. In exile,
virtually in prison, in Aberdeen he continued his pastoral care,
although " . . . afflictions bring the cramp upon my faith. All I can do
is to hold out a lame faith to Christ like a beggar holding out a
stump . . . and cry, "Lord Jesus, work a miracle!" But: "Madam . . .
those who can take that crabbed tree" (the cross) "handsomely upon
their back . . . shall find it such a burden as wings unto a bird or sails
to a ship." "I verily think, that Christ hath said, "I must needs-force
have Jean Campbell for myself," he wrote her, "and He hath laid
many oars in the water to fish and hunt home-over your heart to
heaven."

"I desire not to go on the lee-side or sunny side of religion, or to put
truth betwixt me and a storm," is another famous passage: "my
Saviour did not so for me, who in his suffering took the windy side of
the hill." He writes further to her, in the same letters "Be content to
wade through the waters betwixt you and glory with him, holding his
hand fast, for he knoweth all the fords."

"Indeed our fair morning is at hand," he wrote to another, "the
day-star is near the rising, and we are not many miles from home."

And to the younger son of Earlston: "But God be thanked, for
many spilled salvations, and many ill-ravelled hesps hath Christ
mended, since first He entered Tutor to lost mankind." Again, to
Gordon of Cardoness: "This great idol-god the World will be lying in
white ashes on the day of your compearance: and why should night-
dreams and day-shadows and water-froth, and May-flowers run
away with your heart?" (We, who live so close to a world lying in
white ashes, should appreciate that.) "Build your nest upon no tree
here," he wrote again: "for the Lord hath sold the whole forest to
death."

Tales gathered round Rutherford. As minister of Anwoth he had
taken in a poorly-dressed tramp for the night. When the children were
asked their evening catechism the stranger was given a simple
question: "How many commandments are there?" and answered
"Eleven"—no doubt to the mirth of the bairns. But next morning
early Rutherford went as usual to the grove called "Rutherford's
Walk," and found the man there before him: praying as only a pastor
prays for his own people. When challenged, he admitted he was
Archbishop Usher of Ireland, who had longed to meet Rutherford
but was afraid of his reception, in these times of bitterness.

Rutherford promptly invited him to preach: and when he gave out his text in the pulpit: "A new commandment I give unto you—" Rutherford exclaimed "The Eleventh commandment!"

But there was another side to the gentle, heaven-centred parish minister. "What if conscience toward God, and credit with men, cannot both go to heaven with the saints, the author is satisfied with the former" he wrote at the beginning of *Lex Rex*, a book burned by the public hangman in London, Edinburgh and St. Andrews: "The Law is not the King's own, but is given to him on trust," he wrote: and again: "Power is a birth-right of the people, borrowed from them: they may let it out for their good, and may resume it when a man is drunk with it."

"O man of God, go on, go on!" he had written to David Dickson: but his own criticism of the abuse of power stretched out from the kirk to the earthly kingdom.

Many a head was chopped off for less: and so might Rutherford's have been, had he lived long enough. First he was banished to Aberdeen, from his dear Anwoth; there he complained the people were either Papists or "of Gallio's naughty faith." "When I think of the sparrows and swallows that build their nests in the Kirk of Anwoth, and of my dumb Sabbaths, my sorrowful bleared eyes look asquint upon Christ and present him as angry."

When I last saw Anwoth it drowsed in summer heat. The swallows flickered tirelessly over the old flat gravestones which surround the ruins of the old Kirk, and to eaves over-grown with yellow tea-roses: descendants certainly of Rutherford's swallows. Any man might long for it.

"Arbitrary government had over-swelled all banks of law, it was now at the highest float," he wrote in *Lex Rex* and further refers to "prelates, a wild and pushing cattle . . ." Episcopacy had grown so tolerated that even a man of so fine a mind as Alexander Henderson accepted it. He was presented by Gladstanes to the charge of Leuchars in Fife. When he arrived for installation, he found the church barred and locked against him, and the key hidden. But a window was eventually forced, and he and the other clergy climbed through it.

Some time later, hearing that Robert Bruce was to preach in the neighbourhood, and being curious to hear him he slipped into the back of the church and hid himself in a dark corner. When Bruce, after his usual silent prayer, stood up in the pulpit his eyes seems to pierce the darkest corner as he gave out his text: "Whoever comes not in by the door of the sheep-fold but climbs up some other way, the same is a thief and a robber." The words stabbed Henderson. Perhaps they spoke to some growing dissatisfaction in him. From then on, he rejected patronage, his ministry deepened: and when he was later summoned for not having the requisite copies of the King's Liturgy, his arguments before the presbytery were so fundamental and

56

courageous that he was eventually called to St. Giles, the High Kirk of Edinburgh. The Kirk had found a new leader.

But the greatest thing that happened in Scotland in these lean years was on the bleak ridge of Kirk o'Shotts half-way between Glasgow and Edinburgh, in 1630. It began when the wheel came off a coach carrying a lady who loved to give. As almost always on that desolate road, which runs mainly through bogs and mosses, the rain was pouring down. The minister came out from a nearby manse, and took her in for shelter: but as she found his roof leaked badly, her sympathy went out to him.

She got his manse repaired, and found that in spite of his personal poverty he loved to have the Lord's Table spread as richly as he could, with fine preaching and hospitality, in his wretched little Kirk. Together they planned a splendid sacrament, with all the best preachers in Scotland invited to take part, and invitations spread throughout the countryside.

Anyone who travels that dreary road has seen Kirk o'Shotts, for it sits on the highest, most weather-beaten ridge—where the TV mast is now—with no house in sight. A graveyard spreads round it, and there is in fact a village, sheltering in a hollow behind. The sight may well have been chosen first for a Celtic church for they were often on high spots, like beacons to tribes in the trackless scrub. So, in 1630, it was easy for the crowds to find their way to the kirk: and they came in tremendous numbers, bringing their families with them and camping round about. All Sunday the tables were spread, and the word preached. Bruce, aged now, was one of those who ministered. But the great hour came on the Monday morning, for those who had waited for the Thanksgiving that followed the communion, when the preacher was an unknown young man called Livingstone, Minister of Ancrum: gentle, scholarly, a lover of music, he left a revealing personal diary:- on married love, on worship (he thought "a line of praises worth a page of prayer"), on that memorable Monday in Kirk o'Shotts.

"The only day in all my life wherein I found most of the presence of God in preaching was on a Monday after the communion, preaching in the church-yard of Shotts, June 21st, 1630." He had spent the short, light night in talk and in prayer: but after dawn, as the people began to gather in a great crowd once more, he knew complete terror and despair: and planned "to have stolen away somewhere . . . but that I thought I durst not so far distrust God, so went to sermon and got good assistance about an hour and a half upon the points which I had meditated on (Ezekiel XXXVI 25.26.):" Then, as he ended, something swept over them all: he felt himself "led on . . . with such liberty and melting of heart as I never had the like in public all my lifetime."

As the Holy Spirit swept upon the little churches of the Asian seaports in the days of Paul, so He did upon the people in the church-

57

yard at Kirk o'Shotts. It affected deeply all who were there—even some Glasgow students who had been casually passing by: and its ripples spread through the years. For generations the pulpits were filled by men who had been directly or indirectly influenced by what happened at that Monday morning of "the presence of God." It was known as "the Work at Shotts." In its old sense, the word means "working."

That occasion must have been one of the last of Bruce's public preachings. For some time he had confined himself to a ministry at Larbert, near his own confiscated home of Kinnaird. It was something of a place of pilgrimage, and there is a story of two noblemen who came to hear him: and growing impatient as he hadn't appeared and they had far to ride, they sent the beadle to see if he was ready. The beadle did not care to enter the vestry, but listened behind the door: and came back to say that he must have someone with him: for he had heard Bruce earnestly say "that he could not go, and would not go, without Him: but the other answered never a word."

Now he heard that voice he knew clearly. He had eaten an egg for his breakfast, the homely story runs, and enjoyed it so much he thought he could take another: then called, "Hold, daughter, my Master calls me!" and sent instead for the family Bible. So quickly did the darkness now come down on him that he could no longer see the page, but asked them to turn up the 8th Chapter of the Epistle to the Romans, and put his fingers on the words: "I am persuaded that neither death nor life, nor angels, nor principalities, nor powers, nor things present, nor things to come, nor height, nor depth, nor any other creature, shall be able to separate us from the love of God which is in Christ Jesus our Lord." "Now God be with you, my children," he said in farewell, "I have breakfasted with you, but shall sup tonight with my Lord Jesus Christ."

He is buried in Larbert graveyard where you can see his carved headstone; and its Latin motto: "Christ is in life and death advantage."

In 1633 King Charles I came in a Royal Progress to his northern capital of Edinburgh, Archbishop Laud in attendance, and held a coronation service in St. Giles, Edinburgh, with full Anglican rites. It is said that Laud found one Scottish Bishop deficient in vestments, and sent him out: but otherwise they both seemed to find it a success. So much so that Charles founded a bishopric of Edinburgh—which of course no longer exists—and elevated the High Kirk into St. Giles Cathedral: a name still often used, in the same way that Westminster is still called an Abbey. He also attempted to give Archbishop Spottiswoode, the Primate of Scotland, precedence in the procession over the Chancellor: with the usual argument on these occasions that it was "only for that day." The nobles utterly refused: so Charles took the first opportunity to make the Primate Chancellor also.

This was the King's first visit to the land of his birth: and while much has been blamed on his total ignorance of Scotland and the Scottish viewpoint, he did at least on this occasion see enough to convince him that what the Scots needed was "the beauty of holiness" and the civilising influence of union with the Church of England.

The Scots on their part saw enough to realise with dismay that Charles really *believed* in Bishops. To James they had been—as most things were—instruments of policy—suppressors of dissent. But Charles treated the coarsest of the Scottish prelates with a notable deference. He and Laud are wonderful examples of the High Church mind: they not only knew themselves right, beyond touch of doubt, but knew they could do no better for others than make them right also. They had a call to do it.

Laud thought the whole country an abode of savages: and spoke of his danger and hardship in "the Hilands"—it was in fact the main road between Dunblane and Stirling. If there were religious customs in the country, he would no more tolerate them than a missionary would tolerate the wooden idols of cannibals. They were better off without them.

The first step to re-modelling the Kirk was to print a book of Canons, a replacement for the Book of Discipline. In this, ruling elders vanish, and instead we have church-wardens, or "six chief men of the parish." Something like confession and absolution and something very near transubstantiation came into it: extempory prayer was strictly forbidden, and all worship was to follow the Book of Common Prayer.

School children were to be taught from James' own favourite text book: *God and the King*. Worst of all to the Scots was Charles' own prefatory letter: "We do not only by our Prerogative Royal and supreme Authority in Causes Ecclesiastical ratify and confirm . . . but *command* . . . the same to be diligently observed and executed by our loving subjects . . ." (You can see a copy of this in St. Giles).

The loving subjects were united by anger, by a great and ever-growing resentment. Sunday, 23rd July, 1637 was the day chosen to inaugurate the liturgy, in the High Kirk of Edinburgh. The Dean in his surplice processed in, while a huge crowd watched, tense: he got as far as intoning that he would "now read the Collect for the Day"— "Deil colic the wame o' you!" shouted Jenny Geddes, one of the luckenbooth wifies, hurling her stool at his head. Tradition says she missed—but the riot had begun. Bishop and Dean had to run for their lives, discarding robes as they ran, and pelted with all that came to hand by the whole High Street of Edinburgh. (In the refinements of History Books Jenny is reported as saying: "Dost thou dare to say Mass in my lug (ear)?"—an unlikely mouthful for anyone in a hurry. I give the local oral tradition, which seems to me more convincing). Later, firm and formal protest against both Canons and liturgy was made to the Privy Council in Stirling.

In London, Archie Armstrong was the first to greet Laud with,

"News frae Stirling, my Lord! Wha's the Fool noo?" And Laud, beside himself with rage, had the old man arrested, flogged and sent from court. So ended the last official Fool.

After Stirling, there was what Principal Watt, in his little book about the Covenants, which is surely the best ever written, calls: "a general rally to Edinburgh." "The Tables" were set up: meetings of the nobles, gentry, men of Law, provosts and burghs, ministers and elders. It was decided to renew the covenant not as a church but as a nation. Indeed, it comes as a surprise to see what a comparatively small part the church does have in it.

The National Covenant is in three parts. The first goes back to the *Confession of Faith* of 1581, called the *King's Confession*: which had been signed by James VI and his first love, Lennox; it deals with it in detail and brings it up to date. The second part cites all the Acts of Parliament by which the Presbyterian Church had been established and contrary errors renounced: and it too was a careful and thorough piece of work, entrusted to a great lawyer and a great man of God called Johnston of Warriston. The third part, the actual Covenant to be renewed, was mainly the work of Henderson of Leuchars. But every detail was carefully scrutinised and revised.

In a moment unique in human history, Scotland was entering into a bond with God: and she was anxious that everything should be legally correct and in order.

When the Law of Scotland stands with the Church of Scotland, the nation seems to rise to full stature. At this hour not only were the nobles united with the church, but the lawyers too: and the best of them was Lord Warriston. As a boy, he wrote in his diary, he felt "His wonderful calling me unto the communion of the West Kirk, whereat He gave me many tears (it being my first communion) even while I was drowned in all kind of licentiousness by Sutherland's compagnie . . . as also . . . Prestonpans, Musselburgh, West Kirk, Carnock, thereafter in Foulden, once in Castres and twice in Paris— as many communions, as many comforts."

You can still see the little window above Warriston's Close in the High Street, his "high chamber" where his candle burned late night after night as he gave himself to his reading and his prayers. He had decided after a struggle that he was better fitted for the Law than the Church: but his faith remained the central thing of his life. "God's consolations never run dry," he wrote in one of his Sunday meditations: "are aye tasty and keep men ever fresh, for they are a fountain, not a puddle or pond . . . The restitution of Israel shall watter many nations . . ." Again: "Thou put it in my head to write: Thou hast dited it all: Thou hast made me but a channel to let Thy liquor run through." As Lord Macleod in our own day put it: "We are pipes, not cisterns."

After a struggle with his early ambitions, he decided on "My desire, if it may stand with His pleasure, to live and die with His Covenant, work, and remnant in poor but covenanted Scotland." As Lord Clerk Register he carried in his notebook a private prayer: "O Father, Saviour and Sanctifier, take Archie Johnston—a poor, silly, imprudent, ignorant, improvident, passionate, humorous, foolish, ungrate, diffident body—in unto Thy thoughts and know him by name and surname, and make him know yet that Thou are the Lord God and his God and the God of his seed both in thy words and works."

Foremost among the nobles was the Earl of Rothes, but there were many other great names: Loudoun, Lyndesay, Balmerino, young Mar: Lord Lorne, so soon to succeed as Marquis of Argyll: and his colleague who became his enemy, the young Earl of Montrose, later Marquis, who was the Elder from Auchterarder.

Lord Hope, the Lord Advocate, was a faithful defender of the Covenant. And David Dickson of Stewarton worked chiefly with Henderson on the Church's part. It was a bond of union, and even of loyalty, not of defiance, or rebellion. Does any other nation cherish among its charters agreements with God?

This magnificent document was presented first on Tuesday 27th February, 1638, in John Galloways' house in Edinburgh by Johnston of Warriston: "I read Confession, Acts of Parliament, and Bond to the nobles, by whom two words were changed. After noon with great fears we went to the ministry"—(they met "in the summer-house in the yard" of the Tailor's Hall)—"and after two alterations and a discussion of all objections, we got it approved first by the commissioners (of the presbyteries) then by the whole ministry, except one."

A scribe then set to work on "a fair parchment above on ellne in square"; and the next the nobles and barons convened in Greyfriars church at two in the afternoon. A general fast had been proclaimed. First Henderson preached, then Loudoun spoke and then Johnston produced the Covenant. At four o'clock the signing began, and continued until nearly eight. Presumably scribes got to work on copies that very night: for the next day the ministers began signing in the Tailor's Hall, and the day after various delegates and visitors to Edinburgh.

After that copies went throughout the whole country, and to the London Scots and to the Scots congregations abroad and to Scots regiments serving on the continent. Principal Watt thinks that it was not until April 1st that any general signing began in Edinburgh. Some signed in blood, some could only fit in initials, others added "till death." In the years that followed many honoured their bond in full.

There are many copies still existing: in New College, in the Free Church College, in the National Library, in St. Giles Cathedral beside the tomb of Montrose. The copy taken to Dunblane Cathedral was signed by Montrose, Balmerino, Rothes, Loudoun, Lyndesay, Henderson of Leuchars; and many others including Robert Cadder "schoolmaster in Dunblane" and James Piersone. The last-named had been appointed Dean of the Cathedral by James VI in 1624: so he took charge of the copy of the Covenant after all its signatures had been appended. He had a great-great-grandson who married in Dunblane in 1775: who had a grandson born in 1818 who sold the family property in 1841 and emigrated to Australia, taking the Covenant with him. In 1949 his great-grandson, Dr. Ian Pearson, practising in Tasmania, handed it over to Dr. Hutchison Cockburn of Dunblane Cathedral, visiting Moderator of the General Assembly of the Church of Scotland: and so it came back across the world to its own place again, and you can see it in Dunblane Cathedral today.

"The renewing of the Covenants," both in private and in the church, was kept up as a fruitful exercise of grace for many years: till some miserable old schismatic abolished it, to our country's loss. For, never since the days of Israel of old, had one whole small nation—men, women and even children—stood up as one living soul to call upon their God.

It was, said Johnston, "the great marriage-day" of the nation with God.

It was a moment in the history of man.

CHAPTER EIGHT

ARMY WITH BANNERS

After the marriage day, the marriage settlement. There is nothing else in the world like the General Assembly of the Church of Scotland met, at least in principle, to consider the affairs of the earth in terms of eternity. However corrupt, manipulated, deathly boring—today as in many other days—it can still rise to moments of greatness. As it did in November, 1638: the year of the National Covenant.

Charles I's response to the Covenant was various Royal Proclamations, read out at Town Crosses: counter-acted by Covenanter Proclamations read immediately after. He then sent North his personal friend, the Marquis of Hamilton, to offer terms.

"I give you leave to flatter them with what hopes you please," wrote Charles:" . . . your chief end being now to win time . . . till I am able to suppress them."

To the Covenanters' statement that they would rather die than renounce the Covenant, the King wrote: "I will rather die than yield to their impertinent and damnable demands."

By mid-September he had agreed to a Scots Parliament and to a General Assembly with many conditions, including permanent Moderators. The Assembly was summoned for Wednesday, 21st November, in the vast stone pile of Glasgow Cathedral. Hamilton was the King's Lord High Commissioner. All the King's conditions were voted out.

It was the first Assembly for twenty years, the first free Assembly for more than that. It had to decide on the future constitution of the Church of Scotland. It was, and has been ever since, the definitive Assembly; so it had to be as legally correct as was humanly possible. In Warriston's words: "We will have it thoroughly pledged and judged betwixt His Kingdom and the Kingdoms of the earth."

As in the Dundee Act of twenty years before, there were three ministers and one elder from each presbytery, and one elder from each burgh. There were three or more "advisers" to each commissioner; representatives of Universities; knights, landowners, provosts, town clerks, burgesses and "the best educated clergy in the world." They covered all but the Gaelic-speaking Isles: from Sir Andrew Agnew, Hereditary Sheriff of Galloway in the South-west to Sir James Fraser of Brea, second son of Simon, seventh Lord Lovat, in the far North-east: both being elders. The Caithness men came a month late, which was still good travelling for winter; and they got their expenses.

The retiring Moderator offered a leet of five names: which the Assembly approved. They then voted and Alexander Henderson was unanimously chosen Moderator "by the votes of all, not ane contrair except his own," wrote Robert Baillie, minister of Kilwinning, a true journalist in the original meaning of the word, and a first-rate reporter of his times.

A leet of four names for Clerk was then approved; and Johnston of Warriston voted in by an overwhelming majority. These two men now worked hand in hand. But their appointment was for the duration of the Assembly only. Though Johnston was appointed Procurator—permanent Law Officer—at the end.

They began the agenda with records of previous meetings. The Depute Clerk, Sandilands, could only produce Acts of the Kirk from 1690, from the start of the "permanent Moderators" and other forms of episcopacy infiltrated into the Kirk and gradually tolerated. He swore that his father, the late Clerk, had had no others. It was known that James I had ordered the early records into the custody of the Archbishop of St. Andrews. It was a master-stroke when Johnston produced them complete, from the very first Reformation Assembly of 1560. (And a tragedy when they were destroyed in the fire at Westminster in 1844).

"This day I produced for my first Act the Registers of the Kirk, and can never sufficiently admire and adore the goodness, wisdom and providence of God in preserving them and bringing them to our hands at such a time," he wrote in his diary: "as this was a solid foundation to us . . . In the Great Committee, where my Lord Argyll was sitting, in the Tolbooth, I cleared all their minds that episcopacy was condemned in this church . . . In the Assembly I showed all the warrants and read the very Acts themselves out of the Registers, and answered all the objections." Many had come to dispute for episcopacy, even "resolute to vote for it;" "Yet the Lord made the Acts so to convince their mind that every man's mouth acknowledged that they had been abjured and removed; and when I was reading the roll and heard no word but "abjured and removed" I was stricken with admiration . . . and yit my ears sounds ever with these words, Abjured and removed."

It was too much for the Lord High Commissioner, the Marquis of Hamilton, who warned them even with tears against abolishing episcopacy; and on pain of dissolving the Assembly. By vote, he was totally defeated. So he "discharged this court to listen any longer" and departed. As he went Lord Rothes read out: "In the name of the Lord Jesus Christ, the only Head and Monarch of his Church, we cannot dissolve this Assembly." The Moderator said, "Christ hath given divine warrants to convocate Assemblies, whether magistrates consent or not: therefore seeing we perceive His Grace my Lord Commissioner to be so zealous for his Royal Majesty's commands, have we not also reason to be zealous towards our Lord and to maintain the liberties and privileges of His Kingdom?"

The Bishops were summoned for trial and deposed, mainly for drunkenness, ignorance and neglect. They were a poor lot at best: and all went but two. The Bishop of Orkney, in addition, "curled on the Sabbath." The Bishop of Moray, startlingly, "danced in his sark." "We have been making a tub these forty years," said Bishop Spottiswoode sadly, "and now the bottom thereof has fallen out." Some ministers were also deposed, including Foster of Melrose who "made a way through the Kirk for his kine and sheep, made a waggon of the old communion table to lead his peats in and other excesses."

The Glasgow Assembly also re-affirmed the Reformation principle that no minister could stand for civil office, or take it except in emergency and with the express permission of the Church.

The Marquis of Argyll was not the only one there still hoping some compromise with the King would be possible. It became increasingly clear it was not, and he courageously threw in his lot with the Covenanters, and never wavered, even to the end. It was said to have been one of Henderson's evening prayer-meetings which finally decided him.

The King, and Hamilton, could have saved their breath as far as soothing flattery went. Scots information at this point was excellent; so good its sources are a matter for conjecture. "How did the Scots know," wonders Sir Edmund Verney's descendant and biographer Peter Verney, "that he, the King's own Royal Standard Bearer, was a friend to the Scots?" Is there a clue in the odd fact that Archie Armstrong, King's Fule and good presbyterian, had been on the Spanish Wooing trip with Sir Edmund? Did he send other information?

Certainly the Scots knew the King's intentions fully. Wasting no time, they sent to Sweden for His Excellency Field Marshal Alexander Leslie, personal friend of King Gustavus Adolphus, "with his own Palace on the Balta Sound;" known more familiarly in his native land as "little crooked Sandy, the bastard from Balveny." In the Scottish National Portrait Gallery he is gorgeous in lace frills, velvet and curling love-locks: but his eye goes through you like a bullet. Any spine would stiffen under it.

He not only came, but brought home Scots mercenaries and arms, and in the shortest time had taken effective command. Baillie has a famous description of "the wisdom and authority of this old little crooked solider" whose word was obeyed "like the Grand Sulyman himself," yet who did not issue commands to the volunteers who had brought their men out to serve with him. Instead, he entertained them at his table, and made suggestions. By early summer he had secured the main castles and was ready to march to the Border to await the King and his men.

June in Scotland, with hillsides of hyacinths, riots of

rhododendrons and hardly any darkness, is a month for celebrations. Every 5th June, or thereabouts, all the little town of Duns in the Borders turns out, led by the Provost, a minister in gowns, a Lad and a Lass on horse-back and every other rider available, and all climb up Dunse Law, the hill above the town. Beside the memorial stone and the town's handsome flag, set in the Borestone, the minister takes prayers and gives an address above the champing of bits and cries of excited children. Then, as the psalm is lifted and soars, everything comes into focus. You look past today, past the clothes, the rhodies, the foreign fir-trees, and straight back 340 years to the same little farms below, the same long line of moor rolling towards the coast: where still the road to England runs, commanded by this hill.

Can the singers also see the hawthorn slopes covered with the tents and pavilions of soldiers, from which the singing of these psalms could, said Baillie, often be heard? Every regiment, by regulations, had a kirk session.

For this was "our brave and rich hill," as he called it, where Leslie pitched his main camp on 5th June 1639, with splendid banner flying from this very Borestone. There is one in Queen Street Museum today, embroidered: "FOR CHRIST'S CROWN AND COVENANT." The minister of Kilwinning himself rode between the blossoming trees with two attendants and all the vain-glory of a just cause.

"I found the favour of God shining upon me," he wrote, marching South: "and a sweet, meek, humble yet strong and vehement spirit . . ."

"I carried myself as the fashion was, a sword and a couple of Dutch pistols at my belt; but, I promise, for the offence of no man, except a robber in the way".

"Henderson and others, defamed among us for so many incendiaries, "wrote the English Earl of Stamford, "are, every mothers' sons (weapons laid aside) holy and blessed men of admirable, transcendant and seraphical learning . . ."

For one delicious moment the battle for the two Kingdoms was one: and they were winning it.

The other side thought so too, according to the full letter of Sir Edmund Verney to his family. "Dear Ralph," he wrote on leaving for the North to his son and heir: "since Prince Henry's death I never knew so much grief as to part with you."

As for his army, "there was never so raw, so unskilful and so unwilling an army brought to fight." His heart was not in it. "For my own part I have lived till pain and trouble has made me weary to do so."

Cavalier poet Sir John Suckling brought a troop in scarlet and white to the Border. It was his first view of Scotland ("God and Nature hath placed the beasts in the outfield"): but the troop would not fight.

Parleys began. The Scots were ready, even eager, for battle. "Truly, I think it will come to blows, but do not tell your mother," writes Sir Edmund. Apart from the constant worry over horses, he sends repeatedly for "a Pott" for his head. Later, when things went better, he wrote he would keep it "to boil my porrage in." He was well received in the Scots H.Q., being "well-known as a good friend to our nation," writes Baillie. (How? queries his descendant): He is delighted when he can tell Ralph that he believes he "begat this treaty"—of peace—"but, I pray, take no notice of this unless you hear it from others."

"Baby" Charles, James always called his younger son. There is always more to James than meets the eye, and all of it nasty. Charles had much of the spoilt baby to the end: the very fact of royalty, in his own eyes, gave him god-like status.

So, as the Scots and English negotiated, he made a sudden spectacular entry to Leslie's tent: as if to overawe all by his actual presence. But Johnston of Warriston, who knew a greater majesty, treated him like an ordinary man, arguing and even contradicting. At which the King turned on him in a rage, and commanded him, twice over, to silence.

The Scots held all the cards, and both sides knew it. The Pacification of Berwick let both withdraw without losing face. It avoided war by clever formula, for "anyone could mean by it what they liked." But it settled nothing.

"This day I spoke to an understanding Scottishman and one that is affected to moderate ways," wrote Verney: "he is confident nothing will satisfy them but the taking away of all Bishops, and I daresay the King will never yield to that, so we must be miserable."

But meantime there was triumph. The army marched back singing, with banners displayed. The General Assembly met in Edinburgh within weeks and framed an Act formally abolishing episcopacy forever. It was passed with tears of joy from the old men who had hardly hoped to see this day: but could now rejoice in it, with psalms of deliverance.

This Assembly also passed the first Barrier Act by which any major legislation in the church must go down not only to the presbyteries but to Kirk Sessions—to the very grass roots—for decision.

There was some opposition. The Bishops resiled in advance. The Earl of Traquair, now Lord High Commissioner, complained formally: and informally, of being rabbled by "the wifie at the Nether Bow, and one Little, the barber." The son of the late minister of St. Giles, Balquancal, a very bitter episcopalian, attacked them most. (He died Dean of Durham). To the end Archbishop Spottiswoode maintained James' argument as to: "parity among ministers being the breeder of all confusion . . . and ruling elders a mere human device." He was buried in Westminster Abbey.

Yet there was genuine moderation too. Henderson preached as

retiring Moderator, to the end that "His Majesty might see that this"—Christ's—"government can very well stand with a monarchical government." He declined re-election: "It savours of a Constant Moderator—the first stage of episcopacy; and in truth I have no mind to be a Bishop."

Henderson and Dickson had already travelled North together, with Montrose, commissioned to argue with "the Aberdeen doctors", who clung to a reasoned rather than a prelatical episcopacy. If there were no conversions, there was surely more understanding.

Dickson was now elected Moderator, and his closing message was on the same lines: "Love one another: strive not. Neither insult over those that been of a discrepant judgement from us anent the ceremonies or the government of the church: but let us make a perpetual Act of Oblivion . . ."

As the Assembly ended, the long procession of the Estates rode up the Royal Mile carrying the honours of Scotland, Argyll bearing the crown. Sixty nobles and ninety-eight barons and burgesses met under the oak roof of the Upper Chamber of the new Parliament House: and immediately ratified the Act abolishing episcopacy. The victory was complete.

Too complete. The Assembly also passed an Act making it compulsory for the whole nation to sign the Covenant, especially heads of Universities and other schools of learning: and anyone suspected of leaning towards popery.

One man who may have thought, despite signing, that this breached an invisible line between the power of the sword and the power of the keys was the Graham chieftain, Montrose. By Christmas he was secretly in touch with the King.

Even that architect of the Covenant, Warriston, had his doubts. Normally he wrote crisply and to the point—his letters to Cromwell are models in this way. But in a letter dated Christmas Day, 1639, he wrote to Baillie a long, rambling, personal letter, full of deep philosophical arguments and lawyers' Latin: till he concludes:

"They would remember they should not bauchle the Covenant to the defence of every fantasie; seeing it is a national Oath it must abide a national interpretation in any question whereof the interest is universal . ."

"Now let them consider, if they be so strictly bound to recover that which was never had, and so was never lost . . . As for going to Dunse Law, truly none could have thocht it lawful for private persons . . .

"Brother, I am unweel in my body. I am wearied 'dyteing . . . I wish, and sall labour be all lawful means to recover the liberty of this Kirk (which is all the Covenant can import): but only to the furnishing of grounds for removing of these scruples from people, albeit ignorant and rash, who yet perhaps are zealous and so would be satisfied with reason, before they grow so unreasonable as only to trust to the reason of arms."

BOOK II

DEBATEABLE LAND

CHAPTER ONE

THE CASTE FOR THE DAY

On the evening of Sunday, 14th January, 1968, a large and rather scruffy crowd began to pour into St. Giles. They were mostly students of Edinburgh University, with shoulder-length hair and wrinkled jeans. An English girl was leading the demand for the resignation of their Lord Rector, Malcolm Muggeridge, the preacher that night, for opposing the free hand-outs of contraceptives. Over 2,000 packed in, many standing, mostly hostile.

In the vestry minister and preacher eyed each other, with gleams of understanding. The University Bedellus brought the Rector's gown of office: claret-coloured velvet laced with gold, edged with fur and lined glistering satin. "Do you mind if I don't wear that?" said Mr. Muggeridge. So when he stood in the pulpit in the concentrated glow of light, circled by this huge intent crowd, it was as a slight figure in a light grey suit.

Every chosen word was bell-clear, chiselled by certainty, as he preached, brilliantly, bitingly, on "Another King . . ."

" . . . No doubt long after I am gone someone will be saying on some indestructible programme like "Any Questions", that a touch more abortion, another year at school and birth pills given away with the free morning milk and all will be well . . . Communist utopianism produced Stalin; the pursuit of happiness, American style, produced Lyndon Johnson, and our special welfare variety has produced Harold Wilson. If that doesn't put paid to all three nothing ever will. As for the scientific utopia looming ahead, we have caught a glimpse of that too in the broiler houses, the factory farms, and lately the transplant operations . . ."

"So I come back to where I began, to that other King, one Jesus . . . As far as I'm concerned, it is Christ or nothing . . ."

"And I tell you that wherever the walk, and whoever the wayfarers, there is always this third presence ready to emerge from the shadows and fall in step along the dusty, stony way."

He might have been quoting Peden!

It is no surprise that this very English man should so grasp and cleave to the basic doctrine of the Covenanters.

His own background is so much that of the Independents, the Non-conforming, who have so often been the backbone of England; and who, in Covenanting times, were the Kirk's fellow-pilgrims and comrades-in-arms.

The mass-media of our day, in which Malcolm Muggeridge is so

71

famous, is television. In early seventeenth century it was still the stage, and its language coloured the talk of of all those who found themselves caught up in the violent drama of their times. They were, and knew they were, what Muggeridge, recalling all the tragedies and farces of his own lifetime, calls "the caste for the day."

"Let us play our parts to the utmost of our powers," wrote a Cavalier to a Roundhead friend: "God grant that we get off with honour."

Getting off-stage well mattered a lot: and many men of these times used the phrase. To many, it was the most public act of their lives.

A different production went on in the Palace. "The King loves trinketting naturally," observed Robert Baillie, minister of Kilwinning, who saw and talked with Charles I frequently.

The King was a careful and knowledgeable art critic, collecting paintings and giving support to van Dyck, Rubens and a host of Flemish and Italian masters; and filling his Palaces with statues and antiquities. The Palladian styles of his favourite architect, Inigo Jones, is still admired in some of his buildings: but not those transient masterpieces of his art and Ben Jonson's poetry, the court Masques. These extravagant entertainments, with verses, songs, costumes, complicated plots and satires, grandiose scenery and "devices", were the spectaculars of the age: but for court circles only. They took months to prepare, hours to perform and thousands of pounds to produce. It almost seems as if Charles felt at home in this totally artificial world, where no human or economic reality could intrude. He might have been happy in Holywood.

While the country struggled to live, the Royal households employed an estimated 1,700 servitors, all well fed. Taxes grew and grew, and the army of tax-gatherers, as always, grew with them; until they "dipped in every dish." The Palace of Whitehall, a town in itself, was a focus of this discontent. It is a little depressing to reflect with what continuity it is so still.

In April, 1640, the King summoned Parliament to raise money to crush the Scots. The members were mostly squires and moderate men. Sir Edmund Verney and his beloved son Ralph were among them. An early leader, Sir John Elliot, author of "The Monarchy of Man", had died in the Tower (and been buried there): John Hampden, who had so courageously refused to pay the Ship Money tax, was present, but he was no speaker. It fell to a shaggy, studious young man called John Pym to put the case for the Commons of England. He spoke for two hours: and at the end they voted that "redress of grievances must precede supplies." Charles then dissolved this, the Short Parliament: and turned for help to Black Tom Wentworth, Earl of Strafford, presently trying to subdue Ireland.

Strafford's plan was to send Hamilton sailing up the Forth to take Leith, and to land an Irish Army on the West of Scotland while the King marched North with the main troops. Money must be got, and there was a concentrated effort to raise it from Catholics, Bishops in Convocation, Royalists and the Queen. London crowds demonstrated against the King, and on Strafford's advice two young men were hanged, one being tortured on the rack first—the last time torture was used in England.

The Scots were also having trouble in raising money and men. Warriston was "forfochten" with worry. But a fast, and an appeal, preached from every pulpit, brought a whole-hearted response. Jewellery and plate and provisions were handed in, hoarded home-spun blankets brought out of kists. Hamilton's mother, assisting to fortify Leith with her own hands, vowed to draw the pistols she wore at her belt and fire on him if he tried to land. With good stores and good will the Scots marched to the Tweed Border-line. Montrose, still openly with the Covenanters, was first to lead his men across the river. After a victorious brush with the King's men at Newburn, Leslie marched into Newcastle and occupied the town. This cut off coal to London, and a main source of royal revenue.

Argyll was left to hold the West against the threat of an Irish landing, but some of his Highlanders were in the Scots army—"the nakedest fellows ever I saw," reported a scandalised Englishman. Their huge plaids—the kilt is the surviving half—had to be discarded in battle, when they knotted what shirt they had between their legs and fought with a targe on the left arm, dirk and broadsword in either hand, and in this case also bows and arrows.

The King got as far as York, where there was a Peace Settlement made. By it the Scots were paid £860 a day and occupied the Northern counties. This had to be ratified by Parliament. The English soldiers, "the meanest sort of fellows about London" were not so lucky. Ralph Verney's young brother, Cavalier officer Mun Verney, complained that by winter they were six weeks pay overdue and "notable sheepstealers already."

Another Cavalier, writing earlier to Lady Devonshire, comments: "I am teaching carthorses to manège, and making men that are fit for Bedlam and Bridewell to keep the Ten Commandments, so that General Leslie and I keep two schools, he has scholars that profess to serve God, and he is instructing them how they may safely do injury and all impiety: mine to the utmost of their powers never kept any law either of God or the King and they are to be made fit to make others keep them."

Parliament was called by the King for November 3rd, again for money for the war. This was the Long Parliament that sat for twenty years. The Scots had put in three other peace terms besides the pay: 1). Withdrawal of royal proclamations against the Covenanters. 2). Punishment of "Incendiaries"—troublemakers. 3). "The settlement of uniformity in religion between the two Kingdoms of Scotland and England." The first two were provisionally agreed: the last put to a committee of both Kingdoms.

On the King's suggestion, a conference was held, to which the Scots sent eight commissioners; these included Warriston, Henderson (now minister of St. Giles) and Baillie.

Baillie left his parish, bairns and affairs to his wife—is there a special corner of heaven for manse wives?—and he made his will before he left in her favour. It consisted chiefly of debts owed him by struggling farmers, and by the very look of them, bad debts. He clearly thought so too, for he left her also golden advice: to rejoice if anything ever was paid, but never, never to eat her heart out over the might-have-been. As for the expenses of the journey, he reminds her that it was now all or nothing in the affairs of both State and Kirk. "You must not look to expenses when . . . presently we are either to win the horse or tyne the saddle."

They had a good ride South—the first of so many—finding English inns "like palaces" and particularly enjoying "a sort of little crevishes . . . marvellous dear." Scampi always are.

But their arrival in the big city was sensational. The whole town was already seething, streets in uproar, processions and demonstrations everywhere.

They saw Burton and Prynne march past with Parliament troops "everyone with a rosemary branch" in his helmet—there were no uniforms, and badges were always a difficulty. Bastwick led a whole cavalcade with 27 coaches, 1,000 horses, trumpets sounding, torches, "a world of people."

"God is making here a new world," wrote Baillie.

The Scots, traditional enemies, were now friends and allies.

"Many here are very gracious people. They go far beyond us in private fastings. This Monday is almost a solemn day . . . for voting out of episcopacy . . . All things here goes on as our hearts could wish . . . we were extremely welcome . . . Huge things are here in working; the mighty hand of God be about this great work! We hope this shall be the joyful harvest of the tears that thir many years has been sown in thir Kingdoms. All here are weary of Bishops."

He also saw Strafford, with his "proud, glooming face" go to confront Parliament: and leave for the Tower. Laud was already there.

The King tried a belated stand, offering a mutual Act of Oblivion to both sides.

The Scots had actively helped to draw up the charges against Strafford and Laud, and it was clear that Warriston would be first for the scaffold on any royal list. He refused to the King's face to accept any kind of bargaining. So Strafford's trial before Parliament went on.

An extraordinary amount of eating and drinking went on too during the sessions, as a witness records: "not only of confections but of flesh and bread, and bottles of beer and wine, going thick from mouth to mouth . . ." It sounds like a Test match. Old Lady Sussex, friend of the Verneys, constantly sent Ralph titbits ("perly-cakes and a jeely of pippins") "to comfort you up." They only sat during daylight hours, as a rule; but it was an unaccustomed exercise.

Strafford defended himself brilliantly and the charge of treason could not be made to stick. The House brought in a Bill of Attainder which the King swore on royal oath never to sign. But the pressure built up, the mob rampaged round Whitehall, Strafford himself wrote: "I do most humbly beseech your Majesty, for the prevention of evils which may happen by your refusal, to pass this Bill." In the end Charles did so. Strafford went to the block in May marching "like a general at the head of an army." Old Laud, soon to follow, blessed him through the bars.

By August the Scots Treaty was concluded, their army disbanded and the King set out for Edinburgh. For it was clear that neither side in England could win without the Scots. Charles came to Holyrood on a Sunday, and heard Henderson preach, as Royal Chaplain; but spoilt the good impression by a round of golf in the afternoon. He had come to woo the Scots, and made eager overtures in conversation. But he angered their Parliament by claiming the right to make Royal appointments to all the high Offices of State. Again, it was the hated Warriston who produced old documents, from Hay of Dunfermline's charter-chest, which proved it belonged to the Scots Parliament alone. (A relevant point for future Scots Assemblies).

Before he left in November Charles gave a banquet in Holyrood and distributed titles. The Palace has its gloomy side (I have heard the present monarch's p.p.s. complain of going to bed past a plaque stating "The Queen's secretary was stabbed here"): but it is a splendid setting for a royal occasion. Charles made Leslie Earl of Leven, Argyll a Marquis, Hamilton a Duke and even Warriston a knight and judge: and Henderson Dean of the Chapel Royal.

He had done very well. For the Scots were set on keeping loyalty to their earthly King second only to their higher duty. Some, like Montrose, who signed the royalist Cumbernauld Band at this time, were growing to see the two as identical. There was some dissension among the Covenanter leaders, as "the Incident"—a vague plot and panic—showed. Montrose was briefly imprisoned.

As Charles turned South, the tide was turning in his favour there too. Dissension was growing in the English Parliament, and resentment between it and the people, as it too had to raise money and levy taxes.

Then came disaster. The Irish rose. They acted, not as a conquered people fighting for their land, but as dervishes in a holy war. Ministers were crucified on their church doors, their homes burned and the children who ran out screaming thrown back to burn alive. All the horror of Rome fighting for supreme power with Inquisition, live burnings, tortures, showed up like a grinning skull in the flames. Both Kingdoms reacted sharply against the King and his policy, in

Scotland through the Church, in England through Parliament. Many of Charles' friends and supporters were Papists, and so was his Queen. Strafford's plan to bring in the Irish was not forgotten.

The Queen had cut down her Catholic household, and seen her daughter Mary married to the Dutch Protestant Prince of Orange. But it was too late. Now Pym and Parliament presented a Grand Remonstrance of grievances. There was a rumour that the Queen herself would be impeached. Charles was nerved by desperation to order the arrest of the five most prominent members of the Commons, including Pym and Hampden. But the Lords would not authorise it, nor the Commons give them up. Egged on by the Queen he set off with a guard to do it himself. But he delayed, there was time to give warning. "I see all my birds have flown," said the King, looking round. Yet he still hoped they would be handed over, and bravely demanded them from a city enraged to frenzies. "Privileges! Privileges of Parliament!" the mob howled round his coach, shaking their fists.

The Royal family fled London. The King saw the Queen and Princess Mary embark at Dover for Holland with the Crown Jewels to sell for arms; all of them weeping. Then he set about raising troops, which Parliament was already doing with far greater success. As one Lord observed: " . . . that they who hated Bishops hated them worse than the devil, and that they who loved them did not love them so well as their dinner."

On August 22nd Charles saw his Royal standard raised at Nottingham by Sir Edmund Verney. It was stormy, and the huge embroidered cloth was blown over. Sir Edmund no longer troubled for "a Pott" for his head, nor even put on armour or buff-coat. This beginning of the war was for him the end of all things. His beloved Ralph was compelled by conscience to join the Parliamentary side.

"Brother", wrote Mun to him, ". . . .there be too many to fight with besides ourselves . . . Though I am tooth and nayle for the King's cause, and endure so to the death, whatsoever his fortune be, yet sweet brother, let not this my opinion (for it is guided by my conscience) . . . cause a diffidence of my true love to you."

Sorrowful as the family cleavage was, Sir Edmund's grief went deeper. It was easy for professional soldiers, like Rupert of the Rhine, the King's nephew and cavalry commander, son of Elizabeth of Bohemia; to him, killing English peasants was no more than killing cattle. It was some ease to those who believed in what they did.

"You have satisfaction in your conscience that you are in the right," Sir Edmund told Hyde, later Lord Clarendon, in Nottingham: " . . . and so you do your duty and your business together; but for my part, I do not like the quarrel, and do heartily wish that the King would yield . . . so that my conscience is only concerned in honour and gratitude to follow my master. I have eaten his bread and served him near thirty years, and will not do so base a thing as to forsake him;

and choose rather to lose my life (which I am sure I shall do) to preserve and defend those things which are against my conscience to preserve and defend. For I will deal freely with you, I have no reverence for the Bishops, for whom this quarrel subsists."

In October the two armies met head-on at Edgehill, and fought bloodily, "horse and foot . . . against horse and foot" for a day and a night. It was indecisive. Parliament forces withdrew, so royalists claimed a victory. Sir Edmund fought to the death below the standard, captured only by cutting off his locked hand. It was re-taken by the ruse of a cavalier wearing the orange scarf of Parliament (he was later knighted beneath it).

Ralph sought desperately for his father's body, in the faint hope he might still be alive. But only the clenched hand was found, with the ring the King had given him and he always wore—a miniature of Charles. You can see the ring in Claydon, the Verney house, today.

Who can be certain of hero or villain, goodie or baddie, till the curtain falls?

In Scotland the chief roles in the cast for the day were not, as in the English pattern, the landed gentry: still less the nobles or the red-coats; but, above all, the sober-clad clergy and commons.

They were not for that reason all dull. When young Mr. Blair found, in his first parish, that the congregation bolted for the door without waiting for his benediction—as is not unknown in America even today—he gave out that he had a special announcement to make.

This turned out to be: "Now, the prettiest man and woman among you all, rin first and fastest from the Blessing!"

But he could also preach on the progress of holiness as being an apprentice in Christ's workshop: "He still to them Master of Work."

When Semple of Carsphairn, in the lonely Galloway hills, was called a varlet, he retorted that he was at least God's varlet. "Look not to me," was his call to prayer to the congregation, "but haud up your toom dish with mine . . ." He rather unkindly prayed for one of the Cants, famous preachers of Aberdeen: "Brod him . . . let the wind oot o' him . . ."

He could not endure anything " . . . such as sleeping or rambling looks . . . fighting of collie dogs . . . or the like" during service. "Few durst either sleep, or look about them, or bring dogs to the Kirk." On the other hand he was not boring, even on that unlikely topic, the Covenant of Works, where he was heard to cry to the shade of Calvin: "Come, man, set your foot to my foot, and we shall hough Bellarmine yet!"

Nine months in the dungeons of Edinburgh Castle did not intimidate him unduly ("He is above that guides the gully"), but he was seen to smack his pulpit lovingly on return with the cry: "I parted o'er easily with thee . . . but I shall hing by the wicks o' thee now."

Very different was the young and handsome Willie Guthrie, cousin of the more famous James who was later beheaded. So witty and delightful a companion was he, it was said the very soldiers from the castle sought his company on his visits to Edinburgh. The first people to hear him preach gave him his first call, to Fenwick where there was not yet a church. They built it, but then had to fill it.

For long enough the folk living on that wide moorland South of Glasgow had felt no need for kirk or ministers, and now many avoided him even when he tried to visit. He took up the challenge. He not only farmed his glebe, like all country parsons, but became outstanding at fishing, fowling and curling on the ice. Disguised as a weary traveller he would seek shelter at remote farms, and so gain a footing. He even paid one member half-a-crown to attend Kirk, this being the money he otherwise earned fowling at that time.

Having got them in, he next had to win them over. Here his record of a full, devoted church until the day he was outed speaks for itself. But so too does *The Christian's Great Interest*, the little book he was pushed to publish, and which is still reprinting.

He had a "great pleasure in music," and a splendid voice; but also a sad secret—continual internal pain.

"Penny for your thoughts, Cousin," said James to him.

"There is a poor man at the door, give him the penny! I will tell you, cousin, what . . . I am sure of . . . The malignants will be your death, and this gravel will be mine; but you will have the advantage of me, for you will die honourably before many witnesses, . . .and I will die whining upon a pickle straw . . ." He did die in extreme agony, able only to say, "Though I should die mad, yet I know I shall die in the Lord."

We are all conscripts in that war.

Scots and English were for the moment growing closer.

"Great and good news!" cried an English merchant home from Scotland: "I went to St. Andrews where I heard a sweet, majestic-looking man"—Blair— "and he showed me the majesty of God. After him, I heard a little fair man"—Rutherford—"and he showed me the loveliness of Christ. I then went to Irvine where I heard a well-favoured, proper old man, with a long beard"—David Dickson— "and that man showed me all my heart."

CHAPTER TWO

"DOST THOU SEE YONDER SHINING
LIGHT?"

"Then said Evangelist, pointing with his finger over a very wide field, 'Dost thou see yonder wicket-gate?'
The man said, 'No.'
Then said the other, 'Do you see yonder shining light?'
He said, 'I think I do.'"

So begins Bunyan's *Pilgrim's Progress*, written that century: a century of quests.

The General Assembly of the Church of Scotland met in the East end of St. Giles in 1643, the summer following Edgehill. Six English Commissioners waited upon it, from the Westminster Assembly of Divines: four laymen including the courtier Sir Harry Vane, one presbyterian minister and one independent minister. The Westminster Assembly had been set up some time before by the English Parliament, in despite of the King, to consider the reform of the Church of England, and in particular, Bishops. Now they wanted to see "a nearer agreement with the Church of Scotland." They were seriously considering making the Church of England wholly presbyterian.

"The Churches of England and Scotland may seem both to be embarked in the same bottom," ran their address: "to sink or swim together . . ."

To suppress "papists and prelates" they also wanted soldiers. Both King and Parliament had been making approaches to the Scots for nearly a year, the King doing very well with the nobles. But the suggestion of uniformity in religion had a powerful appeal.

Henderson, in a splendid pamphlet, set forth firm repudiation that the Covenanters had "a presumptuous intention to reform England" or to "touch another free and independent Church and Kingdom." "We do not presume to propound the form of Government of the Church of Scotland as a pattern for the Church of England, but do only represent in all modesty these few considerations . . . Here there is superiority without tyranny, parity without confusion and disorder, and subjection without slavery." But above all, persuasion was to be by preaching only, "without forcing of conscience."

One obscure M.P., Oliver Cromwell, was so impressed by this he borrowed it twice "against that debate."

It was a nicely balanced question whether the Scots' new relationship with England was in support of freedom of religion or freedom of Parliament purely.

"They were for a civil league, we for a religious covenant," wrote Baillie. So finally, out of compromise, the "Solemn League and Covenant" was born. It was duly accepted by both English and Scots Assemblies, and about one-third of the English Lords and Commons swore to it with uplifted hands in St. Margaret's Westminster, in September of that year, where Henderson preached. A month later the Scottish Estates likewise swore to it in the choir of St. Giles "with great joy and many tears." It was then law, and compulsory.

The three main objects of the Solemn League were:-

1) That they would all "sincerely, really and constantly, through the Grace of God . . . endeavour to preserve the reformed religion in the three Kingdoms" (including Ireland) "according to the word of God and the example of the best reformed churches. And shall endeavour to bring the Churches of God in the three Kingdoms to the nearest conjunction and uniformity in religion, Confession of Faith, form of Church Government, Directory for Worship and Catechising: that we and our posterity after us may, as brethren, live in faith and love and the Lord may delight to dwell in the midst of us."

The second point was more selective.

2) "That we shall in like manner, without respect of persons, endeavour the Extirpation of Popery, Prelacy, Superstitition, Heresy, Schisms, Prophaneness and whatever shall be found to be contrary to sound Doctrine and the power of godliness . . ."

3) "With the same sincerity, reality and constancy . . . to preserve the Rights and Privileges of Parliaments and the liberties of the Kingdoms, and to preserve and defend the King's Majesty's person and authority . . . that the world may bear witness . . . that we have no thoughts or intentions to diminish his Majesty's just power and greatness."

In rather confusing support of which Leslie, Earl of Leven, led the Scots Army back over the Tweed into England next January, singing as they went:

"Stand to't and fight like men!
The gospel to maintain!
The Parliament's blythe to see us coming!"

They occupied Newcastle again.

Eight Scots Commissioners now went South to the Westminster Assembly; three elders, including two peers and Warriston, and five ministers including Mr. Baillie.

He sent a constant stream of letters to his cousin, Mr. Spang, minister of the Scots Kirk in Campvere in Holland; generally with requests for books and pamphlets in English, French, Latin:

80

including "a Hebrew Bible and Syriac New Testament, in one volume, both with the points . . . a million of thir would sell in two years!" He also asks information of the whole state of Europe, for Protestant Holland was now the centre for new learning and free speech.

"From that day to Monday," runs his account of arrival, "we keeped in, providing for causey-clothes." London noticed clothes. It had already called the M.P. Oliver Cromwell "that sloven" for his grubby neck-band and village-tailor suit. On Monday, Henderson sent to both Houses of Parliament for the warrant of entry, and three members of the Assembly came to convoy them into it. "Here no mortal man may enter to see or hear, let be to sit, without ane order in write from both Houses of Parliament . . . Dr. Twisse had ane long harangue for our welcome . . . The like of that Assembly I did never see . . . They did sit in Henry VII's Chapel, the place of convocation: but since the weather grew cold, they did go to the Jerusalem Chamber, a fair room in the Abbey of Westminster . . . well hung, and had a good fire, which is some dainties in London."

Besides Dr. Twisse in the Chair ("merely bookish, and not much, as it seems, acquaint with conceived prayer") there were two Assessors, and ranks of forms both sides of the table. "On the lowest we five do sit." The others were filled by divines and M.P.s appointed there. The debates were very long, very formal. "They follow the ways of their Parliament. Much of their way is good, and worthy of our imitation: only their longsomeness is woeful at this time when their Church and Kingdom lies under a most lamentable anarchy and confusion." They sat for nine and a half hours every weekday: besides committees and correspondence.

"... I will talk of things Heavenly, or things Earthly: things Moral or things Evangelical: things Sacred or things Prophane; things past or things to come; things foreign or things at home; things more Essential or things Circumstantial; provided that all be done to our profit."

Now did Faithful begin to wonder: and stepping to Christian . . . (but softly) What a brave companion have we got! Christian: His name is Talkative . . . he is the son of one Say-well and dwelt in Prating Row.

The Assembly sat for years, and exercised Talkatives to the full. The Scots, coming from another Nation and National Church were by their own decision observers, not members. They had a special Committee meeting once a month to press for that elusive uniformity. Their intellectual clothing at least was fully adequate. Besides Henderson, Baillie, Rutherford of Anwoth, there was Robert Douglas, now minister of Kirkcaldy, of whom Gustavus Adolphus had said: "There goes a man who, for wisdom and prudence, might have been counsellor to any Prince in Europe." And there was young

Gillespie, so soon to die of consumption, whose brilliance outshone all the rest, and even put down the great man that Milton, writing at this time, called: "Our admirable Selden," Selden said himself, "that young man, by this single speech, has swept away the learning and labour of ten years."

To begin with, the debates were exciting. The New World seemed almost there. But this wore off. The London fogs gave way to the stifling heat of summer: and the plague continued in cities.

"They can get nothing to any point, either in Church or State," wrote Baillie: "we are vexed and over-wearied with their ways."

They toiled through Apostles, Prophets (now extinct); the duties of pastors (finally agreed): those of doctors and teachers (in which there was sharp division): and reached Ruling Elders, which all the Scots maintained "on the old French grounds . . . to stand on a Divine right; and that ane Ecclesiastic right alone is no just foundation for any officer in the House of God." The English would have none of it, then as now.

"We have been in a pityful labyrinth these twelve days, about Ruling Elders; we yet stick into it," wrote Baillie to Spang: again, "if our neighbours at Edinburgh tasted the sauce wherein we dip our venison at London, their teeth would not water so fast to be here . . ."

"There is shortly," he tells Spang, "to come from the Assembly here letters in Latin to all the Reformed Churches, and among the rest to you in Zealand and Holland." He asks them to be sure to reply in some unanimous way. Gillespie championed Ruling Elders, and independent church courts but there was a more fundamental issue.

The Scots were already "all of one mind" on the "necessity" of coming forward, out of their pews, to sit as a family at the Lord's Supper. "We may not possibly part from it,' wrote Henderson. Baillie agreed. They all utterly rejected the Independents' imitation rite in pews: now forced on us all. By law, new kirks had to have room for a table at the front: for actual use, not altar imitation.

They had finally struggled through Baptism; but now reached this, the un-bridgeable chasm: communicating at a table. Becoming "overtoiled with debate" through "a world of such questions," they were "forced to leave all these things, and take us to general expressions" with "benign expositions." We have indeed all heard them.

Yet the prize was great. In a speech reporting back to the General Assembly Baillie said;

"God has done great things for poor Scotland, wherein our hearts doth rejoice . . . When the Bishops of England had put upon the neck of our Church and Nation the yokes, first of their episcopacy, then of their ceremonies, thirdly the whole mass of a Service Book: and with it the body of Popery . . . to have been freed of these burdens: to have been restored unto the purity of one first Reformation, and the

82

ancient liberty of our Kingdom: . . .we would lately have esteemed it . . . as a mercy above all praise . . ."

" . . . but now behold . . . the Lord has plucked up the root and all the branches of episcopacy in all the King's dominions. That ane Assembly and Parliament of England unamimously (which is their word) abolished not only these ceremonies which troubled us, but the whole Service Book as a very idol—that in place of Episcopacy a Scots Presbytery concluded in ane English Assembly and ordained in an English Parliament: as it is already ordained in the House of Commons; that the practise of the Church of Scotland, set down in a most wholesome, pious and prudent Directory should come in the place of a Liturgy in all three dominions; such stories lately told would have been counted fancies, dreams, mere impossibilities; yet this day we tell them as truths, and deeds done, and great honour to our God."

This was in January, 1645, when victory seemed within their grasp, and uniformity established forever. The year before there had been a battle at Marston Moor between the King's forces and those of Parliament.

"God gave us that victory wonderfully," wrote Baillie to Spang: "There was three Generals on each side: Leslie, Fairfax and Manchester: Rupert, Newcastle and the King: within half an hour and less, all six took them to their heels (this to you alone)."

The man who didn't run was now Colonel Oliver Cromwell with his "lovely troop" as he called them, "who expect to be treated as men." Unlike Rupert's headlong charges, they could check, re-form and return in perfect discipline. But that the battle was not lost before they did was due to the remnant of the Scots standing firm and withstanding the whole brunt. One critic thinks they, as much as any, deserved the name of "Ironsides." Prince Rupert, in his scarlet clothes laced with silver and his Arab horse, must have got away fastest: but among the mounds of dead lay his constant companion—a little white poodle.

Among the Scots wounded was Mure of Rowallan, Renfrewshire, of a very ancient house which ended ruined and extinct for allegiance to the Covenant. He had made Metrical Versions of the psalms, which Baillie thought surpassed all others. These psalms were to form the Book of Praise for the United National Church—what could be better?

"These lines are likely to go up to God from many millions of tongues for many generations," wrote Baillie, pleading for Mure's version. Here is a surviving fragment.

"For me a table Thou does spread
In presence of my foes:
With oil Thou dost anoint mine head
By Thee my cup o'erflows.

Mercy and Goodness all my days
With me shall surely stay,
And in Thy house, Thy name to praise,
Lord, I will dwell for aye."

But here, as at every other point of decision, the Scots were defeated. Turgid torrents of doggerel from Dr. Rous, Provost of Eton, were officially accepted instead.

As the Parliament grew more secure, the English grew more indifferent to the Scots hopes. Uniformity in religion was no longer desirable, even among themselves.

"We have great toil here in the Church Business," writes Baillie pathetically: "we are on the point of setting up Presbyteries and Synods in London; but all the ports of Hell are opened upon us."

The guns were manned by Independents, relatively few but potent. They included Cromwell and Milton who had both at one time sworn the Solemn League and Covenant, and ultimately Bunyan: and a confused host of small sects, surpassing anything the Scots ever attempted: Anabaptists, Quakers, Socinians, Erastians and many, many more.

"The Independents cause much trouble," complained Baillie: He refers to "all the chiefs of the wild and monstrous people:" and to their "hen-wiles"—all taking off in different directions. While the Assembly with "bickerings and strange ruggings" strove to find that impossible unity that would cover them all.

"Then he took him by the hand and led him into a very large Parlour that was full of dust, because never swept . . . But when the man began to sweep, the dust began so abundantly to fly about, that Christian had almost therewith been choked. Then said the Interpreter to a Damsel that stood by, Bring hither the water and sprinkle the room; the which when she had done, it was swept and cleaned with pleasure."

Surely if any man could have sprinkled a little grace on the dusty proceedings of the Westminster Assembly it would have been Rutherford of Anwoth, with whom it was a favourite word. He had returned to his parish for five years after the National Covenant, but spent the next four as a Commissioner to London.

"If grace pay not our debts," he writes to thank his "brother in Borgue" for clerical assistance: "I see not how I shall mak' a reckoning . . . only it is God's will that we put grace to the utmost."

"My heart beareth me witness, and the Lord who is greater knoweth," he explains why he is not going back to London: "my faith was never prouder that to be a common rough country barrow-man in Anwoth: and that I could not look at the honour of being a mason to lay the foundations of many generations in another Kingdom . . . I desire but to len a schoot and to cry Grace, Grace upon the building."

Rutherford's grace did not extend to those "of Gallio's naughty faith." Gillespie, preaching to the House of Commons, denounced those who "cry up that detestable indifferency and neutrality abjured in our solemn covenant . . ." Rutherford was wholly against those who would pander to "the conscience of the idolator"; not to save his soul, but "to make the church quiet and peaceable."

"Every sect cries, give me Liberty," said Cromwell, "but give it to him, and to his power he will not yield it to anyone else."

The Scots knew they were not a sect; they were a Covenanted nation. Any defection from the covenant they saw as an infringement of sovereignty.

Sovereignty to the English meant something quite different.

"Sir," said Cromwell to a Scot, Major-General Crawford, who had turned away a volunteer who would not swear the Covenant: "the State in choosing men to serve it takes no notice of their opinions, if they be willing to serve it faithfully, that suffices."

The difference in priorities cut deep. The Independents wanted liberty for all; but under Parliament, which would set up civil courts to hear appeals from churchmen. The independent courts of the Kirk with its Ruling Elders they viewed with horror.

Milton had come back to England from Italy expressly to aid Parliament in the Civil War. He had been pouring out pamphlets and poetry ever since. As well as his anti-episcopal tracts, there had been one on Education, and the famous one on the freedom of the Press: so full of rolling paragraphs, rich imagery and endless sentences, it deserves to be read by sub-editors pencil-less in Purgatory. Now in one pungent sonnet: "On the New Forcers of Conscience under the Long Parliament" he damned the Scots hopes:

"Dare ye for this adjure the civil sword
To force our consciences that Christ set free
And ride us with a classic hierarchy
Taught ye by mere A. S. and Rutherford? . . .
When they shall read this clearly in your charge—
New Presbyter is but Old Priest writ large."

A. S. was Dr. Adam Stewart, a presbyterian supporter in Sedan, and then Leyden.

Speaking in the House as the Ambassador of another King, Warriston answered him:

"Mr. Prolocutor, I am a stranger. I will not meddle with the Parliamentary privileges of another nation . . . but as a Christian man under our common Lord, a Ruling Elder in another church, and a Parliament man in another Kingdom, having a commission both from that Church and State, and at the desire of this Kingdom assisting to your debates, I entreat for your favour and patience . . ."

"In my judgement, that is before you which concerns Christ and

85

these Kingdoms most and above all . . . I can never be persuaded that (these troubles) were raised, or will be calm, upon the settling of civil rights and privileges, either of King or Parliament . . .

I am confident they have a higher rise . . . for the highest end—the settling of the crown of Christ in this island . . . Until King Jesus be set down on his throne with his sceptre in his hand, I do not expect God's peace . . . in these Kingdoms . . .

" . . . martyrs for Christ's crown are the most royal . . . of any State martyrs: for although Christ's Kingdom be not of this world. and his servants do not fight therefore . . . yet it is in this world, and for this end was he born. And to this end . . . were we born . . . But in a peculiar way it lyeth upon you, Sir, who has both your calling from Christ for it, and at the same time a particular calling from man.

. . . Christ lives and reigns alone over and in his church, and will have all done therein according to his word and will, . . . he has given no supreme headship over his church to any Pope, King or Parliament whatsoever."

It was the perfect reply to Milton.

At the end he was able, as always, to produce the right papers: the original letter of overture from Parliament to the General Assembly of the Church of Scotland, so full of promises and of hope.

He won Parliament's vote, but not its conviction. Presbyteries of a kind were set up in London and Lancashire: but they were still to be subject to the civil law.

At the end of it all, the Metrical Psalms, the poems of the promises, however poor the verse, became the true Scottish praise, and comfort for centuries. Only now, to our loss, are they discarded. So too is that superb document, the *Shorter Catechism*, which the Westminster Assembly commissioned.

The *Westminster Confession*, finally issued, became as "a subordinate standard" the substitute Confession of Faith of the Church of Scotland, and is so still; "a second-rate thing, kept for fear of worse." The English kept neither. Poor Baillie was left begging that "the Covenant at least be approved." He had a desperate longing for Kilwinning: "My heart's at home long ago."

Henderson, who had hoped so much and worked so hard, was broken-hearted. All his suffering and disillusion is in his portrait, now at Yester, from the studio of Vandyke. He had longed for "some quiet little landward charge", but preached that a man's times were not his own.

Throughout this time the King had established his court at Oxford. At first it was something of a picnic: but he soon appointed a Master of Revels, and re-created that unreal world in which he moved so serenely, so much at home.

By now Montrose had finally decided to join him. He knelt and asked leave to raise the Royal Standard in Scotland. After Marston Moor the King graciously granted the request, making him shortly after a Marquis. It seemed the most forlorn hope: but Montrose rallied the clans, was joined with forces of Irish, and began that campaign of brilliant victories and savage slaughters that brought terror to the Covenanters and sent royalist hopes soaring sky-high.

" . . . back come Bishops, Books and all," wrote Baillie despairingly to Spang. It was the final destruction of that grand delusion, the Super-church: and the beginning of a new, more dangerous quest.

"Wherefore, thought I, the point being thus, I am for going on, and venturing my eternal state with Christ, whether I have comfort here or no;" wrote Bunyan in gaol: "if God doth not come in, thought I, I will leap off the ladder even blindfold into eternity, sink or swim, come heaven, come hell, Lord Jesus, if thou wilt catch me, do; if not, I will venture for thy name."

That was a daylight decision, by someone who knew where he was going. But what of all the ordinary folk caught in the mist?

". . . and I was fear'd and confused, thinking I had lost my way," says the Closeburn wife in Hogg's *Tale of the Martyrs:* "and then I came to an auld man, and he says to me, "Is it the road to Heaven that you are seeking, Aggie?" An' I said, "Aye," for I didna like to deny't."

"Then I'll tell you where ye maun gang," said he, "ye maun gang up by the head of yon dark, mossy cleuch, an' ye will find ane there that will show you the road to Heaven." An' I said, "Aye," for I didna like to refuse; although it was an uncouth-looking road, and ane that I didna like to gang."

CHAPTER THREE

THE GOLDEN LEGEND

Like a scarlet sash, a golden thread, through the dust of ecclesiastical debates and civil shifts and compromise runs the Legend of Montrose: the Great Marquis. When all else is forgotten, his greatness is remembered.

His story is a romance of chivalry, ready made. He joined the King not, like others, when all was going well and he might be made by it: but at Charles' lowest ebb, his blackest hour, when there was all to lose, and so little chance of anything to gain. And his success was splendid.

Even old Leven never carried out anything like Montrose's brilliant victories all across the winter-savage map of Scotland. Yet he was no hardened mercenary, but an aristocratic chieftain, writing courtly poetry, welcomed in Vienna and Paris, and ornamenting the small court of exiled Elizabeth of Bohemia in Holland as well as joining that of Charles. His chestnut curls and noble bearing fit perfectly the picture of the hero. In a corrupt age his personal character was noble, in blackest defeat his bearing princely. Perhaps that was what made him so blindly royalist. After Charles' death he could hail him as: "Great, good and just . . . ."

But his flourishes were never frivolous. In servants' clothes, with four stringy horses, he crossed hostile Scotland to an uncertain meeting in the Blair Atholl mountains with the Irish troops and Colkitto's clansmen. He captured all their hearts, and led them out to triumph after triumph.

No country has suffered more than Scotland from romantic novelists. Most are women writing happily for women; but some, as Hay Fleming acidly points out, are historians. They have one thing in common: they write principally for the far greater market South of the Border; and whether lush or factual, whether Walter Scott or the latest codswallop on Mary, Queen of Scots, they are orientated thereto.

I remember as school-girls how we pored over a book on the '45, recommended by the history teacher, written—like many—by a lady who had never set foot in Scotland. It began with the young Highland laird taking that incredible exercise, his customary early morning swim round the point—presumably doing Australian crawl since his arms "flashed." He then threw himself "unconcernedly" down in the heather—prickly but thrilling, since clearly there were no eighteenth-century bathing-suits. The laird was Episcopalian: therefore civilised. The book is still reprinting, hugely popular.

Montrose's admirers have been more restrained. He is not really an episcopal champion. Although his own chaplain, Wishart, became a Bishop and the others with his army were Irish priests, he still claimed to the end to be a Covenanter.

"The Covenant which I took, I own it and adhere to it. Bishops, I care not for them. I never intended to advance their cause," he told the ministers of Edinburgh shortly before his death: "but when the King had granted you all your desires, and you were everyone sitting under his vine and under his fig tree, that then you should have taken a party in England by the hand and entered into a League and Covenant with them against the King, was the thing I judged it my duty to oppose to the yondmost."

This is obscure thinking, and a very negative objective. To fight for Charles was to fight against the Covenant, his fellow Scots and all the English Parliamentarians. "Baby" Charles, as he must have seen, was weak as water and equally unstable. What outcome could he possibly have hoped for? Or was the campaign itself—the glory of it—enough?

Baillie, who campaigned with him, speaks of his desire for command, and of his "more than common pride." Highland pride is quite incalculable: and he was a Chief. The Letter on "Sovereign Power," by him alone or with Lord Napier his brother-in-law and ex-tutor, ran: "And thou, seditious preacher, who studies to put sovereignty in the people's hands for thy own ambitious ends . . . know this, that this people is more incapable of sovereignty than any other known."

There indeed speaks the Chief.

Sentimental affection for Gaelic songs and the pipes makes us forget that the clansmen, properly led, were the most splendid—and ferocious—fighting men in Europe.

Montrose marched east with the Highlanders and Irish troops whose threat had alarmed both Scotland and England for so long. A small army tried unsuccessfully to bar his way, but he made for Perth, calling out the clans. At Tippermuir, near Perth, he met the Covenanting forces for the first time, and beat them soundly. Perth surrendered.

Clan Gordon of Huntly, whose lands had been pillaged by Argyll and clan Campbell the year before, came out to join him in force, and they marched on Aberdeen, of which Montrose was a freeman: and which had supported the King in the past. He called on the town to yield, and when they refused, took it by storm. He then turned loose the clans and the Irish for three days and nights of licensed loot, rape, robbery and slaughter.

Not even Cromwell did that to his own people.

In roadless Scotland no armies moved in winter. But Montrose turned West over the high passes where only clans could go, and swept down into Argyle. Colkitto MacDonald, Lord of the Isles, joined him with more men from the Isles and Ireland, and they ravaged like wolves in the snowy glens. An estimated 895 men and boys were killed "without battle or skirmish." It brings a picture of the lonely croft or clachan, unaware probably of any enemy but winter, any struggle but survival: then out of the dark the yells, the torches, the steel—blood for blood!

Argyll was out-generalled and defeated in his own land time after time. He fled constantly, often in his galley, *The Black Sail*. He fled from Inveraray to Rosneath Castle, he fled from Montrose's great victory at Inverlochy, in February. Gillesbeag Gruamach—"the Gloomy"—had, they said, fear in his soul.

"Only give me leave," ran Montrose's dispatch to the King after Inverlochy, "after I have reduced this country to your Majesty's obedience, and conquered from Dan to Beersheba, to say to your Majesty then, as David's general did to his master, "Come thou thyself, lest this country be called by my name."

The Covenanters were appalled. While the ministers called for fasts and repentance, Montrose swept on. In spring he was back in the East, and captured Dundee in April. In May he won a battle at Auldearn, near Nairn; and in June another at Alford, Aberdeenshire. Turning South, with his invincible army he marched to Kilsyth, near Glasgow, where he met the full muster of Covenanting forces in what was their own home-ground, and cut them to pieces, with heavy slaughter. It was a rout.

Montrose made terms with the city of Glasgow, and agreed not to sack it. This was a disappointment to the clans, and many now began to drift back to the mountains. The raid was over.

In England, the King's war was already lost. The slovenly small country squire with seven sisters and a masterful mother, Oliver Cromwell, had inherited land. He was now a power in Parliament. By his proposal of a *Self-Denying Ordinance* there were whole-sale resignations in the army: and in the elections he emerged Commander-in-Chief. Cromwell used democracy like James had used monarchy: he made it work. And his burning conviction drove him on. "Our rest we expect elsewhere."

He re-made the New Model Army on the lines of his Ironsides, and led them to conclusive victory at Naseby that summer.

Before the battle the King and his troops were so impressive with their banners and trumpets, and Charles himself in full gilt armour on a black Flemish horse, that the Parliament officers withdrew their troops behind the nearest ridge, it is believed to save them from the discouraging sight. The Royalists charged first. Rupert's cavalry crashing through the Parliament's left wing: then Cromwell's troop scattered the Royalists' left, and actually came face to face with Charles and his Life Guards before Lord Carnwath siezed the King's bridle and took flight. The Ironsides re-formed and shattered the

Royalist centre. By the time Rupert got back, the battle was over and lost. Among the baggage captured was the King's carriage and all his papers, including letters to and from the Queen: showing how hard they tried to get Irish troops, Catholic troops, foreign troops of any sort, to fight their own subjects.

Charles did not despair. He surrounded himself, as always with those who looked on the bright side, and would not have "melancholy men" about him. "I am nowise disheartened." he stated: " . . .I hope shortly to recover my late loss with advantage." Rupert tried desperately to get through to him: but he refused to listen. "God will not suffer rebels and traitors to prosper, nor this cause to be overthrown."

He wandered about, playing bowls, reading poetry "as if no crown had been at stake." Finally he resolved to march to Scotland to join with Montrose. He went leisurely through the summer fields, and by York had 2,000 men and felt his position "miraculously good" again. But he was already far too late. His army, which pillaged as it went, was deteriorating daily. Rupert, to Charles' vexation, had been forced to yield up Bristol, their last stronghold. As he turned back he got the news that Montrose had once more met the Covenanters in pitched battle at Philiphaugh: and had been totally, decisively defeated.

We have outgrown the terror of the Inquisition, but thanks to the I.R.A. in this century, we can to some extent understand the terror the Irish gave both English and Scots 300 years ago. The English Parliament decreed, and the Scots accepted, that any Irish found fighting on British soil would be put to death without trial. All Irish prisoners were put to death after Naseby, and also after Philiphaugh. These included the last fifty of Montrose's 300 fighting men, who had surrendered; and, it is said, their camp-followers.

To claim that the ministers either assisted or rejoiced in this is neither credible nor necessary. It is enough that they were committed to it.

When Argyll harried the Gordons, his banner carried the device: "For the Covenant, Religion, the Crown and the Kingdom." The Gordons, when they marched in reprisal, had on theirs: "For God, the King and against all Traitors." Whether as justification or excuse, these slogans were clearly not intended to be taken as a programme. One of the first and most adulatory of Montrose's biographers, his brother-in-law Napier, alleges that the Covenanters carried one embroidered: "Jesus and No Quarter." Though unsubstantiated, and wholly improbable, this has been zealously repeated ever since, the scrupulous adding qualification. For some it is the only thing "known" about Covenanters! Yet it's only "authority" is a wild royalist broadsheet printed in London, as John Buchan admits. The allegation that gentle David Dickson cried "The work gangs bonnily on!" at the post-war executions is equally without proof or credibility.

Was this to embellish Montrose by blackening his opponents? Was it from need to say—as my history teacher did—"One side was bad as t'other"? Or simply an old root of episcopal bitterness?

Montrose as a hero needs no whitewash. He was consistent to the end in nobility of carriage, courage in battle and unstained loyalty to the throne. Even his escape after Philiphaugh has a glimmer of glamour about it.

But what in fact did the hero achieve? One certain thing: he brought upon the common people he despised—on the poorest, the most helpless, on women and children and old and weak—the most wasted and unnecessary wave of suffering the century had yet seen. And in his own country.

At that price, he gave the clans their last successful foray. And if it was personal glory he coveted he has had that in full measure ever since. But who counts the price? Heroes have no warts!

By next spring the only Royalists left in England were broken and beggared men. Parliament was supreme. But Charles, still holding court at Oxford, was hopeful of yet encouraging discord, as the Solemn League grew unpopular in the South and the Scots army grumbled at the lack of pay in the North. He decided to go to Scotland, and set off once more in April, lightly disguised in a plain suit and false beard. He reached the "Saracen's Head" near the Scots H.Q. at Newark in early May. The Scots made him welcome, took him to Newcastle for security, and gave their whole hearts to persuading him to agree to Parliament's new treaty. This offered his restoration and assured peace in return for Parliament's control of armed forces; presbyteries established and episcopacy abolished.

Charles had written to his Queen the year before that he would never give up "Episcopacy or that sword God has given into my hand." The sword had gone, but he remained immovably Anglican. Warriston, who had spent mind and strength and "exhausted his whole patrimony" in labours for the Covenant, both at home and as a member of the Committee of Both Kingdoms in the South, made every effort to get him to sign. "All the Royalists in Scotland could not have pleaded so much for the Crown and the King's just power," wrote Baillie.

Charles, complaining that he was "barbarously baited" by other ministers, asked for Henderson. With him he exchanged long, scholarly letters on their irreconcilable viewpoints, as if it was one of his favourite games of chess. Henderson too was a defeated man. As Parliament grew supreme, it grew indifferent to both Scots and Solemn League. By the end of 1648 it would reject the Covenant outright.

Henderson was also a dying man, and won home, "near unto the High School in Edinburgh," only to his death bed.

"I am near the end," he wrote to Sir James Stewart, later Lord Provost of Edinburgh and later still exiled: "hastening home, and there was never a schoolboy more longing to have the play than I am to have leave of this world."

The ministers had one wholly unexpected ally. The Queen, throughout her married life, had constantly threatened to retire to a nunnery if Charles did not mentally stiffen up. Now his ill-timed stiffening infuriated her. Of course he should sign the treaty, the Covenants, the lot! Her elastic Catholic conscience, which she passed on so fully to her eldest son, Charles II, saw no obstacle at all. None of these agreements need be binding. Besides, since Anglicans, Presbyterians, Independents and all the rest were equally heretics and equally damned, why this niggling and hair-splitting?

Baillie understood him better. "The King took very well with me, I might have had occasion to say to him what I pleased; but knowing his fixed resolutions, I would not meddle at all, neither to preach nor pray before him . . . remaining what he was in all his maxims, a full Canturburian, both in matters of religion and State, he still inclined to a new war; and for that end resolved to go to Scotland. Some great men there pressed the equity of Scotland's protecting him on any terms. This untimeous excess of friendship has ruined that unhappy Prince".

He could not go to Scotland: for the General Assembly, under the dying Gillespie as Moderator, would not have him unless he signed the treaty: and sign he would not.

"What the King or his English Parliament will do next there is no certainty," wrote Baillie. What the Scots did was go home, having at last, after much haggling, got half the back-pay promised to them by Parliament. The King, who had been playing golf with Leven when the English Commissioners arrived, agreed to go South to Holmby House, and seemed restored to his usual serenity by the arrangement. He made a faint joke about the Scots selling him cheap, which remains fossilized in the history books: and ordered Montrose, still trying to recruit, to disband.

The Scots army disbanded, except for two bodies. One went North to harry again the Huntly lands in reprisal for last winter's work in Argyle. The other went to that long peninsula to deal finally with Colkitto's men, the remnant of his Scottish-Irish forces. They were cornered on the southermost tip, on Dunaverty Rock. Of the 800 who finally surrendered, 400 were butchered. Of males, only one small boy was left. Two hundred years later his direct descendant, Rev. McWilliam, sought the Earl of Argyle's permission to gather up the scattered bones and give them Christian burial. General Turner washing his hands as usual, blamed it preposterously on the chaplain, Nevay. But blame is irrelevant. The golden adventure that began so gaily on Duns Law, "our brave and rich hill," came to this ghastly end: and Dunaverty Rock marks its grave.

Charles set off with his escort on what became almost a royal Progress. Everywhere the people, on whom he had brought nothing but misery, hurried to cheer, to kneel, to kiss his hand. The King took it all most graciously; while already planning to encourage new dissensions. Royalty is strong magic. To the True Believer, all of it that glitters is pure gold.

CHAPTER FOUR

THE MONARCHY OF MAN

"Religion stands a-Tiptoe in our land
Ready to pass to the American strand."

So George Herbert wrote at the time; and those of us exasperated by opening our doors to the handsome young men of the Mormons, or to Jehovah's Witnesses, or Christian Scientists or Scientologists or followers of this or that sect, creed or Maharishi, may sometimes feel that the New World has re-exported esoteric faiths back to us with excessive interest.

The *Mayflower* had sailed in 1620, and in the three decades following well over 10,000 emigrants sailed to what Cromwell called the "howling wilderness" of America. With the Dutch they founded Massachusetts and spread to Maine, Connecticut and Rhode Island. Amongst genuine Dissenters were those who had "earned a reputation for holiness by flight." Earlier, Laud had scorned a "universal running to New England and God knows whither." After 1650 the numbers were enormously swollen by prisoners sold as slaves: Dissenters cast out by yet more radical dissent. It was the age of Descartes and Spinoza, Sir Thomas Browne and Charles James Foxe.

English Covenanters, London Covenanters: the terms that once might have suggested revolution now represented reactionaries in face of the fantastical army of Independents. There were only eleven chief English Covenanters in the Commons; the Conservatives, as it were. But they had a fairly large backing both in the House and in the City of London. To curb the Independents they had to get rid of the New Model Army, its backbone. They followed the customary demob. procedure of offering them their bare wages, or the chance to enlist for Ireland—generally considered a quick trip to the grave: and even for that they had to swear the Solemn League.

But these were troops which, as Cromwell had boasted, "expect to be treated like men." In weeks the cavalry had organised themselves into a kind of Union (officers included) and appointed representatives appropriately called Agitators. Parliament, afraid of mutiny, now offered six weeks back pay; but now the infantry had joined in, paying weekly dues, and organising "Assemblies" of its own. These were under the influence of Colonel Thomas Rainsborough, the Leveller, and might be called Army Soviets. He advocated such startling reforms as an almost universal suffrage, and had written: "The poorest he that is in England hath a life to live as the greatest he: and therefore truly Sir, I think it is clear that every man that is to live under a Government ought first by his own consent to put himself under that Government . . ."

Cromwell, with three other M.P.'s, was asked to go down to the Army and settle the dispute. They joined it: "upon a kind of necessity . . . for preventing worse." Indignant, Parliament went back to its first terms. Cromwell and the Army then took a trick by sending Cornet Joyce with his "warrant" of 500 horses to secure the King. They brought him to Newmarket: and there the two men met face to face for the first time. The great gulf between them was now only a trick of time. The King graciously extended his hand: and General Fairfax, the aristocrat, bowed and kissed it. But neither Cromwell nor his son-in-law Ireton could bring themselves to do it.

The Army issued a Declaration that it was not a mere troop of mercenaries but a People's Army: "civilians in uniform."

"As for the thing we insist upon as Englishmen—and surely our being soldiers hath not stripped us of that interest . . .—we desire a settlement of the Peace of the Two Kingdoms and of the liberties of the Subject according to the votes and declarations of Parliament which *before* we took arms, were by the Parliament used as arguments and inducements to invite us and divers of our dear friends out; some of whom have lost their lives in this war. Which, being now by God's blessing finished—we think we have as much right to demand and desire to see a happy Settlement, as we have to our money . . ."

If the fighting men made the peace treaties, would wars cease?

One of their conditions was the election of a new Parliament, purged of the eleven Covenanting Presbyterians. In spite of Cromwell's efforts at compromise, they began to march on London. Parliament called out the city guard and the London mob. In face of chaos, Cromwell and Fairfax rode into London at the head of 1,800 troops and occupied the Tower. The eleven members fled. It was that recurring animal, the military coup.

Charles was brought to Hampton Court, where he settled in most happily. He had his Anglican chaplains, his billiards, his hunting in Richmond Park and, in "a new suit of wrought coloured satin lined with taffeta" he was able to meet his younger children nearby. They were so happy together, it brought tears to Cromwell's eyes to see them. Cromwell came to visit Hampton Court, and the dashing Groom of the Bedchamber took homely Mrs. Cromwell in to dinner.

The conditions now offered by the Army and most earnestly urged by Cromwell to the King for his Restoration, as a constitutional not an absolute monarch, were generous in every possible way, including religious liberty. Yet even as Charles studied these "Heads of Proposals" with apparent approval, except for some minor points to be amended, he had other plans. His hope was, he wrote to a friend at this time, "to draw either the Presbyterians or the Independents to side with me for extirpating one the other", so that he would then be "really King again."

While Charles plotted to divide, Cromwell strove with all his might to unite. He was not "wedded and glued to forms of government:" they were "but a moral thing . . . dross and dung in comparison of Christ." The danger above all was "such a real and actual division as admits of no reconciliation." The aim above all:" . . .let us be united in our doing."

To that aim Charles was a constant hindrance. He was secretly in touch with the Scots, he was constantly intriguing with possible allies abroad. The Thirty Years War on the Continent was ending: there would soon be troops and arms to spare. His hopes were as high as ever.

In early November Charles escaped to Carisbrooke Castle on the Isle of Wight. His flight eased the Parliament situation, and Cromwell may have known about it. Once clear of London the King's plotting moved faster. Three Scots Lords, Lanark, Loudon and Lauderdale, came to him on Boxing Day, and they signed an Engagement, one copy being buried in the garden. In it the King promised to "confirm the said Solemn League and Covenant by Act of Parliament in both Kingdoms . . . provided that none who is unwilling shall be constrained to take it." He also promised to give Presbyterian government in the church a trial for three years in England, and after that to hold another Westminster Assembly and "free debate." The Scots were to send an army forthwith in support of the King; for which they would be paid in full, including outstanding arrears, and there was to be immediate co-operation to suppress: "Anti-Trinitarians, Anabaptists, Antinomians, Arminians, Familists, Brownists, Separatists, Independents, Libertines and Seekers and generally for repressing all blasphemy and schism."

Never in any country but England was there such an outburst of sects and faiths and revolutionary parties—then as in our own day. To the list above can be added as many more, all in some way religious as well as political—especially when most violently anti-religious.

The stage had given way to literacy, and it was an age of small printers and, briefly, no censorship. No country ever had the chance to take such an unfettered look at the human situation and all its relationships—God, society, marriage, money-power, the land—to question all and to speak its mind in total freedom. In *Pilgrim's Progress* only Ignorance knows all the answers. So it was a glorious outburst, an astonishing outpouring of that non-animal quality, in man the animal, that we vaguely call "spirit."

There are echoes in our own age. There were the Diggers ("Friends of the Earth"), Levellers (Marxist Communist): Fifth Monarchy Men (The Charismatic Movement): Ranters (Pop-songs and permissiveness): Familists (Children of Light or Hippies): Adamites (Back-to-Nature nudists): Quakers (pacifists): Shakers (Brethren): Unitarians: congregationalists; Muggletonians (who sound somehow familiar): those who wished to live by every word of the Bible, and those who found it "a mass of improbabilities": (rationalists): those who asked, with earthy words, which layer of sky God sat on ("Honest to God"): wandering Messiahs: workers' co-operatives: Swiss-type cantons, and collective farms: they are all here, in one way or another.

One Leveller pamphlet advocated not only universal suffrage but freedom of religion, and for all conscientious objectors: an old age pension and state provision for the unemployed and the sick. But nationalisation of the land to pay for this Utopia was a different matter, rousing bitter hostility.

The Scots were appalled at what had become of the dream of unity. The more so as Cromwell had now set his face against the Presbyterians who alone still supported the Solemn League and Covenant. If the King had accepted Cromwell's terms then they would have had nothing left: "Only to be quiet and wait on God," wrote Baillie—a fearful prospect.

So the Engagement was welcomed by many in Scotland and passed by the Estates: only a few, such as Argyll, holding out. It was roundly rejected by the Kirk's Assembly, as betraying the Covenant, and the pulpits "sounded loud against it." In Ayrshire "Remonstrants" against it had a small battle with Engagers on Mauchline Moor. The next Assembly summoned eight ministers involved: but Warriston who was now Lord Advocate as well as Procurator of the Kirk, was not there to prosecute them.

"The good Advocate, being resolved in his mind," wrote Baillie, "if he had been put to it, to have pleaded for the ministers and not against them, was with much ado moved by his friends to lurk for some time till the storm went over." He lurked in Kintyre as guest of Argyll. Possibly that was the journey where they sang and discussed Psalm 107 together, "riding from Rosneath to Inverary."

"Praise God, for he is good: for still, His mercies lasting be . . . let God's redeemed say so, whom he from the en'my's hand did free.

He upon princes pours contempt, and causeth them to stray and wander in the wilderness wherein there is no way.

"Yet setteth he the poor on high from all his miseries, and he, much like unto a flock, "Doth make him families."

His position was the more difficult as the Estates had just granted him £3,000: as he "had expendit life and fortune in the service of the public . . . and on the whole progress of the blessed work of Reformation . . ." His wife had tossed sleepless one night, thinking of all their enemies, one by one: and the final blow of the faithful servant threatening to leave because they had too many children (they reared twelve or thirteen) and she wore her clothes too long and then cut them up for the bairns.

He and Argyll held out steadfastly against the Engagement. But Hamilton, Charles' personal friend and chief supporter, had little trouble in raising a large army for the King and marching over the Border. His invasion coincided with risings in Kent, Sussex and Wales; all counting on the breakdown of unity in Parliament and Army.

But the Officers' Council had held a great Prayer Meeting at Windsor, Cromwell present, and passed a resolution that when this, the Second Civil War was over, they would call Charles to account as "a man of blood." On this they were one.

Fairfax put down the rebels in the South, and Cromwell marched North and defeated the Scots at Preston, with heavy losses. Hamilton went to the Tower, and was condemned.

The Remonstrants of the West now rose in greater numbers. Six thousand behind the Earl of Eglinton marched from Mauchline to Edinburgh and occupied the Salisbury Crags, behind Holyrood. Old Leven held Edinburgh Castle in sympathy with them—the Whiggamore Raid, it was called—and Argyll was their spokesman. It was with him Cromwell arranged to march on into Edinburgh in peace after Preston. This was his first visit to Scotland, and he was surprised. "I thought I should have found in Scotland a conscientious people and a barren country." He was disillusioned in both.

Moray House in the Canongate, that elegant building at the bottom of the Royal Mile, was where he lodged. He laid a demand before the Estates to have all Malignants (Royalists) excluded from public office: and Warriston with three nobles brought their full assent. He was banqueted in the Castle, presumably in James IV's great stone banqueting hall, still used; with old Leven in the chair and Warriston and Argyll present.

He had "noble entertainment", he wrote to Parliament: affairs in Scotland were now in a "thriving posture". The Estates had promised to raise 4,000 horse and foot, Major General Lambert, with troops, would stay to hold the country, and Scotland would be henceforth "a better neighbour to England."

On the state of that other Kingdom the Kirk he was silent. To Cromwell the Presbyterian Church was a sect, and an intolerant one: to the Scots it was the core of national life, their identity. Freedom of worship Cromwell extolled: but it was official freedom, freedom under civil law. The idea of an independent church with its own courts, its own values and judgements on earthly affairs, if he glimpsed it at all he totally disowned it.

Back in England he re-defined toleration. Mohammedans, he said, if present, he would not have hindered in their worship. (But six months later several Agitators who had gone too far—mainly Levellers—were shot on his orders.)

Lilburne the Leveller who was acquitted (and cheered), described in his famous pamphlet how, if you asked Cromwell anything, "he will lay his hand on his breast, elevate his eyes and call God to record; he will weep, howl and repent even while he doth smite you under the fifth rib."

The Scots minister Blair summed him up more tersely: " . . .an egregious dissembler, a great liar . . . and a greetin' deevil."

Cromwell gave his own defence to the English critics as to how he could support Royalists against Presbyterians in England, and Presbyterians against Royalists in Scotland:

"I have desired from my heart—I have prayed for—I have waited for this day to see—union and understanding between the godly people—Scots, English, Jews, Gentiles, Presbyterians, Anabaptists and all. Our brethren in Scotland—sincerely Presbyterians—were once our greatest enemies . . . Was it not fit to be civil, to profess love, to deal with clearness with them for the removing of prejudices; to ask them what they had against us and to give them an honest answer? This we have done and no more . . . And we can say through God we have left such witness amongst them, as, if it were not yet, by reason the poor souls are so wedded to their church government, yet there is that conviction upon them that will undoubtedly have its fruit in due time."

He left at the right moment. His very slow journey South gave Colonel Pryde, ex-brewer's drayman, time to occupy London with troops again and purge Parliament of Presbyterians and dissidents by the simple process of not letting them in. The Rump that was left declared "the people are, under God, the original of all just power: the Commons wield that supreme power: the laws enacted . . . bind all citizens alike." In this they included Charles.

That same month, January 1649, the Scots Estates passed the Act of Four Classes, excluding all Malignant Royalists and Engagers from public office: first-class ones for life, fourth-class (mere blasphemers and sinners) for a year: and all had to satisfy the Kirk over the Covenant before re-instatement. Ministers were included in the ban. Argyll and Warriston steered this through. It was a moment of unity for the two earthly Kingdoms at least.

John Knox once wrote that his eyes had long looked for "perpetual concord" betwixt the two nations: which is economic sense. He never meant incorporating union as some historians would twist it: no true Scot ever did.

This concord, Warriston's triumph, lasted six days. Then the English Army and Parliament brought Charles I to trial.

Cromwell hesitated long over this. In the end, his and his alone was the agonising decision. Were all the Malignants to be punished, except the chief? Was his life sacred, and not those of common men? Were all their sacrifices in the past, on battlefield and in prison, to be thrown away? Were all their hopes for the new future to be imperilled

100

now by his failure of duty—his alone? He reached a decision: " . . . we will cut off his head with the crown upon it."

Charles was condemned.

He asked to see his two younger children, Henry, Duke of Gloucester who was only 8, and Elizabeth, 13, who sobbed her very heart out. "Sweetheart, you will forget this," said the King, trying to comfort her. Never, she said: she would remember it all her life. That night she wrote every word and detail in her diary, as any schoolgirl would, and the record remains. She herself died next year in Carisbrooke.

Charles was hurried to the scaffold, through the park and out of the Whitehall window, forbidden to speak and hedged round by pikemen. This, his last appearance in the role of King, and that of the last absolute King, was flawless. "Baby Charles," timid and weak, reached greatness. As the axe fell, a deep groan went up from the people, as if they had indeed lost something.

The Scots lost everything, in claims of government. To this day for all Royal Proclamations from London, seven days are allowed to elapse before they are made public from the Town Cross in Edinburgh. This allows time for a fast horseman to speed over 400 miles. But in 1649 the Estates acted as fast as possible. Charles' head fell on January 29th: on February 6th Charles II was proclaimed King of Scotland, England and Ireland with full honours, to the people standing round the cross in the shadow of St. Giles.

If Scotland could but have a Covenanted King, its Two Kingdoms could be contented at one blow: and grow together in peace and harmony. With glorious hopes both Kirk and State sent Commissioners to the Hague to treat with young Charles, just 19, from whom they expected so much.

"They would only espouse the King's cause," wrote Baillie, who was one of them: "if he would first espouse God's cause."

But, at very first sight, the ever-hopeful Baillie was able to believe everything he had wanted to believe: finding Charles "one of the most gentle, innocent, well-inclined Princes . . ."

CHAPTER FIVE

A COVENANTED KING

"A shoulder of mutton and a whore," was all that Charles II wanted, Cromwell said once. Yet at nineteen he was an intelligent, charming lad of courage and resolution. It was only later that mutton and whores took over, until they became an end in themselves.

Charles had, as even Baillie had to admit, "A great stick" at the *Solemn League and Covenant*. At most, he could agree to it only for Scotland. Secretly, he had just made Montrose "Admiral of Scotland:" but his best hope was an invasion from Ireland. Soon after his father's death he wrote to the Lieutenant-General there, who was planning to unite with the Catholics, that he hoped to join him as soon as possible. He did set out. But Paris, where his widowed mother lived, delayed him two months.

Cromwell-was now "Chief of Men" in England. Within weeks of Charles I's death a Council of State was set up, of which he was Chairman. Two leading Scots Engager peers, Hamilton and Huntly, were executed in March. Hamilton had briefly escaped, been recaptured: and had just time to scribble a note to his two motherless girls: "My most dear children, it has pleased God so to dispose of me as I am immediately to part with this life for a better, so as I cannot take that care of you as I both ought and would . . ." he begs them follow advice in their marriages "and that you think not of ever coming into this Kingdom where your father has ended his days in such a manner." All his estates he left to his younger brother, now with Charles in the Hague.

This month also the English monarchy was abolished, and the country declared a Commonwealth. Cromwell was appointed to lead the Army into Ireland.

"I had rather be over-run with a Cavalierish interest than a Scotch interest," said Cromwell to his General Council of Officers: "I had rather be be over-run with a Scotch interest than an Irish interest; and I think of all, this is the most dangerous."

There was another danger nearer home. It was the Leveller revolt against sending troops to Ireland that had first brought Cromwell to power. Now it broke out again, far more strongly. This time the objection to Ireland was not over the money conditions, but to using "a People's Army" against "the cause of the Irish natives in seeking their just freedoms" which, the Levellers saw, "was the very same with our just cause here in endeavouring our own rescue and freedom from the power of oppressors."

Their three leaders were arrested, and in all Cromwell had six Agitators shot, some in front of their regiments; and including men who had fought all through the wars for freedom and toleration. They had overstepped its official limits: its State permission.

Cromwell was now banqueted by the City of London, and given large grants for the Army. Delays and indecisions had ruined other would-be conquerors of Ireland, before and since; and many there may have wished the same fate for him. But he delayed only for full pay and equipment, sailed to Ireland that summer and carried out a campaign so swift and so savage, it remains a by-word for brutality still. After the extermination at Wexford, which followed that of Drogheda, Cromwell's chaplain Hugh Peters wrote: "It is a fine spot for some godly congregation, where house and land wait for inhabitants and occupiers."

Cromwell repeatedly defended his own efficiency as being "to save further blood." We who claim benefit from Hiroshima cannot well be shocked.

Charles got as far as Jersey, and stayed until all his hopes in Ireland were extinguished. There the Scots Commissioners pursued him, and now he had to consider the Covenant again. He agreed to a conference at Breda, in Holland; and at the same time he sent the Order of the Garter to Montrose, begging him to go on "with your wonted courage . . . and not to be frustrated by any reports you may hear as if I were otherwise inclined to the Presbyterians than I was before I left you. I assure you I am still upon the same principles." Montrose went North, and tried to raise troops in Norway.

"My Lord of Argyll," wrote Charles from Jersey: "I cannot but know how much you are able to contribute to the agreement between me and my subjects of Scotland: and desiring it as much as I do . . ." he begs him to further the sending of commissioners, and "to the moderating of their instructions as much as reasonably you may. It is now in your power to oblige me to a very great degree, and it shall be my care to remember . . ."

To Montrose, ten days later: "I will never fail in the effects of that friendship I have promised . . . and that nothing can happen to me shall make me consent to anything to your prejudice. I conjure you, therefore, do not take alarm at any reports . . . but to depend upon my kindness; and to proceed in your business with your usual courage and alacrity."

Both letters are signed, "Your affectionate friend." He betrayed them both.

To Charles the trip was not wasted. He had long maintained at the Hague the "lovely whore," Lucy Walters, by whom he had his first bastard, later Duke of Monmouth: in Paris he was alleged to have had seventeen mistresses.

In March the Scots Commissioners met Charles at Breda, and offered him the crown and an army, in return for the Solemn League

H

and Covenant sworn by himself and promised for the three Kingdoms: the Irish Catholics and Montrose to be repudiated.

Montrose had already crossed from the stormy Orkneys to the bleak main. On the East Coast of Scotland there were no Celtic clans to rise for battles and booty: only canny folk who shut the door on his rising. His was already a lost cause.

Charles publicly disowned him: and privately offered him money, for expenses. He was cornered at Carbisdale, between the Kyle of Sutherland and the Ross-shire mountains, and defeated. With the young Sir Edward Sinclair of Orkney both of them wounded, he fled into that sub-alpine wilderness. There Sir Edward—and the Garter Star—found an unmarked grave. Montrose, in rags and chewing his gloves, survived to be taken prisoner. The General Assembly decreed a day of thanksgiving.

He was brought to Edinburgh and up the Royal Mile in a tumbril—the equivalent of the dust-cart—and the whole city turned out to see this figure of terror. Like his first master, he was unconquered in defeat. His unshaken dignity awed the crowd to silence, even tears: even, it is said, Warriston, Argyll and his son and heir Lorne—all watching from a balcony; all to go the same way.

His condemned cell became a salon. He wrote poetry—critics say, his poetry was more polished than original: but it fitted the man. He went to the scaffold in a black suit trimmed silver, a scarlet cloak embroidered in silver and lined with crimson: carnation silk stockings, garters and shoe rosettes: a beaver hat (they could cost £200) trimmed silver lace: and his own long chestnut curls.

His courage and dignity never faltered to the end. He was surely the most graceful figure in that sordid place.

His head was stuck on a spike above the Netherbow Port, and his arms and legs distributed "to every airt," as his poem foretold.

As the little ship *Schiedam* of Amsterdam bobbed in the waves at the mouth of the river Spey, Charles finally put his signature to both Covenants: and landed at Spey Bay on June 23rd, a Covenanted King. He rode through Aberdeen (under Montrose's right arm) and on to Falkland Palace.

Provost Jaffray of Aberdeen, one of the commissioners and later a Quaker, was one who had scruples about the constraint of Charles' Covenant. " . . .*he* sinfully complied with what *we* most sinfully pressed upon—. . . *our* sin was more than *his* . . ." But the only one who disowned Charles completely was Mr Livingstone of Ancrum, the preacher at the Work at Shotts "I never delight to hear a man that the most part of all his preaching is what we call on the public and to meddle with state matters," he wrote: "but . . . there are times and seasons wherein a man's silence may bring a curse upon his head." In the general rejoicing, he went unheeded: though he likened the agreement to "a merchant's bargain of prigging . . ."

England gave Cromwell a conquering hero's welcome on his return from Ireland. Even Marvell, that cool poet, wrote a superb Ode for his "Anniversary:"

> "And well he therefore does, and well has guessed
> Who in his age has always forward pressed:
> And knowing not where Heaven's choice may light
> Girds yet his sword, and ready stands to fight . . .
> If these the times, then this must be the man."

Within weeks, he and his weary troops had crossed the Border and made camp in Musselburgh. Fairfax had refused this command and the troops were unwilling. They disliked invading a friendly nation to kill old comrades who had fought beside them. David Leslie, General of the Scots Army, had been Cromwell's lynch-pin in the crucial battle of Marston Moor.

Cromwell exhausted every argument "To all that are Saints and Partakers of the Faith of God's Elect in Scotland" to get them to abandon the King. At the same time the ministers were equally exerted to bring Charles into a more convincing state of grace, with endless sermons. Neither side made progress.

But it was Cromwell, not clergy, who was the loudest in conviction that God was on his side. "These victories and successes are God's rather than ours," he stated after the brutal conquest of Ireland: they were also, he assured Parliament, "seals of God's approbation of your change of Government."

When appointed to invade Scotland: "I have not sought these things. Truly I have been called unto them by the Lord, and therefore am not without some assurance that He will enable his poor worm and weak servant to do his will and fulfil his generation."

The Scots could not rise to such confidence, especially when the Act of Classes, passed to please Cromwell in the first place, had deprived their army of all the best Royalist officers. But for once they were superior in numbers and position. Even without God's categorical assurance, they thought they could win.

"We continue the same . . . to the Honest People in Scotland" Cromwell further wrote to Leslie: "wishing to them as to our own souls." He was "ready to perform what obligation is upon us by the Covenant. But that, under pressure of the Covenant, mistaken and wrested from the most native intent and equity thereof, a King should be taken and imposed upon us; and this be called the cause of God and His Kingdom . . ."—the chief Malignant again supported when all the lesser ones were outlawed—any justice or reason in it "we cannot discern."

The armies skirmished round each other and the city of Edinburgh. Leslie had had a huge defence cut from the Canongate to Leith, which kept the Ironsides out. They went round the Pentland hills, the Braid hills and back down the coast to Cockburnspath. On August 3rd Cromwell wrote his famous last appeal, accusing the Scots of "a carnal confidence upon misunderstood and misapplied precepts, which may be called spiritual drunkenness." It deluded them to believe all they did was established "upon the Word of God." He went on: "Is it then agreeable to the Word of God all that *you* say?" His great cry rings through the centuries: "I beseech you, in the bowels of Christ, think it possible you may be mistaken... There may be a Covenant made with death and Hell."

Charles was not wanted with a "purged" army, so after a brief visit to Edinburgh Castle he was taken back to Falkland. In an attempt to clear up the situation a Declaration was drawn up in the West Kirk (St. Cuthbert's) that same August specifically denouncing Charles' father, mother and grandfather James, their lives and works, the Irish pact and the Papacy generally: and repeating again the terms of both Covenants. Charles was asked point-blank if he would sign it. In Dunfermline, ancient seat of Kings, Patrick Gillespie, minister of Glasgow and brother of the dead intellectual, begged him "in his Master's name" not to do so if he was not satisfied "in soul and conscience:" adding "No, not for three Kingdoms!"

"Mr. Gillespie, I am satisfied with the Declaration, and therefore will sign it," said Charles, not to be trapped into any admission of honesty. At the same time he wrote reassuringly to Ireland "however I am forced by the necessity of my affairs to appear otherwise . . ."

Three weeks later, on 3rd September, his mask for a moment slipped and he burst out to his father's old Secretary of State: "I shall only say this to you, that you cannot imagine the villainy of the" (illegible) "and their party. Indeed, it has done me a great deal of good, for nothing could have confirmed me more to the Church of England than being here seeing their hypocrisy . . ."

An odd word for Charles to choose, in the circumstances.

On that same day, 3rd September, Cromwell's weary army was trapped by Leslie's host between the sea and the hills at Dunbar. Their doom seemed certain. But like Elijah with the priests of Baal, he did not waver. The Scots, over-confident, grew careless. They came down out of the bitter winds to the plain to camp. "The Lord has delivered them into our hand," said Cromwell, biting his lips till the blood ran, drunk with glory. For this blunder some blame the ministers for having purged the army, some (including Carlyle) blame the remaining English officials, some Leslie himself.

The result was devastating. Cromwell silently prepared by night, attacked at dawn and annihilated them. Only dead, wounded and fugitives were left. Thousands were marched South to slavery in the new Plantations overseas, or in the salt-mines, or died of starvation on the way, for no food was wasted on them.

"They were made by the Lord of Hosts as stubble to the sword," said Cromwell: and halted the slaughter only to lead the singing of Psalm 117—the shortest.

The conqueror marched on into Edinburgh, finding munitions in

St. Giles and ministers sheltering in the Castle. He reproved them for not knowing "the mind of God in the great day of his visitation:" as proved by his victory. They had not so learned Christ, they answered, "as to hang the equity of cause upon events." Had not both sides solemnly appealed and prayed he retorted: and was not God's judgement manifest? Then how could they "slightly call it an event?"

He settled in, and had one of his chaplains preach in St. Giles. When the ministers protested—more especially at sundry Ironsides who felt called to clatter up the pulpit steps with their swords and spurs on—he made his classic defence of lay-preaching:

" . . . are you troubled that Christ is preached? Is preaching so exclusively your function? It is against the Covenant? Away with the Covenant if this be so. Where do you find in the scriptures a ground to warrant such assertion? . . . Your pretended fear that error should set in is like the man who would keep all wine out of the country lest men should be drunk . . . When he doth abuse it, judge."

To the Scots, whose preaching was tested, both intellectually and by day to day living with their people, this was shocking. But the Kirk was fatally split. Some were for repentance against "the great and mother-sin of this nation" in watering-down in any way the Covenant. The Resolutioners, the Moderates, were for King and Covenant in a pact with Royalists: the Protesters of the West, the true old Whigs, were for "Covenant first and last." They drew up a document at Dumfries, and Warriston the Whig, and Douglas the Royal Chaplain, fought bitterly over it. Before the Estates, Charles present, it was voted down.

Cromwell marched to Glasgow—Mr. Baillie retreated to the Isle of Cumbrae, leaving his wife to face the Ironsides: but said later their behaviour was faultless.

Cromwell and his Generals went to service in Glasgow Cathedral, where Mr. Zachary Boyd, with considerable courage, "railed on them to their very faces." He might well have been shot, but Cromwell good-humouredly reserved him to hear his own prolonged grace at dinner.

Cromwell had been very ill that winter in Edinburgh, but by now he was in good form again. He was "very familiar" with two of his prisoners, Provost Jaffray and Mr. Carstares, minister of Cathcart and later Glasgow Cathedral. He asked the Glasgow ministers "to give us a friendly Christian meeting," at which debate there was "no bitterness, no passion vented" on either side. "My Lord General and Major-General Lambert for the most part" . . . and for the Kirk, Mr. James Guthrie and Mr. Patrick Gillespie.

Twice he sent appeals to the men of the West to lay down their arms. The second time he sent Jaffray and Carstares. The latter, like his son William who was born that year, was to be a wanderer for most of his ministry. "My dear, I had reason always to bless the Lord that I knew you," his wife wrote: "and this day I desire to bless him more than ever . . ."

When a younger son was born and died she wrote: "Many things are sadder than the death of a child: yet I have my own heaviness for him."

Getting no response to his appeals, Cromwell routed the Westland forces at Hamilton, and finished off Leslie's remnant at Inverkeithing. The Scots had only one card left.

Charles had tried once going off on his own to raise men to follow him; like an unsuccessful election meeting, no one came. He went back to his role of Presbyterian penitent, and being a natural mimic and good actor he did it thoroughly: joining in the national fast that Christmas (while Cromwell ate his Christmas dinner in the High Street): until, as he was heard to say, "I must repent that ever I was born."

Rashly, wrongly, courageously, the Scots decided to take the risk of believing in his sworn word. At Scone, on New Year's Day, 1651, they solemnly crowned him "Charles II, King of Three Covenanted Countries."

CHAPTER SIX

CROWNING MERCIES

The Romans first noticed the black humour of the Picts; that last resource of conquered peoples. Government departments dealing with the Western Isles today may recognise it.

When Edward I of England—"The Hammer of the Scots"—conquered Scotland at the beginning of the 14th century, he demanded from them the Stone of Destiny, the sacred crowning—stone guarded by the monks of Scone. For centuries the Kings of the Picts had been crowned on it, and later Kings of Alba. Its origins were lost in mists of time; but it well may have been brought from the East as the old legend, that it was Jacob's pillow at Beth-el, suggests. One can almost hear the mourning, the bitter grief and wailing, with which was formally surrendered a very heavy square of local sandstone. This was duly transported all the way to London, and incorporated into Edward's famous Coronation Chair in Westminster Abbey, to be part of the solemn coronation ritual of all English sovereigns for all the centuries since. There tourists see it—or one very like it—today.

It may be that Edward himself saw the joke by the following year, for he sent a band of knights to pillage and ransack the monastery of Scone. But of the well-described hollowed block of black basalt, some two to three feet high, covered with sacred hieroglyphics and furnished with rings for transport poles, there was no sign then or since.

In the 20th century some ingenious Scots took away from the Abbey the square of sandstone, to draw attention to Scotland's desire to resume independence. It was inspected and cared for by a monumental stonemason whose tasteful displays of gravestones used to be on show among the dress shops of Sauchiehall Street, Glasgow. He made at least one exact replica. He said he would reveal in his will which was the one handed over and replaced in the Chair in Westminster. But the man is gone, and the joke remains.

If ever there was a black joke, surely it was the coronation of Charles II. Argyll, who arranged it, was promised a dukedom, the Garter and £40,000: the sum being arrears of pay still owing to the Scots army from their last invasion of England. Charles even suggested marrying Argyll's daughter, which was instantly vetoed in Paris.

The coronation took place in the little parish church of Scone, built with stones from the ruined Abbey, with Robert Douglas, leader of the Resolutioners, preaching. The Scots did not anoint their sovereigns with oil as priests and heads of the church, he reminded Charles; but prayed instead for unction from on high. He recounted again how James VI & I had declared his support of the Kirk: "Notwithstanding all this, he made a foul defection: he remembered not the kindness of them who had held the crown upon his head. Yea, he persecuted the faithful ministers for opposing that course of defection: he never rested till he had undone Presbyterian government and Kirk Assemblies, setting up Bishops and bringing in ceremonies against which formerly he had given large testimony."

Surely Charles listened carefully. It was practically a blueprint.

Both Covenants were then read through, and Charles knelt, held up his right hand and swore "in the presence of Almighty God, the Searcher of Hearts" to keep and defend them to the full. He then signed both Covenants, and his full oath attached. Then and then only was he "shown to the people" in the church by the Lyon King, and they acclaimed him.

He knelt again to take the Coronation Oath from the Moderator: and then, robed in purple, was given the Sword of State, and Argyll put the crown on his head. The nobles in turn touched it, and swore allegiance. He was given the sceptre by the Earl of Crawford and Lindsay, and Argyll led him to the throne. Douglas spoke on the meaning of the symbols, a royal pardon was proclaimed: the King now showed himself to the crowd outside who shouted "God Save the King!"

Finally, the catalogue of Scots Kings was recited, the Lords kissed his cheek and Douglas warned that breaking the Covenant brought ruin. Charles appealed to the crowd: "That if in any time coming they did hear or see him breaking that Covenant, they would tell him of it, and put him in mind of his oath."

"Sir, you are the only Covenanted King with God and his people in the world!" Douglas addressed him: "Be strong and show yourself a man!" They all sang Psalm 20: "Deliver Lord, and let the King, Us hear when we do call."

In full robes, with full escort, Charles returned to Scone Palace, and then to Perth, now the only free seat of Government: and bonfires were lit from hill to hill.

Having paid the price, Charles set out to collect. Here he and Argyll parted company. Many distrusted the Campbell Chief for going so far with the Resolutioners—

That Hilander whose conscience and whose eyes,
Played handy-dandy with deceit and lies"—

an allusion to the slight squint which gives Argyll's portrait an irresolute air. But he had done his best for Kirk and King: and when

110

the Act of Classes against the Engagers (Royalists) was repealed in June, he went back to Kintyre. Middleton and Lauderdale, leading Engagers and King's men did ostentatious "penance" in the Kirk, took the Covenants, and then took over the Government.

That spring the Scots State papers and registers were captured: and lying in a leaky ship at Leith, kept Warriston endlessly busy with the thankless task of their recovery and care, as his letters to Cromwell show. They were then taken to the Tower. At the Restoration they were to be returned: delayed for a search for Charles' signed Covenant: and finally shipwrecked and mostly lost at Berwick.

In July the Assembly met—and split. The Protesters were the smaller body, but the more convinced. They fought for Christ's Kingdom only; and produced a pamphlet on *The Causes of God's Wrath* in which Charles figured considerably. They had such men as James Guthrie of Stirling and his colleague Simson, Rutherford of Anwoth and Warriston himself to lead them; and they had the people's support.

The Assembly met in St. Andrews and then Dundee, interrupted by the battle of Inverkeithing in which Leslie was defeated. Cromwell marched on into Perth, as the Estates fled, leaving the door South invitingly open. Charles and Leslie, all the Royalists, some Resolutioner ministers and all the troops, both Highland and Lowland, they could raise—about 20,000 in all—marched over the Border into England.

Charles had counted on support rising to meet them. But from the moment he set foot in England he was known, in all the contemporary references, as "the Scotch King." As such he got little or no help at all. Only a few hundreds joined them as he marched towards Wales. Cromwell saw them trapped near Evesham, and outside Worcester, a year to the day after Dunbar, he fell upon them.

From the Tower of Worcester Cathedral Charles saw his troops being destroyed, and going down he charged and rallied with the greatest courage among them. When they finally broke and fled they ran into traps wherever they turned. All those rounded up were taken on order of Parliament straight to Bristol to be shipped to the Plantations. They starved as they went. Charles, hidden by a Catholic family at risk of all their lives, saw some of them go past. After the first crisis, he hungered for mutton. But his shelterers had not afforded butcher-meat since their eldest son was born, so it had to be secretly stolen. (After Restoration, Charles awarded them and their descendants, a pension "in perpetuity." By the end of the 19th century, recipients included several U.S. citizens and the French Ambassador to Queen Victoria. The Trust is reputed to pay out still).

Charles' escape was a marvel, for he was six foot tall and notably dark. It was not only due to the selfless courage of little people, mainly Roman Catholics, including the disguised Jesuit, Father Huddlestone, who re-appeared at his death-bed: but even more to

111

Charles' own cool courage and skill in mimicry. When troops appeared he would go straight up to them, asking: "What news?" He was in turn groom, lady's servant, pot-boy and Puritan: and played each role with zest. His aide was early suspect, when a smith noticed three of his horses' hooves were shod in three different counties, the last being Worcester. But he reached Brighton and finally crossed the Channel in the coal-brig *Surprise*; being carried ashore on the back of a young Quaker called Carver.

There was a rush to claim rewards at the Restoration. The *Surprise*, re-named *The Royal Escape*, came up-river to moor as close as possible to Whitehall. But Carver asked nothing for eighteen years, when he came to the King with a list of 210 Friends imprisoned for more than six years. The next year he came back and got promises for 471, and 20 other Dissenters, including John Bunyan.

To the end of his life, Charles loved to talk of his escape: and vividly recounted it to Pepys among others. As he got older, it tended to empty the room. But it was his finest hour.

When asked in Paris why he had not tried to get to Scotland, he said, "I had rather been hanged!" Apart from his own views, Scotland was now a beaten and conquered country.

Shortly before Worcester the Estates had been captured by General Monk, whom Cromwell had left holding Scotland, and shipped prisoners to England. This included old Leven, many of the Lords and some ministers including Mr. Sharp of Crail. On September 1st Monk took Dundee by storm, and sacked it with every brutality. One by one the strong points were taken.

Before the bleak fortress of Dunottar, on the far North-east coast, was taken next May, the ministers' wife smuggled out in her clothes the Honours of Scotland, that very ancient regalia used at the Scone crowning. (How on earth did she hide the huge Sword of State?) She hid them all under the floorboards of her husband's little Kirk at Kinneff. Scotland was beaten to her knees. "I do think truly they are a very ruined nation," wrote Cromwell. As for Worcester, he hoped and believed it was "a crowning mercy" to ensure lasting peace in all three Kingdoms.

Next October Scotland and England were declared to be now "one Commonwealth." Scotland was to be governed, under Monk, by eight commissioners sent from England. The Royal Arms were ceremonially torn up at the Cross of Edinburgh, and Charles disowned. Next month, all public meetings were forbidden "of any persons for the exercise of any jurisdiction other than such as is or shall be from the Parliament of England."

Because there was both resentment and resistance, further terms were "tendered"—compelled—at Dalkeith in January. Nominally, Scotland got representation and trading privileges; effectually, she lost all. Even her law, the Court of Session, was subordinated. It was the union England had always desired.

"As when the poor bird is embodied in the hawk that hath eaten it up," wrote Mr. Blair. James Guthrie and other Protesters who preached against it had troops quartered on them.

The state of the church was worst of all; for while full toleration was granted to ministers "of spiritual ordinances according to the order of the Scots churches" it was so also to "others who, not being satisfied in conscience to use that form, shall serve and worship God in other Gospel ways"—papacy and prelacy excepted.

There was strong protest against this "change of the whole fundamental form of government" without consultation. It virtually denigrated the national church from its right to speak for the nation. Moreover, the ministers said, "We dare not add to nor diminish from the matters of Jesus Christ, dearer to us than all things earthly which is so far from being secured" by . . . "general and doubtsome toleration."

But the Assembly itself was split bitterly between the Resolutioners who accepted the situation, and the smaller, thrawn body of the Protesters who held a rival Assembly and declared the other "unlawful, un-free and unjust."

Those who prayed openly for the King were imprisoned; so others did it by allusion. Patrick Gillespie, brother of the brilliant Gillespie now dead, was the only one to pray openly for Cromwell: and was appointed Principal of Glasgow University.

This was the year when Cromwell thought seriously "to take upon him to be King." He had huge plans for England's mercantile expansion, and was already at war with the Dutch, rivals in trade and colonies; especially in the Plantations of the West Indies and America, of which Cromwell himself was commissioner. "The Lord has declared against you," he told the Dutch Ambassador, after a defeat.

He listened to the plea of the Jews from Holland, and opened the door to them: to create "the City" of London. He confiscated land insatiably in all three Kingdoms, he restored and backed the East India Company which plundered India. He was building his New Jerusalem, determined that the people's government should be "for their good, not what pleases them." He even had a scheme to ship several thousand "young Irish wenches" to deprived colonists.

The ineffectual but persistent Rump Parliament was no help. He disposed of it in April with the famous cry: "You are no Parliament, I say you are no Parliament: I will put an end to your sitting . . . What shall we do with this bauble?" (The Mace.) "Here, take it away."

So in its place came 140 "diverse persons fearing God and of approved fidelity and honesty" nominated "by myself with the advice of my Council of Officers." Rous, poetiser of the psalms, was Speaker and five Scots were included. In a burst of joyful faith Cromwell told them: "Truly you are called by God to rule with Him and for Him; I confess I never looked to see such a day as this . . . it may be nor you

113

neither . . . When Jesus Christ is owned this day by your call." They were to take over until "God may fit the people for such a thing," so recently had they been "in thraldom and bondage" to Royal power. He saw at last the Kingdom come, the Promised Land. " . . . You are at the edge of the promises and prophesies."

The "Barebones" Parliament lasted five months, passing such Social-Workery reforms as making marriage a civil ceremony. Cromwell came to refer to it as "a story of my own weakness and folly." However forced to compromise in his setting-up of earthly Kingdoms, the completeness of his honesty—"warts and all"—never falters.

Next July two rival Assemblies met in St. Giles, separated by a thin partition and irreconcileable convictions. There were some 750 Resolutioners to 150 Protesters. At the same time there was a rising of some of the clans in the far North-west, led by Glencairn. They were defeated at Dalnaspidal: but the rising gave the English C-in-C the excuse to suppress Assemblies altogether. Baillie was there.

Dickson had preached on Peter and Paul, urging unity. Robert Douglas then took over and spoke eloquently against schism. This ended at 4 p.m., and the prayer of Dickson constituting the Assembly was almost finished when there was a clatter of hooves and shouting of orders: and with the heavy tramp of booted feet on stone a troop of musketeers, fully armed, matches blazing, marched into St. Giles. Lieutenant General Cotterel, in command, leapt on a bench and his English voice rang out: "Gentlemen, I am commanded to ask you by what authority you sit here: if you have none from the Parliament, Commander-in-Chief or Judges, you are to go with me."

The Moderator asked non-members to leave, then answered firmly: "We sit here by the authority of Jesus Christ and by the law of this land, whereby we are authorised to keep General Assemblies from year to year, according to the several Acts of Parliament; and every Assembly meets by appointment of the former."

Cotterel ordered them to go "or else he would make them rise on other terms." Dickson craved time to constitute the meeting and appoint the next Assembly, but the soldiers stood-to (attention), and an officer rudely shouted him down. So out between the files of armed men the ministers went like prisoners, through the West Port and across Bruntsfield Links to the unconsecrated graves of criminals (Montrose among them) where the roll was called.

"When he had led us a mile without the town," reported Baillie; "he then declared what further he had in commission. That we should not dare to meet any more above three in number: and that against 8 o'clock tomorrow, we should depart the town . . . and the day following, by sound of trumpet, we are commanded off town under pain of present imprisonment. Thus our General Assembly, the glory and strength of our Church upon earth, is . . . crushed and trod under feet."

"Take from us the liberty of assembly," Knox had said, "and you take from us the gospel."

So far from being the Puritanical tyrants of "history" books, the ministers had been struggling against rising tides of chaos, as countless contemporary records show. "Patrick Leslie, Lord of Lindores, was never mairrit but had above sixty seven base children . . ." "Marjorie Ramsay, Countess of Buchan, confessed the sin of immorality with the parish minister" . . . The Earl of Eglinton, having appeared in Kirk on the Stool of Repentance, announced that it was the best seat in the house and sat on it thereafter. The evidence suggests that the ladies no more minded the cutty-stool than those who pose smiling on the steps of the Divorce Court today. Even more rife was the problem of violence.

Baillie, at a titled wedding-party in Kilwinning, had to cope with the characteristic syndrom of drink, daggers, murder and feud. Now what little authority the Kirk had had was abolished.

The Protesters Assembly was also dismissed; but Cromwell recognised that they had "the root of the matter in them," and made overtures with grants for the universities. Guthrie and Warriston were irreconcileable, he was told: but others more reasonable.

The versatile Mr. Sharp, minister of Crail, he was told, "is devoted to your service." Mr. Sharp gained his freedom in the South after less than six months in prison, where others served two years or more: presumably assisted by such offers of devotion. Cromwell had already noted approvingly his continual busy-ness, calling him "Sharp of that Ilk." He later concluded that he was an atheist.

Cromwell sent again for the Scots Protester ministers, holding a public debate between them and the Resolutioners, led by Sharp. Sharp sent home to Edinburgh his own full and flowery version of it. But the Protesters were in no way won over. Before the Protector in Whitehall gentle Mr Livingstone who had refused to take part in Charles' II's coronation, prayed: "God be gracious to those whose right it is to rule in this place, and unjustly is thrust from it . . . let our prayers be registrate in the Book of Life . . . as to thir poor men that now fill their rooms, Lord be merciful unto them . . ."

"Let him alone," said Cromwell to the indignant congregation: "he is a good man: and what are we but poor men in comparison of the Kings of England?"

But one result of this mission was that Cromwell gained one of its elders, a man he had long admired, even coveted: Warriston.

The Covenant, Warriston's life-work, bound all who swore it in loyalty to the King on earth as well as in Heaven. But Cromwell and Warriston were like to like, in character, courage and integrity: and a world away from a Stewart monarch. Warriston knew he would be tempted in the South: his wife and children were almost destitute again. He accepted office under Cromwell, and sat in his House of

115

Peers. The Rev. James Guthrie, a good friend, wrote letters of prophetic warning against it.

" . . . and whereas I thought I was following the call of God's Providence," Warriston wrote in his diary later: "The truth is, I followed the call of Providence when it agreed with my humour . . . and seemed to tend to honour and advantage; but if that same Providence had called me to quit my better places and take me to meaner places or none at all, I had not so hastily and contentedly followed it." Was he the first of that endless line of great Scots to fancy their gifts have fuller play in the South?

In Cromwell's last years he was surrounded by peace, and courted and consulted by rulers across all Europe and even from Asia. He fought hard to consolidate, turning from creating the Puritan Captain General with his pocket Bible in his holster, to creating the Puritan Captain of Industry, the good churchman with his armament of capital: as unmistakeable and more enduring a figure. He had come to believe now it was the fighting, not the victory that was the mark of grace—as Rutherford had said long since: "Duties are our, events are the Lords':" Men must be doers always, said the Lord Protector now, saved not by their works but by their doing. And "We are English, that is one good fact," said this man, born Williams.

His devastating peace extended to Scotland where General Monk was Commander-in-Chief. By next spring even the Highlands were crushed into order, and a chain of forts built clear across the country: five main ones, and lesser ones between to link up, on the Roman pattern. Superb pre-historic brochs at Glenelg, thousands of years old, were among the casualties, providing stones for the forts and for huge hideous barracks.

At the Cross of Edinburgh Monk announced Scotland's formal incorporation in the Commonwealth under Cromwell as Lord Protector. Her Monarchy and Parliament were thus abolished, her Law declared subservient, the cross of St. Andrew received into the arms of the Commonwealth. It was a Roman peace.

Without Cromwell's restraining hand the Ironsides reverted to traditional procedures. "They send in all their plunder and spoil to the ships: yea, they spoil Kirks"—for firewood—"and then put their horses in them," wrote Mr. Blair. (Though firewood indeed was scarce, and horses were precious.) He complains that they looted Holyrood Chapel, and Greyfriars, Lady Yester's and College Kirks: also the High School and a great part of the College of Edinburgh.

"Our noble families are almost gone," wrote Baillie: "Lennox has little in Scotland unsold: Hamilton's estate except Arran and the barony of Hamilton, is sold . . . the Gordons are gone; the Douglas's little better; Eglinton and Glencairn on the brink of breaking; many of our chief families' estates are cracking."

The Earl of Traquair, once the King's Treasurer and Lord High Commissioner to the 1639 Assembly, could be seen "in an antick garb" begging in the High Street of Edinburgh: doffing his old cavalier's hat for "groats, maiks, fardens."

"Of a long time no man in the whole Isle did mute," wrote Baillie to Spang in Holland: "all were lulled up in a lethargic fear and despair . . . as our miseries, without a Kingdom wholly, without any judicature to count of our own, without a church well-near, are great, so we expect they shall increase . . ."

There was one more twist to the black jokes of Scots coronations. In the 18th century Sir Walter Scott, that ardent Royalist, re-discovered the Honours of Scotland in an old chest in Edinburgh Castle in time for the State Visit he organised of George IV. (For this he even got Prinny into a kilt—with tights).

This century they were borne up the Royal Mile for the coronation visit of the present sovereign: whose chosen title of "Elizabeth II" the Scots had deeply and loudly resented. On this occasion of splendour in St. Giles, with the Lyon Court, the Judges the Thistles, the Royal Bodyguard of Archers, the coronetted peeresses, and every imaginable gown of grandeur, one little figure walked in in coat, hat and shopper-sized handbag.

Cursiter, Royal Limner, painted out the bag in the official scene hanging on Holyrood stairs: but the Scots have not forgotten. This time the joke was on them.

CHAPTER SEVEN

THE POWER AND THE GLORY

"Sometimes they strew his way
And sweetest praises sing
Resounding all the day Hosannas to their King:
Then "Crucify!" is all their breath
And for his death they thirst and cry."

Samuel Crossman (1624-1683) who wrote that hymn had lived through it all.

When Cromwell died on "his" day, 3rd September 1658, he was buried in purple, the crown he had not worn beside his corpse as he lay in state. When Charles returned eighteen months later the corpse was dug up—"a little, fiddling thing"—and hanged.

Eager republicans and dissenters became the most fanatical monarchists and episcopalians, ardently gathering missiles to stone the scapegoats. Yet, as Crossman would appreciate, the pyramid was not reversed without machinery, nor the mob counter-drilled without stage-management. As with Holy Week, a great deal of behind-the-scenes organisation, busyness and contacting, had to take place. Every cog had its part; Judas was vital.

Johnston of Warriston had been elected to the ruling Council of England, after Cromwell's death, and then to the pinnacle of power as its Chairman. But the Model Army, which had "idolised themselves" now also crumbled. "Never was a pack of men so seen more deserted of God and emptied of wit, sense, reason, common honesty and moral trustiness . . . They could . . . break Parliaments but . . . settle nothing." So he wrote: a perennial discovery.

Now the rising tide of Royalists forced him to hide for his very life.

He fled, unpaid, with his pregnant wife, who for once reproached him: making his heart "near to bursting with anguish and grief." But they reached Scotland.

Had either of Cromwell's elder sons survived, perhaps he might have founded a dynasty. Richard Cromwell, declared Protector, was unconvincing, he did not last; although he survived to old age. The year after Cromwell's death the wheels were already turning. General Monk, ruler of Scotland ("a sensible man with no fumes of religion about him," said Clarendon), decided he would lead, not wait. He summoned his officers to Greyfriars Kirk, and called for volunteers to march South with him to "restore order." They all offered their swords. On New Year's Day they marched over the Border. When he arrived in London he sent for "Mr. Sharp, his good friend." With his aid he had already drawn up and issued a vague but impressive declaration on preserving popular liberties and so forth. Monk, as Bishop Burnet put it, "steered with a strong tide."

Sharp went back to Edinburgh to re-assure the ministers. He did this so successfully that they stinted themselves to raise money to send Sharp posting South again at top speed, carrying all their hopes and dreams. They earnestly charged their "dear brother James," as Baillie called him, to see that the Church of Scotland was "guaranteed in her freedom, privileges and legal judicatories." Assuring and re-assuring them with every breath, he hurried off, and sent a stream of long reports, full of encouragement: telling nothing. "The Lord having opened a fair door of hope," he would write: "We may look for a settlement upon the grounds of the Covenant, and thereby a foundation laid for security against the prelatic and fanatic assaults."

When the frustrated ministers, unable to make out any plain facts among his verbiage, wanted to send other envoys to find out for themselves what was happening, Sharp, backed by Monk, quickly forbade it. "If we be quiet, our business would be done to our mind."

No doubt it was his delicate choice of word that led Monk to guarantee "Presbyterian government not rigid." The word seemed odd to the Scots. Sharp admits a little more. "I sméll that moderate episcopacy is the fairest accommodation," he writes: and goes on soothingly "we shall be left to the King, which is best for us." As for "the epithet of rigidity, the carriage of (Presbytery's) true friends hath given sufficient proof of the causelessness of that aspersion."

The King was now poised for his triumphal entry, no longer as a suppliant at the back door, but ready to be received in full power and glory.

And Mr. Sharp, spokesman and representative of the Church of Scotland, went over to Breda for the final arrangements. To the ministers in Scotland he was their gallant comrade, putting the case for the Covenant courageously before the King himself: a belief he fostered with every letter, mentioning his exhaustion in the good cause. To ambitious Lords he was a willing tool—"our caynd, honist, Sherp friend"—as described by Lord Rothes, dissolute and greedy. Lauderdale assured the King: "God hath made him as happy an instrument in your service all along as any I know of in this country." Sharp was also a devoted go-between for Monk, who wrote: "Nor need I say anything by so knowing a bearer . . ." Most significant of all is the private description of him as "the only person capable to manage the design of setting up episcopacy in Scotland."

By the final *Declaration of Breda* Charles offered a general pardon to all, except those whom Parliament might exempt. The statesman of the Restoration Settlement was Hyde, later Lord Clarendon, the historian: whose daughter Charles' younger brother James first seduced, then secretly married, later constantly betrayed: but

119

I

Clarendon himself remained loyal until discarded. Although it was said his daily query: "How do the grandchildren?" became an irritation to the King.

Sharp had five interviews with Charles in Breda, in which they seem to have arrived at full understanding. He had many instructions sent from Douglas, Wood and other ministers, which he ignored. He wrote them further pages of verbosity, obscuring more than they revealed, stressing his toil and tribulation on their behalf. He "found his Majesty resolved to restore the Kingdom to its former civil liberties, and to preserve the settled government of our Church."

Charles was proclaimed King of three countries in London on May 8th, Edinburgh on the 14th and Dublin shortly after. He landed at Dover on the 25th, and was met by Monk and the army, the general "prostrating himself" and offering his sword: which was returned with the Garter (and later the Dukedom of Albermarle). The ministers of Dover "gifted the King a large Bible with golden clasps . . . joyfully received." He entered London on the 29th, his birthday, and spent the night with my Lady Castlemaine while the city was "in glory," said Pepys, and mad with joy. It was roses, roses all the way—"bells, bonfires, balls and masques . . ."

Scotland's bonfires burned as high, or even higher. For had they not, at long last, a Covenanted King to rejoice all their hearts? If the coronation at Scone had been a shabby affair, they made up for it now. In splendid fireworks, the muckle great De'l chased Cromwell right up Edinburgh Castle rock and out of sight. At the Tron in the High Street of Edinburgh, traditional bonfire stance to this day, Jenny Geddes herself, in a transport of celebration, burned "her Chair of State, and all her creels, baskets, creepies and forms." Who could do more?

Charles even took time off from his mistresses to issue a pious Declaration against "all prophane, debauched and dissolute persons, especially drunkards . . ." This seemed a good beginning, and revived Presbyterian hopes. Everyone knew Charles had signed and sworn coronation oaths and both Covenants at Scone. On the other hand, the English Coronation oath bound the sovereign to uphold prelacy, so there was a delay in the English crowning while the whole question hung in the balance. "We were up and down in our hopes and expectations," wrote a minister in Scotland. Their very lives depended upon it.

But Bishops were restored to vacant sees in England, and dissenting parsons outed. The Synod of Ballymena sent Mr. Blair, who had been ministering there, to petition the King about the Covenant: but he found in London he could not even see him until the very word was erased. He got little comfort from Charles, and none in Ballymena on his return.

Argyll, whose son was already received at court, ventured to attend: although he did not ask for the dukedom, the Garter or the gold promised at Scone. He was instantly arrested in public and taken to the Tower. Warrants went out for Warriston and two other supporters of the Covenant and Cromwell: Sir James Stewart of Goodtrees, former Lord Provost of Edinburgh, and Sir John Chiesly. The last two were caught, but Warriston was warned as he rode home, and turned his horse immediately for Leith. He reached Hamburg, fell seriously ill, and was bled into childish weakness by an English doctor, either through stupidity or treachery. His wife and children meanwhile were deprived of all possessions—such as they had.

While the Resolutioner ministers waited anxiously for the outcome of all Sharp's great labours, the Scots had petitioned to have their own Parliament again: and the Estates met in Edinburgh on 23rd August. At the same time, by ill-luck, the Protesters had convened a meeting nearby, to send their independent loyal greetings to the King and to remind him at the same time of his obligations under the Covenant. This horrified the Estates, and in panic they sent three times to make them disperse and tear up their paper: which they refused to do. About a dozen were then taken prisoner to Edinburgh Castle, including James Guthrie, Semple of Carsphairn ("God's varlet"), two ministers of Edinburgh, and the ministers of Scone, Kirkliston, Burntisland, Methven, Oxnam, Mordington: and Kirko of Dunscore, an elder. Defiant at first, cold and jail-fever wore them down, and the sickest were eventually allowed out to house-arrest in the High Street. Warrants were issued for others, including Patrick Gillespie (the Provost of Glasgow went bail for him). The King made Mr. Baillie Principal of Glasgow College in his place.

On the last day of August Mr. Sharp—"one loving brother"—at last came back to Scotland to report. He bore an impressive letter from the King himself, replying to a loyal address by the presbytery of Edinburgh. It began with a long, fulsome account of Mr. Sharp's own skills, genius and high spiritual qualities—("the bearer and, it was thought, the penner of it," murmurs one diarist). It goes on to speak re-assuringly of the good qualities of most of its ministers, and the intention of His Majesty to "discountenance prophanesses and etcetera" and to protect and preserve the government of the Church of Scotland "as it is established by law." Copies were sent to all the presbyteries. In Fife the whole synod was invoked to hear it and to frame a reply.

Here there was a slight snag. Someone wondered if they might not mention the Covenant? Luckily, it was Sharp's own synod and for once he was there, eloquently to plead against such discourtesy to His Majesty.

The Church had many enemies at court, he warned them all—"Yea, even many unnatural sons" of the Kirk itself, against which he had had to struggle. His advice was taken, he was thanked and praised—and as it was not fulsome enough the Moderator was asked to do it twice: (but did it as "slenderly and wershly" as before). Blair had returned from Ireland to teach in St. Andrews: and suddenly saw through "the knave and his tricks," and how he had deluded them all. It is the essence of a Judas to be an "in" man.

Shortly after this Sharp got Blair outed: and he himself was appointed to St. Andrews: not because he meant to leave Edinburgh, that outpost of the South, but because he needed the doctorate, that went with the place, to be a Bishop.

The Provost and Town Clerk of Glasgow were now imprisoned in Edinburgh Tolbooth, and Provost Jaffray of Aberdeen, turned Quaker, among others summoned. The Estates condemned Guthrie's *Causes of God's Wrath* and Rutherford's *Lex Rex*, and they were burnt by the hangman at the Cross, and below Rutherford's windows in St. Andrews, where he was Principal of St. Mary's. A guard was sent to arrest him and take him to Edinburgh; but he was too ill to be moved.

"Tell the King," he said, "I have a prior summons to a higher court and judicature, where the judge is my friend: and where few Kings or great ones ever come."

The Senate met to vote him out: Lord Burleigh said, "You have voted that good man out of College, but you cannot vote him out of heaven."

His last words were, "Glory, glory dwelleth in Emmanuel's land."

The charges against all these men were of "embroiling the Kingdom," and they were threatened with transporting to Barbados as slaves. Sharp publicly claimed to have interceded for James Guthrie: but privately wrote to Lauderdale, urging extreme measures against all those "hair-brain rebels." Later he urged the liquidation of "Guthrie, Gillespie, Rutherford" in order to "daunt the rest of the rebels." He claimed that Guthrie had "justified the murder of the King." Lauderdale was willing to listen, as the King's servant through and through. Both he and Middleton, now the King's Lord High Commissioner, later threw blame on Sharp for his persecuting zeal, and relish for torture.

Plain greed, not prejudice, was their own mainspring. Lauderdale, who hated "damned insipid lies," had "a selfishness that never slept." Middleton had risen from the ranks, by devious means.

At Christmas, Argyll was brought from London to Leith by boat: and with him a Quaker, Lord Swinton. (The Friends were believed Puritan revolutionaries by the South, secret Papists by the North). Argyll went to the Castle, Swinton to the Tolbooth with Guthrie and other Protesters.

On Hogmanay, Middleton, with Mr. Sharp as his Royal Chaplain, was installed in the Palace of Holyroodhouse. On New Year's Day he rode with the Estates and the Honours of Scotland in full panoply up the Royal Mile to Parliament. The first day was taken up with the Oath of Allegiance. "I acknowledge my said sovereign only supreme

Governor of this Kingdom over all persons and in all causes," ran the kernel of it: ". . . and shall never decline His Majesty's power and jurisdiction, as I shall answer to God." This Oath was obligatory on all holding public office. Attempts to insert "civil" before "supreme authority" failed.

The second day made arrangements, by Charles' command and at his expense, for the "funeral" of Montrose. The arms and legs were retrieved from four cities, the rotting bones dug up from the Burghmuir, his heart was restored, though its case—made from his sword-point—was lost: and finally the head taken down from its pike above the Netherbow. (It was thought to be his: there had been a rumour of someone rescuing it earlier). Kinsman Graham of Gorthie, with Hay of Dalgatie, took it reverently down, kissing it (and dying four days later). A coronet was placed on the skull: and all swathed in purple the remains lay in state while the "mourners" caroused on the free wine—"mair like a bridal," said a contemporary.

Most of them had helped to bring Montrose down, and had rejoiced at it. Middleton was vice-regal Chief Mourner: although his own father had been run through by Montrose's men as he sat in his chair: and he personally had given Montrose's house to the flames and shot his servants. Few there had not cried "Crucify!" at the right moment: and would do so again.

The bits and pieces were finally placed in an ornate tomb in St. Giles under a life-size of effigy in white marble: and flanked today, with the irony of ignorance, by a signed copy of the Covenant.

As this, the Drunken Parliament, "drunk higher, they resolved to venture" on a clean sweep by Act Recissory, of all statutes previous to 1633, Charles I's coronation in St. Giles. They also repealed the Acts re-establishing Presbyterianism, and passed one forbidding all assemblies and the renewing of "the Solemn League and Covenant, or any other Covenant . . . without His Majesty's warrant . . ."

In March Charles made a witty speech to the English Parliament, in which his urgent need for supplies was lightly brought to their notice. (In the years ahead his speeches became shorter and sharper, until they were little more than howls for money). "I have the worst luck in the world if, after all the reproaches of being a Papist whilst I was abroad, I am suspected of being a Presbyterian now I am come home . . . I am as zealous for the Church of England as any of you can be . . . as much in love with the Book of Common Prayer . . . and have prejudice enough for those that do not love it . . ."

Acts remitting all "unlawful" Parliaments and their works were now passed: leaving the legal position of the Church of Scotland still doubtful. But in preparation for the King's coronation in Westminster Abbey in April an Act was passed in Scotland the month before in which the King duly resolved to maintain Reformed Protestant religion "in its purity of doctrine and worship as it was established in this Kingdom during the reign of his Royal father and grandfather of blessed memory."

The Scots woke up to find the iron yoke of Episcopacy back on their necks. Jenny Geddes had burned her stools too soon.

Jenny is never forgotten, whoever else may be. The Scottish Reformation put its own particular stamp on Scotswomen. On the one hand the need that they too should read their Bibles and teach their children the deep questions of the catechism made them literate and intelligent people. On the other hand the fundamental tenet that it was the man who was priest and king, whether in his own house or in the larger "family of God" of Church or community, inhibited both aggression and loquacity. Mary Slessor could outface any naked savage: but felt faint if a minister tried to join her audience. I have heard an English woman doctor refer bitterly to "the place of THE MAN in Scotland." But it does not mean that all women were crushed to silence.

Even witch-trials, which seemed to revive with the revival of episcopacy, were affected by the change of education. The last witch to be tried at Menteith was a young woman called Barbara Drummond. She was accused by an ungrateful patient, Geill Finnie, of curing her of pains and dumbness by witch-craft. The full Presbytery was convened, and Barbara summoned for trial before them. She "told the presbytery expressly that she would answer them no more Interrogators anent anything without she had her Procurator."

When the trial was resumed and Geill Finnie deponed the usual gruesome string of accusations, designed to raise horror and loathing in the hearers so that often the Pannel was condemned unheard, Barbara merely commented: "Ill must they die that says so!"

Asked outright if it was true she could fold her tongue in her mouth like a snake, she retorted: "Ye may fold your tongue, an ye like it!" The court, instead of shuddering with horror, was shaken with laughter. She was hastily remanded to prison.

Relief was short. Even there she contrived to make her presence so felt the records say plaintively she was "troublesome to the town, in time of hairst"—an added aggravation.

Fortunately the Clerk to the Presbytery, the Rev. Robert Kirk of Balquwhidder, was an expert on the subject of the occult. He had published an authoritative little book, *The Secret Commonwealth of Elves, Fauns and Fairies*—still pleasant reading.

He visited the prisoner frequently, either to assist with her personal problems, or possibly to compare notes. Her situation was an increasing embarrassment: and it must have been a merciful solution when she suddenly disappeared. Mr. Kirk as it happened also vanished at this time. You can still see his wife's tombstone in the graveyard, where Rob Roy Macgregor is buried: but there is no mention of the minister on it.

The congregation maintained that, in the course of his researches, he had been stolen away into Elfland. Ill must they die, Barbara might have said, who doubted it.

More characteristic of the Covenant women were the fourteen little girls in Pentland who, in an age when statesmen could scarcely spell, drew up a dignified and impressive Children's Covenant for themselves. Or Miss Janet Fimister, middle-aged Edinburgh spinster, who attended the gallows, straiked the corpses, and taught herself to read, write, and discuss theology with exiled ministers in Holland. Or Lady Caldwell, who spent three and a half years as a prisoner in Blackness Castle.

Grizzel Home of Polwarth was only twelve when her father sent her with a message to Baillie of Jerviswoode in the Tolbooth. It must have been a frightening journey up the High Street, full of soldiers and gibbets, pyots and corbies busy at the bloody heads and hands overhead; the prison full of gaunt, unkempt men.

But there, for the first time, she met young George Baillie. "He was the best of husbands and the delight of my life for forty eight years, without one jar betwixt us."

She helped hide her own father in the family vault, slipping out at midnight with food stolen from table. Once, to the horror of nine hungry little brothers and sisters, she managed a whole sheep's head.

She persuaded the curate to kill his dogs, whose barking was a risk. Finally, they all escaped penniless to Holland, where she slaved to keep them: sitting up two whole nights a week to get it all done. "She went to market, went to the mill, dress't the linen, cleaned the house, made ready the dinner, mended the children's stockings and other clothes," wrote her daughter, Lady Murray, later. And young George Baillie was at her side, carrying the shopping basket through the stout mevrou's in the market and jotting down her songs as they went. Her best-known, still sung, is: "O werena my hert licht, I wad dee!" "Good Breeding, Good Humour, Good Sense were her daily Ornaments," says her tombstone: but her portrait laughs out provocatively. One brother was in the Prince of Orange's Guard. They returned with William.

Then there was Duchess Ann, with the great heart and brain, and a face even Kneller paints as homely. In her book, "*The days of Duchess Ann*", Rosalind K. Marshall gives her story.

Ann was the elder of the two little orphan daughters to whom the first Marquis of Hamilton had written from the Tower, just before his execution. God-daughter of Charles I and brought up at his court, Ann was sent North at nine to her stern old Covenanting granny—the one who had helped fortify Leith with pistols in her belt. They were kindred spirits.

When the younger Marquis of Hamilton had died of wounds after the battle of Worcester, Ann inherited all, at 19: a string of titles to lands and castles from the Isle of Arran in the Clyde across Scotland to Bo'ness on the Forth. In actual fact, she possessed "a little hut in the woods," a few cows and one or two unpaid servants. All the rest was in the hands of Cromwell's men.

She paid court to Monk, and through him to Cromwell. She married the young Earl of Selkirk, who renounced his Roman faith in writing first; and sent him to Charles II's court in suits of velvet and brocade, encrusted with gold and silver lace—clothes were all-important at the Restoration. She herself wore "douce-coloured dresses" run up apparently by the estate upholsterer (though her riding clothes were velvet).

She got her husband made Duke of Hamilton, and bit by bit re-built her entire Kingdom. She fostered good farming, industries and trades, and above all schools and Kirks. Her communion cups are still in use at Dalserf. Her husband constantly pleaded for moderation in the Scots Council: and she sheltered Covenanters on the run, especially after the Battle of Bothwell Bridge. She also employed Quaker gardeners, when no one else would: and helped episcopal widows and orphans.

She lived long: to see her work wasted by a worthless heir: her savings lost in Darien, and her country's independence at the Union. She pulled herself out of despair, and began again with her grandchildren. Her words ring down the years, "A given-up battle is never won!"

The Covenanters needed such women.

CHAPTER EIGHT

NO CROSS, NO CROWN

If you have to kill a human life, which is the best way? The quickest? Do those who cry, Bring back hanging! stop to picture the usual slow strangulation? Or the nerve-severing drop that can jerk off a whole head?

The Maiden, the Scots instrument of execution now in the Museum of Antiquities, Queen Street, Edinburgh, was one of the most efficient, and therefore most humane ways of killing ever invented. A modern journalist who had seen executions in many countries said so of the guillotine, which is on the same principle. An immensely heavy, weighted, triangular blade shot down between two oiled uprights and the head fell in the basket, all in seconds. A headsman with axe and block frequently took several swipes to be even partially effective.

Beheading was for the upper classes. Lesser criminals were hanged, which was much slower. With hands tied, they climbed a steep ladder which the hangman then turned over, sending the condemned spinning into space. If their struggles were prolonged, friends swung on their legs. Hangings were usually down in the Grassmarket in Edinburgh: beheadings were always in the High Street, near St. Giles, on a high scaffold.

The "Heart of Midlothian," marked with studs in the paving—and spat on traditionally for luck—is said to show the spot.

The horrible "three-fold death for traitors," specifically invented by Edward I for William Wallace, remained an English institution: but was brought into Scotland with episcopacy. The tortures of the Boot and later the thumbscrews—invented by a Bishop—were used in Scotland only under episcopacy.

Apart from the Castle dungeons, the Tolbooth at St. Giles' West door was the capital's main jail. Its site too is marked in studs. There in the month of May, 1661, both the Marquis of Argyll and Mr. James Guthrie, formerly minister of Stirling, were held for trial: and execution.

The records of Argyll's trial are missing, but a full account was left by Sir George Mackenzie, later known as "Bluidy Mackenzie," destroyer of the Covenanters. At this moment he was simply an ambitious young advocate of 25, already an author: and later a founder of the Advocates Library. So well did he defend Argyll, as being the one made scapegoat for many, he might even have got him off. But Sharp and Rothes had gone South to confer with Monk, Clarendon and Lauderdale.

At the last moment a courier arrived with letters Argyll had once written to Monk during Cromwell's reign, upholding the "Tender" of terms he had been forced to take at the time. Only young Montrose chivalrously refused to vote for his death. Argyll said: "I had the honour to put the crown upon the King's head and now he hastens me to a better crown than his own."

"My Lord, God has been with you," said Guthrie to him as he went out to die: "he is with you, and God will be with you."

Mackenzie had bluntly told Argyll beforehand that there was a fear he would show his besetting timidity on the scaffold. But he was now composed. "My Lord, keep your grip siccar," whispered one of the ministers of St. Giles as they climbed the steps to the Maiden. "Mr. Hutchieson, I am not afraid to be surprised by fear," he answered, holding out his wrist to his doctor, who found his pulse perfectly steady.

In his last speech he proclaimed his unswerving loyalty to the Covenants and to the Throne.

His head was put on the spike vacated by that of Montrose, and his body lay first in the Magdalene Chapel below the Bridges, then was taken to the Campbell vault at Kilmun. His memorial in St. Giles, a modest plaque, is opposite the tomb of Montrose.

Guthrie's execution was postponed for a couple of days, as Coronation Day was a public holiday. Bishop Leighton, now Principal of Edinburgh University, took occasion to give a dinner in honour of the King's Commissioner, the drunken ex-pikeman, Middleton. He had even written a Latin Ode in his honour, and "broke glasses" with him in a mutual toast. "Saintly" Leighton he had been called, because he cared nothing for wealth, ambition, drink or women. He engaged constantly in prayer, and gave all his money to the poor. He too had sworn the Covenants, and been an ordained minister of the Church. His father had been flogged, branded and imprisoned for years without trial for writing a *Plea Against Prelacy*. His own creed was doubtless sincere: but so was his determination to see nothing, know nothing, of the bloody-minded cruelty and tyranny with which it was being enforced. He deplored persecution— he called it scaling heaven with ladders fetched out of Hell—but never once did he raise a protest in public. He could be called a Holy Willie as much as a saint. But at least he was the best, as the most humble and least self-seeking, of the new prelates. His creed of total pacifism, possibly springing from a childhood horror of suffering, was the logical alternative to resistance.

Guthrie too had children, and the condemnation had reached out to sentence little Sophia and Willie and his wife to "perpetual beggary." When Lord Tweedsmuir objected, he was later fined and imprisoned himself. Guthrie defiantly cried that "he hoped his head would preach more on the Port than ever in the pulpit." The nickname of this "little man who would not bow," as Cromwell had called him, was "Sickerfoot."

He had always been good with children, and now he took them into his confidence. "Willie," he said to the child on his knee, "they will tell you, and cast up to you, that your father was hanged; but think not shame of it, for it is upon a good cause."

James Cowie, Guthrie's man, spent the last night with him, and took charge of Willie next day. He was shocked to find that when other children ran at the beating of the drums, Willie was still absorbed in some dreamy play. Reality came later. He would be seen standing on the causey staring up at the heads on the Port. Did he look amazed at the ravages of heat and hoodie-crows on the loved face? When found hiding in a cupboard he could only say, "I've seen my faither's face!" He was a brilliant scholar, but Death called him early.

With Guthrie another Covenanter was hanged: a soldier, William Govan, who had been cheered as a hero when he brought back Montrose's standard in triumph after Carbisdale. He had to wait his turn at the gallows-foot.

Guthrie's last speech was long and rousing. He "durst not redeem my life with the loss of my integrity; I judge it better to suffer that to sin," he told the crowd. As he went up the ladder he said: "Art thou not from everlasting, O Lord my God." Before the hangman turned the ladder over he raised his bound hands, tore the napkin from his face, and shouted: "The Covenants! The Covenants shall yet be Scotland's reviving!"

Govan had a last comment to make on Middleton. "The Commissioner and I went out to the fields together for one cause. I have now a cord about my neck, and he is promoted to be His Majesty's Commissioner; yet for a thousand worlds I would not change lots with him—praise and glory be to Christ for ever!"

Guthrie's headless corpse lay in St. Giles, where a student, later the famous surgeon George Stirling, strewed it with herbs. The story went round that blood from the head dripped down on to Middleton's coach as he drove back to Holyrood Palace: and could never be scrubbed out.

That same month Patrick "Soople" Gillespie was brought to trial: but he had many friends and was acquitted. "Well, if I had known that you would have spared Mr. Gillespie, I would have spared Mr. Guthrie," is reported as Charles' passing remark.

Most of the other Protesters, ministers and elders, were evicted, imprisoned or fled. The minister of Scoonie was evicted, Robert Traill banished and his wife in prison for writing to him: Maxwell of Monreith and Kirko of Dunscore fled to Ireland. It is believed to be Kirko who was shot on Whitesands, Dumfries, after secretly returning. Sir John Chiesley was ruined and imprisoned for ten years:

Lord Swinton, turned Quaker, was also ruined and left in the Tolbooth.

Sharp went down to court in July, but this time without any commission from the Edinburgh presbytery. In spite of all his pious prevarications, the truth was growing clearer. Not only were Bishops restored in England, but Bishop Jeremy Taylor had evicted all non-episcopal ministers in Northern Ireland ("the most of them Scotts") because, not being ordained by a prelate, they could not be ministers at all.

On Sharp's return, the presbytery of St. Andrews sent two ministers, Forest and Blair, to reason with him.

Blair, after a wrecked attempt to reach America, had returned from Ireland. He was now teaching in St. Andrews. Blair was a Royalist as well as a Covenanter. At the Scone Coronation he had been one of the preachers. "There are some that say, Give us religion well-secured, come of the King what will," he had said then: "and there are others that say, Give us the King well-established on his throne, become of religion what will: but, blessed be God, there are some, both ministers and others, that wishes well both to religion and the King, giving to God what is God's, and to Caesar what is Caesar's."

This was the Moderate, or Resolutioner, viewpoint, which had seemed so acceptable to all then. But it was so no longer. The talks were a failure; it was then Sharp marked Blair down for eviction.

It was not easy to get men of any standing to be Bishops. Alexander Burnet, later Archbishop of Glasgow, was offered a choice of diocese. Sharp himself made a bid for Robert Douglas, offering him high office: and being flatly refused. As he reached the door Douglas called him back: "James, I see you will engage: I perceive that you are clear, you will be Bishop of St. Andrews: take it, and the curse of God with it."

On September 6th the Lord Lyon proclaimed the King's will at the Cross of Edinburgh: the establishment of Episcopacy throughout Scotland. Gilbert Burnet the diarist, chaplain both to Charles II and to William, and latterly Bishop of Salisbury, called Sharp "The spirit that moved the whole engyne" . . . He was a nephew of Johnston of Warriston.

The Duchess Ann's husband, Duke of Hamilton, and brother-in-law Lord Crawford, protested in vain. Then Sharp, with Fairfoul and Hamilton—two previous Bishops—went off to London to receive consecration from the fount of ecclesiastical honour. Leighton was already there.

As parish ministers, Sharp and Leighton had been fully ordained already. But the English Bishops insisted that it must be re-done. In 1610, when Spottiswoode was made an Archbishop by James VI & I he had refused this, and the English Bishop Bancroft supported him: declaring it ridiculous to suppose that all the Reformed Church ministers in the world were illegal. But Sharp and Leighton were

130

servile enough to accept: and kneel; and return to consecrate others. Not, it seems, all tacitly conforming ministers. There was some kind of "episcopal blessing," like a modern "rite of reconciliation" possibly, where the necessary episcopal finger reached the scalp. How Hromadka, the great Czech preacher of our own day, laughed at that!

But for the war-weary Scots, many like Baillie himself devoted Royalists, it was no laughing matter. It was after all a very low-key episcopacy, with little change in services, and complete inter-communion. More than half the Kirks' ministers conformed.

Yet even those who did, like Robert Douglas, who still defended the King, and Dickson, began to see that the Protesters had, after all, been "truer prophets;" that the encroachments of prelacy, however mild, ate the heart out of their faith. For it was now a State absolutism, with the King sworn Head of the Church, and the Bishops his officers. Free speech died with freedom of preaching: and with it the gospel, Knox had insisted.

In Edinburgh only one minister conformed, nicknamed The Nest-egg. Throughout the South-west, hardly any did. In Ruthwell, the minister held his charge through fifty four changeful years on the classic plea: "Wha would quarrel with their brose for a mote in them?"

Rejoicing for the Restoration had so swiftly turned sour that in two years "Restoration Day" was a mere legal compulsion. On 29th May, 1662, Mr. Donald Cargill, minister of the Barony Church, Glasgow, found a large congregation at his mid-week service; and asked them, Why they were there?

" . . . we thought once to have blessed the day when the King came home again; but now we think we shall have reason to curse it: and if any of you come here for the solemnising of this day, we desire you to remove." As for the King: "Woe! Woe! Woe! unto him! His name shall stink while the world stands for treachery, tyranny and lechery!"

Within days the soldiers were at his door: but he opened it himself in his landlady's mutch and apron, unrecognised. He preached at street corners and in pends, but by October was formally banished "be-North the Tay." So began a long ministry on the moors, preaching on the run across the country. Someone saw him preach through a hot June day on Tinto-tap on "two drinks from a bonnet." It is only lately that they have blown up "Cargill's Loup" across the River Ericht, to end the temptation to the reckless. When Cargill himself was congratulated on making "the rare loup," by which he escaped arrest he said, "Aye, I ran all the way frae Perth for it!"—15 miles.

A young graduate, Hugh McKail, was preaching his trials for license in St. Giles at this time. He was consumptive, with the brilliant good looks that often went with that disease. On the last Sunday before the non-conforming ministers had to leave Edinburgh, he reviewed the history of the Kirk, and concluded that "the Church in all ages has been persecuted by a Pharaoh upon the Throne, a Haman in the State, and a Judas in the Church!" He was lucky to escape first to Holland, then home to hiding-places.

In spring Sharp came back to Scotland with his fellow-bishops, riding in a grand new coach with a crest and six outriders in ecclesiastical purple livery.

He preached in St. Andrews on the text: "For I determined not to know anything among you save Jesus Christ, and Him crucified."

He rode out of St. Andrews with an escort of fifty horses. Then "The Earl of Wemyss met him with a great train and conveyed him to Burntisland." In the first week of May, six (Highland) Scots Bishops were consecrated, with the magic touch and the words, "Receive ye the Holy Ghost!" Sharp, now Archbishop of St. Andrews, had brought back the full panoply of lawn sleeves, rochet and tippet: and no doubt croziers and crucifixes in plenty. Leighton shunned all these ceremonies. He seems to have mollified his conscience by rejecting all the trimmings and ostentation of Episcopacy while accepting its principles. This did no good to the Covenanters, and irritated his colleagues who thought it "looked like singularity and affectation."

This "Coronation Day" the hangman tore up the Covenants at the Cross, and in Stirling, where Guthrie had been a loved and respected minister, and where they will still show you his pulpit, it was a drunken carouse. Robert Douglas had prepared to preach to the Estates in St. Giles, but Sharp claimed precedence, and at the last minute forced him to give way.

That summer Act after Act went through, to finish off the Covenant men. There was compulsory billetting of troops, "fines" for all declared liable, their names on secret lists. Middleton, constantly fuddled, passed them indiscriminately, pocketing the cash. That was his first blunder. The second was when he followed up the Drunken Parliament with a Drunken Council in Glasgow, where it was enacted that all ministers who would not accept re-appointment by patron and bishop would be evicted and outlawed. Fairfoul, now Archbishop of Glasgow, thought ten might go; Sharp estimated a dozen, Middleton perhaps forty. In all over three hundred went—an enormous demonstration.

From now on Middleton was on his way out, Lauderdale on his way in. Eventually Middleton was made governor of Tangier—it was part of the new Queen's dowry—and fell drunk off a balcony to his death.

Lauderdale was fully as gross and coarse personally—Charles had a special fastener for his snuff-box to keep his filthy fingers out of it— but he was a man of real ability, and surprisingly good education. Warriston had esteemed his gifts: and Baillie, who was indebted to him for the Principalship of Glasgow University, trusted him.

But Lauderdale was on the make. He saw that the King wanted two

things in Scotland: his own supremacy, and the Covenanters'
extirpation.

The first he achieved very well. He was the main architect of the
system whereby "the Lords of the Articles," chosen by the Crown,
chose all the legislation: the Scots Estates had only to assent. As he
himself put it: "Nothing can pass in the Articles but what is warranted
by His Majesty, so that the King is absolute master in Parliament
both of the negative and the affirmative."

The representatives of the burghs were also chosen, the Lord
Advocate pointing out that basic flaw in democracy: "If the burghs
had liberty to choose whom they pleased to represent them, factious
and disloyal persons might prevail to get themselves elected."

Clearly this was a collision course with the doctrine propounded by
Rutherford in *Lex Rex* long ago: "Power is a birthright of the people
borrowed from them; they may let it out for their good, and resume it
when a man is drunk with it."

When Charles I had said they would leave him no more power than
the Doge of Venice, Rutherford had later said that; "the Duke of
Venice to me cometh nearest to the King moulded by God." And "A
limited and mixed monarchy, such as in Scotland and England,
seems to me the best government . . ."

Now its limits were being legislated out, and as an essential part of
that programme Presbyterian government in the kirk must be
abolished too. Here Lauderdale proceeded at first with more caution;
so that Baillie, who still thought of him as a man of the Covenant, had
written the year before an impassioned plea against the setting-up of
Episcopacy. "I tell you, my heart is broken with grief," he had written:
but Lauderdale had not even troubled to reply. As Principal, Baillie
had been forced to receive "His Grace" Fairfoul of Glasgow, the
Commissioner and the Privy Council: and to offer them the sack and
ale Middleton drank so excessively. Baillie's world, which had
seemed so bright and hopeful, with his own appointment, the
Covenants sworn and the King come home again, was all crumbling
about his ears.

Bitterest drop in the poisoned cup was the realisation, at last and in
full, that "dear James" Sharp, whom he had once trustingly called
"the most wise, honest, diligent and successful agent of the nation in
the late dangers of our Church" instead and in fact "piece by piece, in
so cunning a way, has trepanned us." The shock was terrible.

Once he had pleaded to Sharp to help "old friends out of beggarie
and dyvorie."

Instead, he now saw he had brought on them all "a fearful
persecution . . . of the old Canterburian stamp." Too late they were
in the trap. With appalling clarity he saw the darkness coming on the
land. "I care for no vanities . . . God be merciful to our brethren who
has no help of man, nor any refuge but in God alone." Death was not

the worst of ills "in these very hard times." He turned his face to the wall and died in August, 1662.

There is no portrait or memorial of him, except his letters and journals, now so shamefully out of print. So vivid, so natural are they that when his voice breaks off you miss it like a friend.

From now on, as the last curtain rises, the issues are stark and clear. From now on the knock would come to every Manse, to every door in the land. Conscience could easily cost not only men's and women's own lives, but that of the innocent.

From now on the verb "to lurk" is much used; it meant to live homeless, to find what shelter one could: risking—probably condemning—a friend's whole family by asking shelter or bread. The decision "to suffer rather than to sin" was wholly individual: and inescapable.

Yet from now on a great host, a vast unarmed army of astonishing diversity, arose in Scotland: sick and whole, youths and aged, rich and poor, girls and mothers, labourers and University professors, boys and men; for the next twenty six years they were continually defeated, continually depleted: stripped and starved, beaten and slain. But never wholly extinguished.

K

BOOK III

THE KING'S PEACE

CHAPTER ONE

THE KNOCK ON THE DOOR

"I'm banish't! Oh I'm banish't!" wept the child in the pony-panier at the Brig-en' o' Dumfries.

"Wha's banish't ye, ma bairn?" asked a passer-by.

"Bite-the-Sheep has banish't me!" she sobbed: with reason. For as the family crossed Devorguilla's Bridge—the graceful span is still standing—they took the cold, weary road to the hills: where one little girl of the family died.

The kirk and manse of Troqueer, which they had been forced to leave, cannot look so very different now, at least in position. It stands on a little bluff above the river, as if on a Celtic site, and was one of "Trois Choires" of Norman foundation, the other two being Devorguilla's Sweetheart Abbey (New Abbey), and Lincluden. Dumfries has crept out to it now, yet there is still green grass and trees looking out on the shining river, where the Rev. Mr. Blackadder walked to clear his mind in the manse garden before his last service.

Usually Galloway, tilting South, is a land of rich colour: but this was one of its dowie days, a "grey Gallowa" day, when the sea-mist billows up from the Solway, filling every glen to the brim: ghostly, woolly stuff, muffling sight and sound. All the minister could see that day was the hump of Criffel in the background, rising through the vapours "like an island in the ocean." Then, in that dense silence, the Sabbath bells began to speak, one by one, from far and near and farther off, each one a voice he recognised; bidding farewell.

Before his last sermon ended, the dragoons of General "Bloody-Bite-the-Sheep" Turner clattered up and ordered him out of the pulpit. He told the people to go: but they followed him to the manse, where he finished preaching from the stairs, and blessed them for the last time. Out of the nineteen ministers of Dumfries Presbytery sixteen refused to resign their calling until re-appointed by the Bishop and patron: and were banished. Out of sixteen ministers in the Stewartry of Kirkcudbright every single one went out.

Most went on preaching secretly in households that could be trusted. Some went further. Gabriel Semple of Kirkpatrick Durham, new young minister of that tiny hamlet, and Welsh of Irongray, son of Josias Welsh of Temple Patrick in Ireland and grandson of Knox, "began the Sunday after they were expelled in Corsock-wood, where they lodged a year. They wrocht to each others' hands; for while the curates were pursuing the one in the country, the other was preaching in the woods."

137

Neilson of Corsock, "a meek and generous gentleman," sheltered many. He sounds a typical easy-going, warm-hearted Galloway man. As well as planting curates in the empty kirks, and having them backed by soldiers, Sharp had taken care to attack that heartland of the Church of Scotland, the elders. Among others, Gordon of Earlston was ordered first to Edinburgh and then out of it "away from the fanatic wives" who were supporting him.

Women in numbers had run after Welsh, at the end of his last communion service in Irongray. He was outed by a papist laird, Maxwell of Munches—that beautiful estate near where the little town of Dalbeattie now stands: but it was done mercifully.

For years collections were taken "against the minister's home-coming:" but Welsh, on the run for twenty years with a top price on his head, was never to return.

Gilbert Burnet describes the curates now forced upon the parish kirks "by a sort of hue and cry," as being hirelings "unstudied and unbred"—the very dregs.

One such curate, the usual ignorant, uncouth North-east country bumpkin, was brought in in Welsh's place. Drying their tears, the Irongray women met him with such showers of stones that even supporting soldiers retreated. Their leader, Margaret Smith, was taken to Edinburgh under arrest, tried and condemned to be transported to Barbados; but she "told her story so innocently," she was reprieved.

Another women of that parish, Helen Walker, was the original Jeannie Deans—in spite of the cottage in Holyrood park.

Some men were not only evicted, but specifically exiled. There was no longer an open door in France, where the Huguenots were increasingly persecuted. But the independent Netherlands, which had had to fight so long and so bitterly for their own freedom of conscience, gave them refuge. The year 1976 saw the 3rd centenary of the Scots kirk in Holland. Without the welcome, even before that year, many more men, perhaps even the Kirk itself, would not have survived. Arts and science, banking, above all freedom of mind and speech, had fled from the Italy of the Popes to the Holland of Erasmus. They valued the "Truly Erasmian" qualities: which Erasmus had once called "truly Dutch:—of kindliness and moderation." Many Scots slipped back and forth from Leith and Bo'ness: but some spent the rest of their lives there.

Two exiles who mattered most were both Galloway men, influenced by Samuel Rutherford. One was that John Brown of whom he had written: "I never could get my love off that man. I think Jesus Christ has something to do with him." A brilliant scholar, his first and only charge was the tiny village of Wamphray in Annandale. From there, in his late fifties, he was taken prisoner to Edinburgh for preaching in defence of the Covenants and defiance of Episcopacy. Five weeks in the foulest dungeon brought him to the verge of death.

Then he was exiled for the rest of his existence. In Holland he wrote and published a steady stream of works on the Two Kingdoms, and the doctrines of the Reformation, which were smuggled back into Scotland and kept alive the great issues. He claimed, with Knox, the right to resist tyranny, by force if need be.

His colleague was a much younger man, McWard of Glenluce, who had been a student of Rutherford's at St. Andrews: and who, in Holland, published the first edition of Rutherford's marvellous "Letters," which are still reprinting. He was himself a Professor of Humanity at 21 or 22, and was then called to the "outer High Kirk" of Glasgow Cathedral.

But it was in the Tron Kirk of Glasgow that in February, '61, he preached on Amos: 32, and said: "I do this day call you who are the people of God to witness that I humbly offer my dissent from all Acts which are or shall be passed against the Covenants and the work of Reformation in Scotland: and I pray that God may put it on record in heaven."

He was lucky to escape to live out his life in Rotterdam and Utrecht, acting as *locum* and "second minister" to the Scots Kirk there. He did slip back once or twice in secret. In 1669 he slipped back to marry the widow of the former Lord Provost of Glasgow.

"Christianity is the soul cast in that blessed mould of dis-conformity to the world and conformity to Christ," he wrote.

Charles II once demanded their lives from the Dutch government specifically, along with that of another exile, Colonel Wallace. But after a short stay in Germany, all three returned to live and die in the freedom of the Netherlands.

So did gentle old Livingstone of Ancrum, the preacher at the Work at Shotts. He commended humility to his flock: "It fitteth the back for every burden, and maketh the tree sickerest at the root when it standeth upon the top of a windy hill." He reminded them above all, "We have not sought yours, but you." He must have guessed he would not return. All his last words to his sorrowing people were pleas for charity and long-suffering: for tolerance towards the curate thrust upon them: for blessings on the King and both Kingdoms. His old friend and colleague Blair, virtually a prisoner now in Kirkcaldy, thanks to Sharp, wept as he saw his ship sail away past.

Holland was civilisation. For having some of Brown's writings in the house James Guthrie's widow and daughter Sophia were exiled to one of the Shetland Isles. So was Mr. Smith, the minister and dominie of Soothaik and Coen (the mapmakers anglicise it to Southwick and Colvend today). He had been caught taking a service in a house in Leith, and was brought to trial before a tribunal, with Archbishop Sharp in the chair. When he addressed him politely as "Sir," this was not sufficient for His Grace: and he was asked if he did not know whom he addressed? "Yes, indeed," he said, "a former colleague and brother in the ministry!" For this he went first to a dungeon with a raving maniac: and having survived, to the Shetlands where he lived for four years alone on a rocky island with "nothing but barley for his bread, and his fuel to ready it with was sea-tangle and wreck."

Even abroad, not all were safe. In a room in Rouen old Johnston of Warriston sat at those daily devotions he never missed. Perhaps he gave thanks that his life's partner, mother of all his brood, had come over from Leith to be with him in his continuing weakness.

But a woman is easy to follow. A knock came to the door, and Crooked Murray the spy broke in with a French warrant and a guard, arranged by Charles. They carried him to the Tower of London where one of his daughters came to look after him. Then he was taken to Edinburgh, forced to walk from Leith up to the Tolbooth—a long way for a done, old man—and brought to trial. Utterly broken, he flung himself on his knees before the Council, sobbing, begging for mercy: or at least for time, because "his memory was lost, he remembered neither matter of law nor matter of fact, nor a word of the Bible." His nephew Gilbert Burnet said, "he did not know his own children." But Lauderdale pushed on both sentence and execution.

Resigned, he told a friend he dared not doubt his salvation, he had so often seen God's face in the hour of prayer. He was hanged opposite "Advocate's Close," the building, still standing, called after him, where he had spent such endless days and nights of work and study for both the Law and Church of his country. He apologised to the crowd that he could no longer remember the long speech that he had meant to make, and had to read one. "Pray, pray! Praise, praise!" he said to them all repeatedly: and they were the last words he spoke.

His younger son, then a child, studied law in Utrecht and became Secretary of State for Scotland and, like his father, Lord Clerk Register. He retired to Twickenham where he entertained the Prime Minister, Sir Robert Walpole and sometimes King George II, living to nearly ninety. Warriston's daughters remained Covenanters and mostly married Covenant men: one, the son of Baillie of Jerviswoode, who went to the same scaffold in old age.

Scots Law was now also subservient. Such lawyers as had resigned in protest had given in and returned. The Kirk was desolate. In Aberdeen and Edinburgh there were more masses said than sermons, noted a diarist. But in spring the exiles in Holland, chiefly Brown and McWard, brought out the *Apologetical Narration* of the whole struggle: and it ran like wildfire through Scotland.

The gist of it was that by giving in and obeying the Government, the ministers "should quite undo and betray their posterity." Whereas by resisting they would be "keeping up some footsteps of a standing controversy." . . ."if there were but this much of a standing difference betwixt the people of God and the common enemies of Zion to be seen, posterity would in some measure be kept from being deceived, and would see the interest of Christ not killed nor buried quickly, but living, though in a bleeding condition."

It was "a damnable book," Sharp wrote to Lauderdale in London, giving an alarmist report on the "Westland Whigs," who might combine with the Irish and rise. As well as burning the book at the Cross, a whole string of new, more repressive measures were brought in. The Twenty-mile Act, which sought to exile ministers further away from their parishes: the Bishops Dragnet, which combed out all those not attending to hear the curates preach, and fined them savagely: more free quartering for the soldiers, and encouragement to loot. General "Bite-the-Sheep" Turner was sent to Dumfries with 127 Foot Guards, and summons issued for eleven ministers, including Welsh, Semple, Blackadder and Peden of Glenluce.

Blackadder's family were lurking in the hills in a remote farm while he searched for a place to hide them, and his younger son left an account which can stand for all the others.

"Turner and sodgers came to search for my father . . . about 2 o'clock in the morning. They gave the cry, "Damned Whigs, open the door!" Upon which we all got up, young and old, except my sister and the nurse with the child at her breast. They shouted to bring candles and fire, or they would roast nurse and bairn and all in the fire and mak a braw bleeze!" They drew their swords and hacked stools and chairs to throw on the fire—"and they made me hold the candle to them, trembling all along, and fearing every moment to be thrown quick into the fire. They went to search the house for my father, running their swords down through the beds and bed-clothes; and among the rest came where my sister was, then a child and as yet fast asleep, and with their swords stabbed down through the bed where she was lying, crying, "Come out, rebel dog!" They then ransacked every corner, threw all his father's books and papers on the floor or into creels. Then, "up to the hen-baulks," and wrung all the cocks' and hens' necks, one by one, throwing them down: and so with all the salt-meat and all the meal: "all this I was an eye-witness to, trembling and shivering all the while, having nothing but my short shirt upon me."

Finally, he managed to slip out, as if in play, between the two sentries with drawn swords, and ran half a mile in the dark "naked to the shirt." When he got to the next clachan, the Brig-en' o'Mennihyvie, (Moniave), every door was shut, and all asleep. So he climbed to the top step of the Town Cross and there slept, exhausted by terror. An old woman looked out as darkness thinned, and saw a white object: "Jesus save us! What art thou?" He was Mr. Blackadder's son, he said: "There's a hantle o'fearful men, wi' rid coats, has brunt all our house, my brither and sister and all the family!" "Oh puir thing!" says she, "Come in and lie doon in my warm bed . . ." And it was the sweetest bed that ever I met with."

The children were scattered to other farm houses, but these too were ruined one by one by soldiers. At his, the Peeltoune, "the puir mither begged but ae lamb for meat to the bairns but could not get it. The meat they were not able to eat, they destroyed; threw down the butter kirns, and hashed down the cheese with their swords, among the horses' feet."

Blackadder took his family to Edinburgh, and hid them in the attics and wynds of the Cowgate, under the very nose of the Castle garrison. In moments of alarm the children were dispersed among other families. But through poverty, danger and the long heart-sickness of hope deferred, their education was not neglected. The eldest son, William, graduated in medicine at Leyden, and was doctor (and agent) to William of Orange. Adam, the racy narrator, was a well-doing merchant who brought home a "Sweds" wife. Robert, the most scholarly, died while studying theology at Utrecht. Thomas, another merchant, emigrated to New England. The surviving daughter married and raised a large family. And the baby the dragoons had threatened to throw on the fire became Colonel John Blackadder of the Cameronians, one of Marlborough's distinguished commanders, Governor of Edinburgh Castle and a prominent elder in the General Assembly.

They might stand as a model manse family; but the only manse they had was the rabbit-warren of tenements below the High Street.

CHAPTER TWO

THE WESTLAND MEN

Rain fell in torrents all the autumn of 1666, day after relentless day, bringing flooding and misery to man and beast. On one of these short, black November days some refugee elders—Maclellan of Barscob in Balmaclellan and three others—ventured out of hiding and came down to St. John's Town of Dalry, near Barscob, to look for food. On the way they met Corporal Deanes and three soldiers of the fine-raising garrison of Dalry, driving some prisoners to thresh the corn of a poor old farmer called Grier, to pay his fine for non-compearance at the curate's service; Grier himself having hidden. They could only pass on, helpless.

But as they broke their fast at the Clachan ale-house the cry went up that Grier was found "bound like a beast," and that the soldiers were going to strip and torture him on a red-hot grid, to find if he had any hidden savings. They rose up and ran, and found them at it. There were high words, and swords drawn. Barscob crushed his clay pipe, loaded it in his pistol and fired, grounding Deans (who afterwards claimed a pension for it). The other soldiers surrendered.

When they got back to Balmaclellan they found that a conventicle—an unauthorised service—had been arranged there: and clearly they would be held responsible. Since it was too late to turn back now, they rounded up the local garrison of 16, with one trooper killed in the process, and set out to muster at Irongray. By now they had 54 men on Galloway nags led by Barscob, and 150 on foot, led by Neilson of Corsock.

Torrential rain held them up till Thursday dawn, when they all marched over Devorguilla's Bridge to Baillie Finnie's house—the General's H.Q.—and called on Turner to surrender. "Bloody-Bite-the-Sheep" appeared at the window in nightcap, night-gown, drawers and socks, crying for quarter, which was promised by Neilson. He then came down between two rows of drawn blades and primed pistols. A mysterious Captain Gray, who had been egging them on, was about to shoot him when Neilson stepped between: "You shall as soon kill me, for I have given him quarters." Gray later vanished. Could he have been Colonel Blood, the Irish adventurer and informer, who was known to be with the Covenanters at this time? He was in every national conspiracy, always escaping, pardoned (and rewarded) by the King: even for the attempted theft of the Crown Jewels from the Tower! A double agent, we would call him today.

Turner was led on a little nag with a halter to the Town Cross, where the muster loudly and publicly proclaimed their unswerving loyalty to the King, as well as to the Covenants: and their determination to uphold both with undying loyalty. Then they drank His Majesty's health, with cheers of "three times three."

They then held a council on Nith sands, opposite Troqueer: repeating again that they were not a rebellion, but a protest. To make it effectively, they decided the best way was to take Turner a hostage to Edinburgh, and there demand a fair hearing and redress of all their grievances. They took the troopers' swords—their only arms of note—and set out on the long road up Loch Ken.

Their every move was known, and a proclamation was issued against them, urged on by the prelates, which was virtually "a command to the scaffold." General Dalziel, home from the Muscovite wars, mustered 2,500 foot and six troops of horse and set out on Saturday to intercept them. The Covenanters had now reached Dalmellington.

Dalziel was a callous old soldier, whose eccentric appearance embarrassed the King on his visits to Whitehall: small boys hooted, even in the royal parks. In an age of velvet and brocade, long hair and periwigs, he wore a tight "jockey coat," his own bald head and a beard uncut since Charles I's execution. He did not rush upon the Covenanters, but kept a parallel course, by Glasgow, Kilmarnock, Mauchline, Strathaven, while their numbers and hopes were still growing.

Welsh preached a rousing sermon on their first Sunday on the march: and by the end of the first week they were in Ayr. Here they were joined by Colonel Wallace of Auchans, a veteran of Cromwellian wars. He began to put them into some order, and to teach them the rudiments of drilling. There were now about 700 men who could march in step. Between them they had about 60 muskets, 40 pairs of pistols and 20 lbs. of powder. Besides the swords they had scythes and clubs:

"Some had spears and some had pikes:
Some had spades which delvyt dykes"

—so ran a jeering ballad. Some 32 of the outed ministers had joined them: but Peden of Glenluce, who distrusted even this slight military showing, left them again and went to Ireland, where he worked in the fields by day and prayed in the barns where he dossed at night.

Two young brothers Gordon of Knockbrex, that loveliest creek in the Solway, friends of Rutherford, joined them here: and they got word that Muir of Caldwell and Ker of Kersland in Renfrew were bringing out bands to join them. But, owing to Dalziel's strategy, they could not break through his lines to join the main body, and in the end gave up and went home. They were accused, ruined and exiled

144

just the same. Ker died in Utrecht after years in prison: and Dalziel got the Caldwell lands.

From Ayr they marched through Coylton where two of their scouts were caught and hanged; then Ochiltree, then to Cumnock in the bleak hills. A disastrous march in a downpour took them over the Ayrsmoss, by Muirkirk and Douglas. "I never saw lustier fellows than these foot were or better marchers," is Turner's tribute. They camped for the night in St. Bride's Kirk, Douglasdale, among the graves, and held a council there.

By now it was clear that the prelates had roused the Council in Edinburgh and the King in London, and, so far as possible, even the Scots people against them. Not only were they "Whig rebels" but it was alleged that 40 Dutch ships had made landfall at Dunbar. England was at war with the Dutch: and Mr. Pepys in London was thoroughly alarmed about it. Their chances of having their grievances heard, always remote, were now hopeless. Yet to turn back would not only not save their lives, it would ensure that their families were victims also.

They soberly decided that the Lord could work by few as by many: and if they failed and fell, they "reckoned a testimony for the Lord and their country a sufficient reward for all their labour and loss."

Heartened by this decision they marched on into Lanark for their second Sunday, their manpower now at its estimated height of 1,000 men with four or five officers. Here they had two tremendous services, the evicted minister of Tarbolton preaching at the Tolbooth, and Semple to the horsemen at the townhead: and both lots renewing the Covenants, sworn with uplifted hands. From there they marched out by noon over to Bathgate, within reach of Edinburgh. But Lanark's steep street was not quiet for long. By Sunday afternoon it clattered with troops again as Dalziel and his trained men marched in.

From now on the Covenanters' numbers shrank. Some gave up from sheer exhaustion, some from despair: some were actively discouraged from joining. One who gave up sorely against his will was the young consumptive preacher, Hugh McKail, who had come out of hiding to join them. His enthusiasm was such he got men to hold him on his horse: but eventually collapsed and had to be left behind at the end. One old man who went the whole way was known simply as "the Guidman." He seems to have been that perennial character that C. E. Montague, the First World War writer, once described as being born "a shipwreck below par:" requiring black disaster to make him blossom into infectious gaiety and good spirits.

That disaster surely came in their last night-march from Bathgate and Newbridge across the bogs and hags to Colinton churchyard, on the outskirts of Edinburgh. The rain had now changed to cutting sleet. They tied themselves together to keep going: "rather like dying men than soldiers going to a battle." At Hunter's Tryst they stopped.

Edinburgh was in a panic nonetheless. It shut its gates, mounted the strictest guard, and armed even the College of Justice. The Covenanter envoys tried in vain to gain any access. A bold minister called Veitch—one of four sons of a Lanarkshire minister—tried in disguise to get through the ports, at risk of his life, to raise help inside and so force a hearing. But it was all hopeless. Dalziel's terms were total surrender only. They had tried their utmost, and failed.

They withdrew down the Pentlands to Flotterstone: and there on a little hill at Rullion Green they prepared their last stand: lit their campfires—it had turned hard frost and bitter cold—and sang their psalms: Psalm 74 especially:

> O God why has thou cast us off?
> Is it for evermore? . . .
> Unto thy Cov'nant have respect
> For earth's dark places be
> Full of the habitations
> Of horrid cruelty.
>
> Do thou, O God, arise and plead,
> The cause that is thine own . . .

As the short day reddened to sunset Dalziel and his troops marched down the glen from Currie. Though hopelessly outnumbered, the Covenanters made the most of their position, and for a while held them off.

In the first skirmish two ministers, McCormick and Crookshank, were killed. Then "they mixed like chessmen in a bag," wrote General Drummond. Barscob and his 80 gallant nags withstood the shock of charging regiments of horse; and the white hill dyed red. Finally, Dalziel on a fresh horse, and fresh troops with guns blazing, and full panoply of drums and trumpets, swept them away.

As they fled Captain Paton of Meadowhead Farm near Fenwick, a veteran who had fought with Gustavus Adophus and on Marston Moor, turned and fired a silver button, wrenched off his jacket, at Dalziel who was wearing proof-armour. The General swerved and it killed his servant. At once Paton was surrounded but he hacked his way out, crying "Tell your Master I cannot sup with him tonight!"

By clear moonlight the wounded and fugitives were hunted down, the dead stripped. More than fifty were killed, as many caught. Maxwell of Monreith got clear on his good grey nag, and never halted until over Tweedsmuir, and so home—100 miles—where the horse was honourably retired. One wounded man got along the hills as far as Dunsyre—a weary journey—and sought help at a farm. They dared not take him in, but hid him under bushes. He asked, if he did not live, to be buried in sight of the hills of home he had tried to reach. Next morning farmer Adam Sanderson of Blackhill, finding him dead, hastily buried him.

But when the hunt had died down the corpse was carried by pony to the highest point of Blacklaw Hill behind, from where you can see the faint blue peaks of Ayrshire hills, and again buried. Victorians, verifying the story, found scraps of red cloak and silver coins with the bones: and the grave is still marked.

The Kirk Session Minutes of Penicuik record 3/4d. paid to the bellman "for making Westlandmans' graves." These were the lucky ones. The captives were packed into Haddo's Hole at the back of St. Giles, and told they were pardoned only as soldiers—not as citizens.

One who was doubly lucky was an Ayrshire farmer called John Nesbit of Hardhill. Badly wounded and left for dead, his body was stripped where it lay. But in spite of the loss of blood and the cold he crawled off and survived.

The Nesbits had a long history of dissent. Fifty years before Knox and the Reformation, the teaching of Wyclif had come into Ayrshire: and this family was one of those who followed it. In a secret chamber dug below their farmhouse they had a family treasure—a precious hand-written New Testament.

Naturally John was a Covenanter. From this time forth he was also a refugee. In time his wife and children also were driven out. His wife survived four years in the homeless hills: until the day when he heard she was gravely ill. He found them in a roofless sheep-fold- " . . .no light or fire but that of a candle, no bed but that of straw, no stool but the ground to sit on." His little daughter was already dead, his wife dying: and his two sons delirious with fever, and did not know him. He helped carry his dead, dig their graves and bury them, before vanishing again. The two boys surprisingly survived, though at one time beaten and threatened by soldiers to make them tell where their father was. The elder became Sergeant James Nesbit of the Cameronians, and left a Memoir.

The prisoners taken to Edinburgh must have shown up as miserable, wretched creatures, after all they had suffered and the poor treatment they received. The records suggest they were viewed far more with horror than as heroes. No one wanted to share their fate, no one wanted to know. Some twelve hundred were penned in a corner of Greyfriars graveyard for five months without shelter. Blackadder risked bringing food.

"This rabble," as a letter from Sharp and the Council to the King described them, "should be extirpated as traitors:" and "those principles which are pretended as the ground of this rebellion are so rooted . . . it will require more vigorous application . . . as may secure the peace of the Kingdom." Archbishop Sharp signed this first.

Ten men were hanged together on one gallows in Edinburgh, their heads struck off to be nailed up in Lanark, with those of four hanged at Hamilton, including Parker of Busby, whose sword was kept in the

147

family, and Christopher Strang of Kilbride. "Our Right Hands stood at Lanark. These we want, Because with them we swore the Covenant," as the memorial tombstone put it. The young Gordons died in each others arms and one was beheaded. (The severed skull of a young man was dug up near Knockbrex Castle centuries later). Thirty-five were taken back to be strung up near their own doors. Neilson of Corsock and young Hugh McKail, who had never got to Pentland but was caught in the rout, were reserved for torture.

"Having a full account of the happy success you have had against the rebels in Scotland," wrote the King whom the Covenanters had toasted, to Dalziel on December 5th, "I could not but give my hearty thanks for it myself, by letting you know how well I am satisfied with your conduct and zeal in my service . . ." "Your very loving friend . . ."

The Duchess Ann was one of the many who wrote on behalf of McKail: and his cousin Dr. Matthew and the minister Robert Douglas swallowed their pride and went to plead for him to Sharp: and were repulsed. Ostensibly it was to find out if there was a Dutch plot behind the rising: but McKail's sermon in St. Giles was not something Sharp would forget. It was believed there was a pardon which he held back. Turner, now free, appealed in vain for Neilson, as he had promised.

Go down steps at George IV Bridge, Edinburgh, and you will find the Laigh Hall, traditionally the torture chamber. Used now by lawyers, its rough stone walls, with high small windows, hold perpetual chill. Here the iron cage was fitted to Hugh's spindle shank and Rothes asked the questions while the mallet-man drove eleven blows on the iron wedges, till the knee-joint was cracked and crushed. McKail bore up with courage till he was carried off unconscious.

But Neilson had not only the stout bones of a countryman: he had probably never imagined the reality of the evil that now overwhelmed him. His awful screams could be heard all over the city.

McKail kept up what sounds a rather feverish gaiety until his hanging four days later: his cousin Matthew sharing his cell and going with him to the scaffold, where he was "wholly unable to walk or stand." There he gave his Testimony, long and carefully written.

"Although the market and price of truth may appear to many very high," said a young probationer Robertson, looking round the crowd in the Grassmarket before he was hanged: "yet I reckon it low . . ."

These Testimonies were important as more than last words or sermons: they were the dying men's way of staking their deaths against the people's reluctance or indifference. As he struggled up the ladder, Hugh broke into unprepared words: "Now I leave off to speak any more to creatures . . . now I begin my intercourse with God . . . Farewell, father and mother, friends and relations! Farewell the world and all delights! Farewell meat and drink! Farewell sun, moon and stars! Welcome God and Father—welcome sweet Jesus . . .Welcome blessed spirit . . . Welcome glory! Welcome eternal life! And welcome death!" As he swung jerking into space, Dr. Matthew flung his full weight on the thin legs to shorten the agony.

"So to bed—and with more cheerfulness than I have done a good while, to hear for certain the Scots rebels are all routed," so Samuel Pepys wrote in his diary on December 3rd: "—they having been so bold as to come within three miles of Edinburgh, and there given two or three repulses to the King's forces, but at last were mastered—300 or 400 killed or taken, among which their leader, one Wallis, and seven ministers (they having all taken the Covenant a few days before, and sworn to live and die in it, as they did) and so all is likely to be there quiet again . . ."

But Mr. Pepys was wrong. It was not the end but the beginning.

L

CHAPTER THREE

DESERT PLACES

The very voice of the solitary places is in the long call of the curlew. "Where about the graves of the martyrs the whaups are crying," wrote Stevenson, that lover of Covenanter histories, when in Samoa: "My heart remembers how!" There is an old tradition in the moors that it was lucky to trample on the nests of the peesweeps, another moor-bird, lest their startled calls betray the conventicles.

That word, conventicles, was first invented by Government officials to describe the spontaneous and unique form of worship that seemed to grow straight out of the heather.

It might be thought that a people hard pressed even to live in those times had more than enough of religion, let alone sermons; for they were constantly fined if they did not attend their church to hear a curate, and as constantly pillaged by mercenary soldiers if suspected of taste for any other sermons at all.

Yet unasked and unsought, always at risk and often suffering, these huge crowds of generally poverty-stricken people would make their way through bogs and up hillsides for no other reason than to hear the gospel preached: by men who took no money and stood to die for it.

An eyewitness describes a "countryman with a blue bonnet" standing beside the preaching-tent, or booth, and "hearing every word as if he had been sucking it off the preacher's mouth."

It was as if, pushed to the bitter edge of existence, they had a famine-hunger for something to make sense of it all: for some vision above and beyond the daily struggle for brute existence. Not an escape: an answer.

Secretly, Blackadder slipped in and out of Edinburgh and going West travelled round in a wide circuit, from Tarbolton and back to Fenwick, preaching at meetings that steadily grew, only by word of mouth. When he preached round the Calders, or in "The Black Dub of Livingstone" or at Calder House where Sandilands, Lord Torphichen, kept up the noble tradition of his family which had supported Knox, then he would make his weary way home again by night rather than put anyone at risk by giving him shelter.

At one point Sandilands was, briefly, taken prisoner; and as the people fled the soldiers got "great booty of cloaks, plaids and Bibles."

How did the outed ministers live? Adam Blackadder records that once Mr. Welsh and Mr. Gabriel Semple rode in to Edinburgh to visit, and his mother cried in despair that she had "neither black nor white to give them." But as they smoked pipes together (long clays, presumably) a whole sheep was handed in.

There was nothing of the "bloody-minded bigots" of fictitional history about these men. They were sober, godly pastors of all ages and the highest standard of education. Many came from well-to-do homes, some had parents of rank. Blackadder might have claimed the baronetcy of Tulliallan, had he chosen.

Nor were the dragoons necessarily English invaders and persecuters. They were just as likely to be Scots mercenaries home from the Continental wars, where they had learned to steal or starve. All the King's men in Scotland, the chief persecuters, were Scots. Some were graduates. Turner was a son of the manse.

One lie put out about the Covenanters then, still circulating today and still believed by the fanatically-minded, was that their secret meetings were to plot rebellion. For that reason Blackadder disliked the usual house-conventicles, and in spite of the added risk of spies and soldiers, much preferred to preach in the open.

"While you kept your preaching so quiet, we thought you were at some worse turn," said an outspoken Fifer to him: "but now we see, and God forgive you that you did not acquaint us sooner. Whenever you have the like again, let us know, that we may have a share of it."

Whatever they got, it could not possibly have been the comic rantings and ravings described by Sir Walter Scott for English readers. The people must have seen that these men had something that they themselves needed and wanted.

"I care not to trample all things under my feet, that they may be so many footstools to help lift my heart to heaven," said Welsh, preaching his farewell sermon to his people in Irongray on Romans 8: "I care not to bear all the crosses and afflictions on my shoulders, so be I may win to yonder glory. I care not how difficult and hard and how rough the way may be for I must be at it—I must be within that New Jerusalem, the City of the everlasting God."

Here is Blackadder speaking as ambassador of the heavenly King to a huge crowd gathered in "a green and pleasant haugh by the waterside."

". . . Shall we take back this word, that ye are content to take Him in all the terms that ever He offered himself to you . . .? Shall we tell Him these good news, that here we have found out a willing people . . . that is, willing to follow Him through the wilderness, and to bear His cross and witness for Him . . .?

"Come away, poor man and woman that is glad to close the bargain: thou that hast been as it were putting thy hand to the pen, and yet dare not seal it: He loves that thou should . . . Seal it with thy hearty consent! Or say with Thomas, if thou can say no more, "My Lord and my God."

They were conscious of being, not a dissenting body but part of the universal Church as much as they were part of the natural world.

"The principal remote cause of the civil republic is God the Author of Nature," wrote Brown in Holland: "The principal remote cause of the Church is God the Author of Grace." There was but one Visible Church in the whole world. All particular creeds were but branches in various degrees of purity: "Since the purest churches under heaven are subject both to mixture and error . . . yet though the people should withdraw from communion with the greatest part of the church which is now corrupted . . . they remain a part of, and a part in, the Visible Church."

, "Bread, wine nor water me no ransom bought!" wrote John Bunyan, imprisoned in Bedford jail for preaching the gospel at this time. And again: "Methought I saw with the eyes of my soul Jesus Christ at God's right hand. There, I say, is my righteousness . . . for my righteousness was Jesus Christ himself, the same yesterday, today, and forever."

If the Bible was the people's only book, they had the more reason to study it constantly: and could see reflected in Israel's history their own stumbling search to find their Creator and His Kingdom where they belonged. They sought not a national home but an eternal one: and since this was their guide-book and passport, they must know it well.

The hangman of Irvine was a stray from Strathnaver called Sutherland, who had been turned out in his 'teens to find his own keep. By droving and starving, riding back horses and garotting witches, he had made his way to Ayrshire, where he found folk friendly; and there he learned not only to speak English but reading, writing and independent opinions. When Rullion Green prisoners were sent back there to be hanged, he spoke with them: and finding them honest, godly men he point-blank refused to do the job—furthermore quoting copious Bible texts to his betters till they were nearly demented with rage.

On this one rebellious cog at the very bottom of the social scrap-heap their own civil obedience, their fortunes and possibly even their own necks, depended.

"Confound it, ye shall be hanged!" roared the Lt. General.

He would be the worse confounded, said the hangman calmly: for "the Lord hath chosen the foolish things of this world to confound the mighty . . ."

"Tell us quickly, who put these words in thy mouth?" shouted the curate.

"Even he who made Balaam's ass to speak . . ."

He would be flogged, tortured, branded and shot, they said: while he continued steadily to recite Scripture. They brought lead and melted it in front of him, to pour on his hands—which would discharge him from any hanging at all, he pointed out, (with text). "The Provost rounded in my lug, not to be afraid of the country folk: he would give me 50 dollars and I could flee to the Highlands, or anywhere." He answered loudly, "What, would you have me sell my conscience? Where can I flee from God? Remember Jonas fled from God, but the Lord found him out and ducked him ower the lugs . . ."

He was put in the highest stocks for the night: then told next day he would be rolled downhill in a barrel full of nails: to all of which he could reply with chapter and verse. Finally, he was blindfolded and tied to a post for a mock execution, carried out in the liveliest manner. Still he was obdurate and still he spouted Scripture, piously, patronisingly; unbearably.

Authority, defeated, fell back on offering life to one prisoner to hang the rest. They agreed it would be the youngest, and well filled with brandy. But afterwards they made him hang the Ayr men as well: and he is said to have died "in distraction."

Other dirty weapons that had served their purpose were now discarded. Lord Rothes was "de-courted." Turner and Bannatyne, persecuters of the west, were dismissed. General Turner, like so many other Generals, settled down to write his Memoirs, in which he appears—don't they all?—a rather jolly dog. A Glasgow graduate, he had been Leslie's Adjutant in the Bishops' Wars, and then turned mercenary on the Continent. He makes the classic defence: "I had swallowed without chewing, in Germanie, a very dangerous maxim . . . which was, that so we serve our master honestly, it is no matter what master we serve."

Bannatyne went back to mercenary wars on the Continent: and walking on the ramparts of beleagured Angers uttered famous last words, "Cannonballs kill none but fey folk!"

Defoe was later to call Turner "a butcher . . . rather than a General." But the Scots said he was "a saint to Bannatyne." Of young Grierson of Lag, a fresh persecuter, a Covenanter wrote: "A great persecuter, swearer, whorer, blasphemer, drunkard, liar, cheat, and yet out of Hell."

Even Sharp found the upper class cooling. A bitter young "stickit minister" Mitchell, had taken a shot at him, when alighting from his carriage in the High Street: but wounded the Bishop of Orkney—Blair's old assistant at St. Andrews'—instead. Sharp now made an approach to the rising star, Lauderdale: "coldest friend and violentest enemy;" but Lauderdale produced a letter Sharp had once written to the King running him down in favour of Middleton.

Charles knew very well the kind of men he was using to suppress in Scotland that religion "not fit for gentlemen." He shared the amusement when courtiers replaced a goblet of "the King's choice syllabub" with horse-piss, which Lauderdale loyally drank. Dalziel was welcomed, however grotesque, or brutal. The "Muscovite" never married, but left his loot to illegitimate children: so beginning the legend that his name was so cursed, no direct heir would ever inherit. (This in turn so moved a 20th century Dalziel lady that she is said to have arranged an exorcism—but unfortunately by a Bishop).

153

These men were materialists rather than Royalists, putting any earthly king above all. The Act of Supremacy now passed did exactly that. "The Church as to her ecclesiastical being is annihilated and there is no more a Church as such," wrote Brown, the watchdog in Holland: "for that company is now metamorphosed into a formal part of the civil polity and is like unto any other company of merchants, tradesmen or the like."

Even Bishop Alexander Burnet of Glasgow objected to this Act so strongly that he was virtually deposed: and eventually the pliable Leighton was made Archbishop of Glasgow by the King instead.

Lauderdale and Leighton combined to offer the Covenanters a carrot, called the Accommodation. This was backed by the first Act of Indulgence, by which outed ministers could return to their kirks and manses on easy terms. It was a shrewd move. Although only 43 accepted they included such men as Robert Douglas, the royal chaplain, now in his seventies; they took a wedge out of the Kirk's united witness and weakened it.

Once accepted, Lauderdale began to tighten the screw: and an Act Anent Deponing made informing of relatives and neighbours not only a duty but compulsory. Weir of West Calder, of that little square kirk on Main Street, had returned: he spoke out, was again outed, imprisoned and exiled (but eventually returned).

The Act of Indulgence was followed in a year by "a clanking Act" against conventicles, as Lauderdale called it: which made anyone attending liable to total confiscation and even death. Yet for a while the clanking was greater than the actual persecution. The Covenanters came to call those years The Blinks; the sunny interludes. In them conventicles reached a high tide that was sheer poetry: and which, to use a phrase from Sir James Stewart of Goodtrees writing in Holland "will never be forgotten as long as Scotland is Scotland."

Gaelic, without English, barred the west: but from the far North-east of Ross and Cromarty down through Scotland to the Borders and over to Northumbria conventicles flourished and spread. Hog of Kiltearn, a Gaelic-speaker to some extent, had been born in Tain: when outed he preached all round the Black Isle and Dornoch Firth—that area whence came the first martyrs of the Reformation, Patrick Hamilton and George Wishart. With him was Fraser of Brea, in the Black Isle; whose father had been an elder at the Glasgow Assembly.

In Perthshire, Fife and the Lothians, Clydesdale, Ayr, Galloway and Dumfries, the psalms went up from a thousand throats. Most tireless of all, Welsh preached up and down the Border hills and glens: once, in a hard winter, he preached in the middle of the frozen Tweed, so that neither Scotland nor England need bear the blame.

In June, 1670, when there is scarcely darkness all night in the north, word went round that the meeting-place was Hill o'Beath, a rounded hump near Kinross.

"On Saturday afternoon people had begun to assemble," wrote Blackadder: "many lay on the hill all night." Barscob had come with nine or ten Galloway men. Blackadder "slept all night in his clothes" at Inverkeithing, and rising early made his way to the top of the hill. As a great crowd steadily gathered, rumours and tension gathered with it. There were militiamen on the fringes: unexplained characters who would have led off horses: the local curate's sons with "14 or 15 fellows at their back, who looked sturdily."

Blackadder would let none be put out. He took a turn in watching for trouble in the morning, then began to preach. A lieutenant of militia, dismounting, got to the front and listened for a little: then tried to leave. Objections threatened to become a scuffle. Blackadder broke off to ask: "What is the matter, gentlemen? Let me see Sir, who will offer to wrong you . . . we came here to offer violence to no man, but to preach the gospel of peace: and Sir, if you be pleased to stay in peace, you shall be as welcome here as any. But if you will not, you may go. We compel no man."

He got his horse and left. The service ended and the crowds streamed off into the dusk. Then the militia were seen coming back in force: but some of the men who had both weapons and horses drew up in a show of strength, and they retreated again. The peace held.

At Kirkcudbright, Carrick and Glendevon there were vast gatherings. The price on Blackadder's head was now 1,000 merks. Once, when the sheriff and his men rode up, a bonnet and plaid were thrown on him and the crowd closed ranks. The dragoons' captain did not attack: and was cashiered. Once when Welsh was in desperate need of shelter he went to the house of a disaffected man and offered to lead him where Welsh was, in return for bed and board: and next day led him into the heart of a conventicle and made him listen to the sermon. Once when Peden, that lone prophet of the hills, saw the dragoons coming upon him he prayed: "Lord, cast thy cloak around puir auld Sandy this aince mair"—and the scarf of Galloway mist swept round and swallowed him up.

Is it surprising that some heard psalms where no voices were? Or saw True Thomas's "milk-white steed with a blood-red saddle"—prophecy of persecution—at the edge of the crowd? Even in our "dregs of days" there are places that seem to hold a different light, as if on a deeper focus. Such as the vale of Assissi and the woods outside it: the white bays of Iona; and Eynhallow, holy isle of Orkney, where birds are curiously tame and seals swim in the bay with you. So too in those hidden hollows of the Covenanters, if you can climb and clamber to them: those "desert places" R. L. Stevenson wrote about, "in the vacant, wine-red moor."

Climb past Maxwelltown Farm with its famous ponies, above Shawhead, Dumfries, and you come upon an unexpected green amphitheatre rimmed with heather. The guide-books talk of "stone tables," but there are only long, radiating lines of dry-stane dykeing, which skilled hands would knock up in no time, needing only trestles and cloths. Here Blackadder preached on Isaiah: "Neither shall the covenant of my peace be removed:" and he and Welsh, the other preacher, broke bread and shared cup with 3,000 souls. The whaups rise wailing from your feet as they did then; underlining the silence.

At East Nisbet in the Merse of East Lothian they held a communion service on a heavenly summer day—"one of the days of the Son of Man"—days which, Christ told his disciples, they would long to see again. More than 3,000 people came forward with their lead tokens—seals of understanding. "From the Saturday morning when the Work began until the Monday afternoon when it ended" all was perfectly organised. Scouts were set, guards chosen for duty; two long tables set on the grass beside the river, a short one across the head: in "families" of a hundred at a time they came forward, and all was done "decently and in order." This in spite of Lord Home ("as ramp a youth as any") having boasted his horse would "drink the wine and trample the elements."

Nor was it all grimness and gloom for the young. "In the month of November 1674," wrote Adam Blackadder after one of his father's conventicles: "forty-six of the inhabitants of Stirling were all denounced to the horn, and proclaimed his Majesty's rebels . . . and me, the poor apprentice, amongst the midst of them. All the rest fled out of the town in disguise—most of them in bonnets and Highland plaids. I would have been for running too, but my master discharged me to leave the shop." "For," said he, "they will not have the confidence to take up the like of you, a silly young lad."

"However, a few days thereafter, I was gript by two messengers early in the morning, who for haste would not suffer me to tie up my stockings, or put about my cravat, but hurried me away to Provost Russel's lodgings—a violent persecutor and ignorant wretch.

The first word he spake to me (putting on his breeches) "Is not this braw work, Sirr, that a wice man be troubled wi' the like o' you?"

"Ye have got a braw prize my Lord, that has claught a poor 'prentice."

"We canny help that Sirr, we must obey the King's laws."

"King's laws, my Lord!" says I, "there is no such laws under the sun!" (For I had heard that . . . masters were bound for their servants . . .)

"No such laws, Sirr!" says our sweet Provost, "Ye lee'd like a knave and a traitor, as ye are . . . Away with him!"

He was put "within iron gates" in the Tolbooth "where I lay about five weeks, and was never merrier in all my life, with ten or twelve more of my fellow-prisoners for the same alleged crimes."

"While I was in prison, the Earl of Argyll's two daughters-in-law, Lady Sophia and Lady Henrietta, and Lady Jean his own daughter, did me the honour, and came to see me; where, I remember, Lady Sophia stood up upon a bench, and arraigned before her the Provost of Stirling: then sentenced and condemned him to be hanged for keeping me in prison: which greatly enraged the poor fool Provost, though it was but an harmless frolic . . ."

Elder brother William came with an order for his release, which the Provost, possibly still enraged, refused to grant. William had to return with letters threatening to put Provost, bailies and all in prison if the orders were not carried out before midnight: this being backed up by "two or three mosquetaires" which he had privately provided. As late as possible the Provost sent a bailie to say, "Adam, the Lord Provost has been pleased to grant you your liberty."

"I smiles in his face, and says to him: "I believe, Sir bailie, it's a forced putt: but I'm in no haste . . . I'll e'en stay till I sup with my brethren, and give them my foy before I go"—upon which the bailie was dirt-feared lest I should have stayed . . . he immediately took a sixpence out of his pocket and says to me, "Weel, Adam . . . ye are free to go whenever ye will."

Surely there was never a truer church of Christ than the kirk on the moors, where the door was free to all! Climb today to these solitary places and push the heather from the stones. They say that this man, or men were shot for resisting "Tyranny, Perjury and Prelacy"—odd things to find among the whaups! But we get no choice where we resist "the bloody gully of absolute power:" whether on the moors or the battle-field, or the picket-line: only by how much. If the right to dissent is the fundamental human freedom, the strength to leave the herd must be more than human.

They got what they came for, these men and women who toiled out, under threat, to lift the psalms among the hills: the bread they broke together the bread of life, the cup they shared, hand to hand, the fellowship of suffering and wine of joy: and the rough, scarred hand on the table with theirs the hand of Christ.

CHAPTER FOUR

TWO-EDGED SWORD

A thousand years ago a Northumbrian poet wrote of a bleak rock amid the waves, with "hoovle-poovle of gannetes" and singing of far-wending swans: and it is believed to have been the Bass Rock. Gannetries are few in Britain, especially those in the path of whooper-swans' migration. They were valuable in the days when meat was scarcest in spring, for their edible nestlings. Take a spring excursion today from North Berwick round the black volcanic plug of the Bass, some five miles out into the wind-licked seas, and you will still find the hoovle-poovle snowfall of nesting gannets.

You will find also that the only access is by one small landing stage: and that the dank cold is perpetual, even in summer. In winter, it made survival a feat. Was it Lauderdale, made Captain of the Bass, who thought of the Crown buying it for £4,000 as a prison for Covenanters, in 1671? It held well over fifty, some for years: and they included a Papist priest and an episcopal curate who had publicly called James, Duke of York, "a bloody man." But mainly the prisoners were outed ministers or those caught sheltering them: or even those persistently attending conventicles. Cells were small and damp: suffocating when given smokey fires. Food and water were very poor, walkable paths "about 60 feet." But you could write, given total resolution. Even the wife of Gordon of Earlston, allowed to join him there, wrote some "Soliloquies."

Gilbert Rule, minister of Alnwick in Northumberland, was there: arrested for "preaching in St Giles Kirk and baptising a child, although with consent of the episcopal incumbent." When apparently dying he was released, studied medicine in exile, returned to Berwick and became Principal of Edinburgh College in 1688.

Another near casualty was Hog of Kiltearn, who took "the bloody flux." He refused to petition the Council, so the doctor did it for him: and some would have released him on the plea that he did not travel round nearly so much as the others. But Sharp maintained that he could "do more harm from his armchair" than others on the move: and ordered him down to the lowest dungeon. His man wept as he helped carry him down: but, whatever the reason, he recovered there and afterwards would thank "Good Dr. Sharp."

Two Campbells of Cessnock were there: Urquhart of Kinloss: John Dickson of Rutherglen, who survived seven years: Mitchell, who had shot at Sharp, was eventually recognised and arrested, tortured in the Boot: sent to the Bass, and later taken back to be hanged: Mossman:

158

"Bass" Spreul, apothecary of Glasgow (six years and tortured in the Boot): John McGilligan, minister of Fodderty and Alness in Tain (two spells of three years): Henry Erskine was sentenced to the Bass, but reprieved to exile: he beguiled his children's hunger with his fiddle.

Alexander Shields, author of *A Hind Let Loose*, who made a rare escape when taken back to the Tolbooth, in women's clothes: Major Learmonth of Lanark, a leader at Rullion Green, who had hidden on and off for sixteen years in a self-made "air-raid shelter" until betrayed by his own herd, died there in his eighties: and nearly all the preachers were there except Welsh, who was never caught. Blackadder died there.

For "Prophet" Peden, who took the earth for his pillow for twenty-five years, privation was no hardship: but confinement was. He speaks in a letter of how they were allowed out once a day in pairs: 'to breathe in the open air, envying with reverence the birds their freedom; provoking and calling on us to bless Him for the most common mercies."

Even here his legend grew, for it was said that when one of the guard's trollopes taunted him he warned her that judgement was at hand: and on her next trip up the path a great gust of wind shot up her skirts and carried her out to sea . . .

Peden believed in the Lord's judgements, but not in armed risings. He confessed guilt that he had not gone on to Pentland to die with his brethren: yet at no time did he support fighting the Lord's battles with sword and gun.

Another original thinker was Fraser of Brea, also in the Bass. He was a friend of Independents and Quakers and wholly pacifist. He was against the rising mood of rebellion that the long and bitter persecution brought, as he wrote in his Memoirs: "Some hot-heads were for taking the sword and redeeming themselves from the hands of oppressors . . . but I opposed rising in arms all I could, and preached against it and exhorted them to patience and courageous using of the Sword of the Spirit . . . that their strength was to sit still."

Fraser's father, a second son of Simon, Lord Lovat, died when he was ten. At thirty-three Fraser was ordained by a "Field Presbytery," and his direct and popular preaching made him a target for Sharp and his "special treatment." While in the Bass he wrote a work on the Atonement that, like Edward Irving's 150 years later, was suspected of heresy: but to him showed the love of God, and that towards all men everywhere. When it was finally published, 100 years later, it split the U. P. Kirk in half. "Now I could bake my own bread", he wrote, on discovering personal prayer.

Blackadder was "jumbled in his own mind" about the use of force to defend conventicles; though he remained firmly against armed rebellion. "Our trust was in the arm of Jehovah, which was better than weapons of war or the strength of hills," he wrote of that

159

communion by the Whitadder. But it was seldom as simple as that. Some stragglers, both men and women, had been caught and suffered after Hill o'Beath: and little piles of arms began to appear at the fringes of the congregations. His own belief was that "the Lord called for a testimony by suffering rather than outward resistance," but he was too gentle a shepherd to force this on others. The plain fact was that when the cry "the soldiers!" arose, little bands of rough-riders and volunteers had only to snatch up arms and take up their positions for the threat to melt away: and the flock was safe. It was an almost unanswerable argument on the other side.

Balfour of Burleigh, a pugnacious little bonnet-laird known everywhere as Burly, was the chief organiser of these watch-dogs in Fife. He was one of a widespread group which included his brother-in-law, Hackston of Rathillet: King and Kidd, two militant chaplains: young Welwood and Thomas Douglas, a fiery preacher: Hamilton of Preston: Cargill, once of the Barony Kirk: Henry Hall of Haughhead in Teviotdale, a very active elder: and a new voice, Richard Cameron, who saw the indulged ministers—"The King's Curates"—(the others were the Bishop's curates)—as a greater menace to a living Church than the dragoons themselves.

Cameron himself came from a conforming family, and as dominie and precentor under the curate in Falkland, must himself have conformed. But he had heard both sides and made up his mind. He was licensed to preach by Gabriel Semple, Welsh and other outed men in Henry Hall's house.

They sent him to preach in Annandale, that hideout of all the lawless men. When he protested at such a flock for an untried preacher Welsh clapped him on the shoulder with the commission: "Go your ways, Ritchie, and set the fire of Hell to their tails!" Those who turned up at his first conventicle got more than they expected. His text was, "How shall I put you among the children?" and his sermon began "Put you among the children! Offspring of thieves and robbers!"

His licensing without a set course of training was held irregular by two presbyteries, and they insisted that he should moderate his preaching against the indulged ministers. This he refused outright to do, and left for Holland that same year.

Yet already the name—his name—Cameronian—began to be used for the hill-men and the militants, who outright rejected the authority of Charles.

For who now believed in a Covenanted King? The first men of the Covenant had sworn allegiance to an earthly as well as to their heavenly King: and might not consider his defection an excuse for their own. Covenants, unlike contracts, could be one-sided. They might well share Rutherford's view: "I am not of that mind that tumult of arms is the way to put Jesus Christ on his throne." But Rutherford had also accepted Knox's view, now much revived, that rulers drunk with power should be restrained like lunatics. The exiles in Holland argued the case on paper. Since Charles was an apostate King and usurper of the sacred throne, the opinion gained ground that it was not only a right but a duty to resist, even depose him.

They were carried on by the rising tide of distrust and contempt for Charles, now at its height. The Sixties had brought England the Great Plague, the Great Fire and the great insult of the Dutch sailing up both Thames and Medway. The Seventies saw Charles' secret treaty with the French at Dover, promising to make Britain Roman Catholic: and his disastrous wars with the Dutch that made England "hundreds of thousands of pounds more bankrupt than before." as Sir Arthur Bryant put it. He had virtually pawned the nation to the bankers. His annual cries to Parliament: "This obligeth me to move you again for a supply" . . . "I am highly concerned to commend to your consideration and care the debt I owe the goldsmiths . . ." and so on, fell on increasingly deaf ears. He had denied his secret treaty, but the rumours persisted.

Further Acts of Indulgence favoured the Papists as well as Dissenters: including the heir to the Throne, James Duke of York, now an avowed Catholic. Charles' interest in the navy and science was fitful, his extravagance to his mistresses and bastards—six made Dukes—was illimitable. By 1678 the Popish Plot alleged by Titus Oates caused a panic that led to the execution of thirty five Roman Catholics, including seven Jesuit priests and old Lord Stafford, who was over 80. By 1679 Parliament voted to exclude the Duke of York from the succession, and to remove Lauderdale from Government: but they failed in both.

Holland had also had its crisis. In 1672 the greatest army in Europe, the French, with its famous generals, invaded the United Provinces. President de Witt had been murdered. The people turned to the dour little orphan of 22, William II of Orange. He put himself at the head of the troops and swore to die "in the last dike," and let in the sea. The invasion was literally washed out. Now Holland's trading prosperity grew greater as England's faded. The Scots must have seen William as the last great Protestant champion of Europe. In 1677, as one of Charles' conciliatory gestures, he was married to the Duke of York's daughter Mary. So he had at least an interest in the throne of Britain.

For three generations there had been a Scots Brigade in the Netherlands. Fairfax, Monk and two Cromwells had at one time served in it; but its main strength was from Scotland.

Scots were Williams' agents later: some even now. William Carstares, son of the Cathcart manse and that minister who was Cromwell's prisoner, was a student at Utrecht where he first met William and became his friend. Carstares was caught in London distributing the "Account of Scotland's Grievances" and letters in cipher were found on him. He was sent for trial to Edinburgh, and spent four years in jail; and then lurked in London and Ireland before going back to Holland again. Dr. William Blackadder was also in the Prince of Orange's confidence later on.

Blackadder himself preached a sermon of comfort at this time to a big conventicle on Falla Moor: on the text: "When the Lord turned again the captivity of Zion." He said: "Sirs, your common by-word is good: "All is not lost that is in peril." He spoke of Gods' times and seasons which, more than all, divide the Two Kingdoms. "Your guessing can be of no use . . . we have guessed it would come this way and that way, this year and that year . . . and we have wished and desired that God would take this way and that way of delivering his people. . . . beware of limiting God to your own times and seasons: but follow your duty and let God take his own way."

In 1677 there was a conference of ministers, both indulged and outed, in Edinburgh: and Blackadder pleaded hard for peace among the brethren, for brotherly co-operation wherever it was possible. He was met with cries of "Divisive! Divisive!" Persecution had stiffened resistance. He was voted down by those who would cut themselves off completely from the compromisers: and they were now the voice of the people.

The year before, Welsh and Ritchie Cameron had held a great open-air communion at Maybole. Now, "swords sold well at Maybole Fiar," noted a diarist. More were said to be coming in from Holland.

"Many a man in Galloway," wrote Dr. Matthew McKail a little later, "if he have two cows, will sell one and buy a pair of pistols."

In 1678 came one of the meanest episodes of all Scottish history: the invasion of the Highland Host.

Politically it was brilliant, well worthy of Lauderdale. It aimed to satisfy the dispossessed remnants of the clans whose lands the great landlords were mopping up: and at the same time, without any outlay for arms or ammunition, to destroy the very subsistence of the independent Lowlanders: to make the rich farm lands of the West bear nothing but "windlestraes and sandy laiverocks, rather than rebels to the King," as Lauderdale put it.

Glenlyon today is a dream valley, green and sweet, with a clear river through its trees: and almost empty of all human habitation. Guarded too by padlocked gates.

The Macgregors of Glenlyon were one of the clans promised booty by swarming into Clydesdale and Ayrshire and taking under written license all they could carry, harry or drive. So the word went round. The clans mustered at Stirling in January, the hungry month, and ravaged for a month or more. Every horse and pony was taken, every implement or kitchen tool, every thing living or liftable. They left the Lowlands to face the year with bare hands and empty bellies.

As the last of the looters reached the Clyde, on the way back to the mountains, the tide was up, and the ford too deep. They had to cross the bridge. Glasgow students barred their way and made them drop their booty. But "it was but rugg coats and horn spoons and the like." There was nothing else left to take.

On top of stripping the poor, there were the official fines of heritors and others, all duly listed. From the Cumbraes throughout Ayr the staggering total of £137,500 is given.

There was no armed opposition to the Highlanders. There was indeed an extraordinary restraint. They too were victims: and the pity is they could not speak to each other.

Had there only been a common language they might even have made common cause against what are called from this time, so accurately, the "managers" of Scotland: those who farmed their own country for the benefit of bosses in the South. It was a miracle there was no rising: and a disappointment to Lauderdale. "Would God they might rebel," he said: so that he could "bring in an army of Irish Papists and cut all their throats."

The law in Edinburgh said nothing to all this. "They were not minded to be martyrs." Others had less choice. When Borland of Brig o'Kilmarnock was fined £100 and pillaged, his minister Wedderburn, author of a treatise on Divine Grace, tried to intercede: and had his chest cracked by the butt of a soldiers' musket, from which he shortly died.

The debate between resistance, even with arms, and open rebellion hung in the balance. Those who were "conveners of meddlers," as Blackadder called them—especially young Hamilton of Preston— held meetings "before the times were ripe, to consider the propriety of rising in arms, and thereby did no good to the cause by making the people restless and the executive more rigorous."

By that September a returned Highland mercenary, Graham of Claverhouse, had been given a troop of horse to harry Covenanters: and Bishop Paterson of Galloway steps into history as the inventor of a double thumbscrew of particularly fiendish design, especially made for his Presbyterian brethren. You can see it in "John Knox's House" today.

The temper of resistance was rising. Major Johnston, the sheriff's man in Edinburgh, who made the arrests, was beaten up in the spring. At a big conventicle near Whitekirk in Lothian a soldier was killed in a scuffle: and a man named Learmonth, though completely innocent of it, was seized and hanged. At another conventicle in March the soldiers were driven off and Dalziel himself slightly wounded.

Bishop Leighton had gone home to Sussex in 1674. He died, as he had wished, at an inn, and was buried beside his brother Sir Elisha in a very English Church. Before he left Scotland he despaired of episcopacy there: and made his final judgement that all religious differences were but "a drunken scuffle in the dark."

Sharp, though unpopular, was still viciously active and in

November 1678 he set up schemes and sent letters to Lauderdale, all planning renewed and more repressive persecution.

In the spring of 1679, a year of decision, twenty men met in Fife, led by Burly, to pray and to consider direct action. They resolved that the local Sheriff Carmichael, not only a persecutor but a man who had gone on from robbery to rape, must die, to protect their families. Next morning, the 3rd of May, they set out early to waylay him as he hunted hares with his dogs on the hillside. But he got warning and slipped off. Towards noon they gave up and were about to disperse when they saw that extraordinary sight in Scotland, a coach and six, with five servants in purple livery, lumbering over the ill-made roads to St. Andrews, whose towers showed 3½ miles away. It was Archbishop Sharp himself: delivered into their hands.

They held up the coach, slashing harness, horses and servants, dragged out Sharp, who was riding with his daughter, flung all his crimes in his face and, in spite of his hysterical pleading, cut him down, and shot, stabbed and killed him. Hackston alone held aloof, sitting his horse with his cloak about his face, neither sharing nor resisting. Then they all rode for their lives.

The dam had burst. Three weeks later Burly, Hackston and Hamilton were at a great conventicle in Avondale, near Bothwell, where Thomas Douglas preached. Then they rode into Glasgow to a secret meeting with Cargill and Spreul, where a manifesto was drawn up. On Saturday, 29th May, the compulsory day of rejoicing for the Restoration, they rode into Rutherglen, on the edge of Glasgow, as dusk fell, singing psalms; beat out the bonfires and brought out the Provost and baillies to hear them read their Declaration. By it they were "adding their testimony to the martyrs" against all statutes overturning the work of Reformation: establishing episcopacy: renouncing the Covenants: outing ministers: imposing the Restoration Day and royal supremacy and authorising Indulgences: and this they fixed to the Town Cross before they all rode off.

The very next day, "the last Sabbath in May," Blackadder was preaching on Falla Moor, deep in the trackless moors south of Edinburgh, still pleading for patience and long-suffering. "When ye came forth with swords in your hands, to defend the worship of God, it is well: but whatever you endeavour with your hostile weapons, I would have you trust little to them." After the service some "honest men" came to complain: the people, they said, "needed a word of exhortation and upstirring, and not to cool their ardour as you have done." He would be the first, he told them, to defend the gospel; but could go no further.

It was already too late. Next day, June 1st saw the militants holding another conventicle at Loudon Hill, two miles from Darvel. But they had not been long engaged when the warning was given: Claverhouse and his troop of horse were moving against them. Thomas Douglas, that very upstirring preacher, shut his Bible with the words: "Ye have got the theory—now for the practice!"

The congregation became a Council of war, and Hamilton, as their nearest, and hottest, laird was voted to lead. "I, being called to command that day," he wrote later, "gave out word that no quarter should be given." In truth, they had nowhere to put prisoners if they took them.

They drew up all the armed men and horses they had on Drumclog Moor. Claverhouse (a unique speller) had once written of his commission: "For my owen pairt, I look on myself as a cleanger." With enthusiasm he rode to the challenge. Walter Scott, who carried his adulation to the extent of transferring the song "Bonnie Dundee" from the town to the man, had a famous portrait showing a face of almost girlish beauty, framed in the curls of a vast black wig. Eye witnesses insist he had buck teeth, dark skin and short red hair of his own. His breastplate in Blair Castle proves he was small and slightly mis-shapen. But on one thing friend and foe agree: he was a superb horseman. Later, he was seen to ride his coal-black charger "Satan" along the narrow parapet of the Nith at Dumfries and at the end rear it up and whirl round "on a sixpence."

At Drumclog he was not so lucky. The moor, as the Covenanters knew and he did not, was deep peat. His troopers bogged down in it and his own horse, wounded by a thrust from a pike, bolted for a mile. When he did get back his troops had fled. A young divinity student of St. Andrews on holiday, a born soldier called Cleland from Douglas, is credited with teaching the Covenanters to fire, then fall flat so that the soldiers' bullets whistled past. Only one prisoner had been taken alive, and there is no note as to whether he was young or old, Scots or English: only that his fate was being debated when Hamilton, flushed with victory, rode up: and insisted that, as orders were orders, he must be despatched. So he was killed.

In Holy Trinity parish church, St. Andrews, there is one of the most grotesque baroque monuments in Europe. It shows Sharp, ex-minister of Crail, persecuter and sadist, kneeling in angelic robes of white marble, hands folded in prayer, before the object of his adoration: a white marble Bishops' mitre. His achievement was to give the Scots not a mere resistance to episcopacy but a lasting abomination of the very name of Bishop.

On Drumclog stands a splendid memorial, commemorating those who fell that day, the Covenanters' one victory under arms. It marks also a small defeat for that other King whose mercy was for all.

CHAPTER FIVE

CAMERONIAN

The Covenanters marched into Glasgow on June 3rd, two days after Drumclog, several thousand strong. They came in two divisions, one up the Gallowgate and one over the Townhead. But neither divided nor united could they get into the centre of the town, barricaded and defended both by regular soldiers and artillery: they had none.

They marched back to Bothwell Bridge on the Clyde, which was now defended by their only cannon, a little brass gun someone had prudently lifted from Douglas Castle in the by-going. Thousands more flocked in from every quarter: the men of the West with Welsh and Cargill: Ure of Shargarten, ex-episcopalian minister, with the Stirlingshire contingent of 200: men from Fife and from the Lothians, even from Perthshire. Many of the outed preachers were there, including by now Blackadder: some accounts say also his eldest son, William.

If Cleland at 18 was one of the youngest fighters, old Captain Paton, now into his sixties, must have been one of the oldest. Since Pentland he had been lurking, but slipping back to Meadowhead from time to time. Once he caught a grazing horse and rode calmly through his pursuers as they sought a man on foot. Once Cargill baptised twenty six bairns in his barn at one service. Now he was back in the battle line.

So great a gathering brought, for three short weeks, the light of hope: a false dawn of deliverance. They were weeks filled with debate and division. The Moderates could not accept the Rutherglen Declaration and drew up their own which repeated the original Covenant position: a free Presbyterian church: a lawful King: free Parliaments and Assemblies: and they fixed this to the Cross at Hamilton on 13th June. This sent Commander Hamilton into a towering rage: and he spent his time defending the militant position, where a Cromwell or a Leslie would have concentrated on welding his forces together, and arming and drilling them.

Charles put his eldest and most beautiful bastard, the Duke of Monmouth and Buccleugh, in charge of a well-armed force, to suppress the Covenant men. Monmouth, authorised to be lenient to all but the slayers of Sharp, came north to Bothwell at top speed. A deputation went to him with drum and flag of truce, to propose the terms of the Hamilton Declaration, coupled with a desperate plea against persecution. These would be considered, said Monmouth, "if they laid down their arms first." "And hang next!" said Hamilton.

By 22nd June there were 10,000 well-armed troops drawn up before Bothwell Brig. The Covenanters held off the first attack: but "scarce any" had powder and ball for a second shot. There was no one to lead a charge for that hand-to-hand fighting where homely weapons had a chance. Even so, Ure and Hackston held the bridge with desperate gallantry until the crucial barrle of gunpowder for the little cannon arrived: and it held only raisins. They had been betrayed. "The Lord took both courage and wisdom from us," wrote Ure later.

Hamilton was blamed for everything: but the rout was total. Claverhouse and his troop took full revenge for Drumclog, cutting down defenceless men, even after surrender. Monmouth alone showed mercy consistently, refusing to kill prisoners, or to pursue them into Hamilton Park close by, where the Duchess Ann sheltered hundreds, refusing troops who might "disturb the game." Twelve hundred men were taken prisoner on the field, and any known ringleader was a hunted man for the rest of his life.

"Our people are fallen and fled . . . they are hashing and haggling them down and their blood is running like water." said Peden that day—23rd June—in the Borders. Taken prisoner that spring, along with others, they had been shipped from Leith to be sold as slaves in London, for the West Indies Plantation. But when the English merchant captain found, on conversation, that they were decent godly people, and not the desperate criminals he had been promised, he would not buy: nor would the original trader feed them. So they were turned loose to walk home, and Peden was still on his way.

Old Gordon of Earlston was also late for the battle, but caught and killed in the rout: and buried at Glassford, Lanarkshire. His son, young "Bull" Earlston was there, but escaped by throwing on mutch and goonie and rocking a cradle.

Burly, young Cleland and Cargill were all wounded but escaped, the first two to Holland, where Cleland spent six years studying law in Utrecht: Burly to Rotterdam, where he was coldly received. Cargill had had his spell in Holland and preferred to take his chances lurking in the hills, as did old Paton.

Welsh escaped to London, and to a certain house in Wapping kept by a Scots widow, who must have been well-known as offering refuge. It seems to have been a Whig area—the leader of the English Whigs, Lord Shaftesbury, had a hired gang known as "The Brisk Boys of Wapping." English Whigs were a long way from Scottish Covenanters: but Welsh preached to the Independents, who heard him gladly; and when in this alien corner he died eighteen months later, far from the clean air of the moors, like his exiled grandfather, a great crowd came to his funeral.

Fraser of Brea, released from the Bass to exile in '82, knocked on this same door for shelter. He stayed, and married the lady. But, after

167

four-and-a-quarter years of deep joy, she died: and his touching and original treatise on marriage is her memorial.

Welwood, the young preacher, died in the hills. King and Kidd were both caught. Kidd was first tortured, then both were hanged and beheaded. They went to the scaffold hand-in-hand, making little clerical jokes on their names, before giving their testimony. Blackadder escaped, and next year took William to Holland and entered him as a medical student in Leyden. While there Blackadder preached for fifteen successive weeks in Rotterdam, to great appreciation.

As the prisons overflowed, most of those taken at Bothwell Brig were herded into Greyfriars graveyard in Edinburgh, and lay there three months without shelter, and little and rotten food and water. Batches were regularly cross-examined: "Would they pray for the King?" "Was the Archbishop's death murder?"—questions designed to confuse rather than elucidate. The hangings seem almost random. These five were hanged on Magus Moor, although they had no connection whatever with Sharp's death:

Andrew Sword, weaver, from Borgue: who sweetly sang, "O taste and see that God is good" under sentence.

James Wood, Newmilns, had never even seen a Bishop, but praised the Lord he died a martyr.

John Waddell, New Monkland, was ready to be "a hingin' witness" for the gospel.

Thomas Brown, a shoemaker, said it was his first and last visit to Fife. He had risen for the gospel, and laid down his life for Christ.

John Clide was "a poor ploughman laddie" whose mother wept bitterly at the gallows foot.

Their bodies were hung in chains, to rot and be eaten by vermin.

John Stevenson, minister near Girvan, passed four winter months in a haystack and often, in old Dailly Kirkyard "made a grave my pillow."

Ure of Shargarten, who lurked for nine years, slept all winter in the woods of Balquwhan, sometimes frozen to the ground.

William Veitch, who had narrowly missed Rullion Green, escaped to England, changed his name to Johnston and lurked in Newcastle. When his wife joined him they settled at Stanton, near Morpeth, farming and teaching. Discovered and denounced, he was brought to trial in Edinburgh in '79.

"Had he taken the Covenant?" asked Bishop Paterson. They could see by his age he could not "when you and the other ministers tendered it," he said. He was sent to the Bass: then brought back for what seemed a capital charge. His agent, young Gilbert Elliot, went off to London and with various "sordid intrigues" obtained his pardon: and made his own name.

Years later Gib Elliot, now Lord Minto, came on circuit to Dumfries, and found the Rev. Mr. Veitch of St. Michael's officiating.

"Ah Wullie, Wullie!" said the Judge, "Had it no' been for me, the pyots had been pyking your pate on the Netherbow!"

"Ah Gibbie, Gibbie!" said the minister: "Had it no been for me, ye wad hae yet been writting papers for a plack the page!"

The Third Indulgence offered an escape to hundreds to save their lives by "taking the bond." At the last, when only 257 prisoners who refused completely to do so were left, they were shipped in a leaky old tub, packed like herrings in a barrel, with little in the way of provisions. Ostensibly, they were bound for America.

But recent research makes plain that this was a coffin-ship, never intended to go so far. She took twelve days to reach Deerness in the Orkneys, where on 10th December, the storm rising, the captain battened down the hatches and she drove on the rocks. Captain and crew made it to the land: and thrust back into the sea survivors who had struggled out of the broken ship. Yet a few did survive to tell the tale: and it is commemorated on the tall monument at Scarvating, the most northerly memorial of the Covenanters: and recently in Old Livingstone Kirk.

"I perceive Lauderdale has been guilty of many bad things against the people of Scotland," remarked Charles, when he had read the full reports: "but I cannot find that he has acted any thing contrary to my interest."

Charles was fully aware of all that was going on in Scotland, and his personal letters of thanks to Lauderdale are almost fulsome: "assuring you of my constant kindness" . . . "your abilities and faithfulness" . . . "ever your true friend" . . .

Monmouth's mercy, long remembered in Scotland, was replaced by the cold savagery of Charles' brother and heir, James, Duke of York: installed that December as Lord High Commissioner in the Palace of Holyroodhouse. Partly he had been sent to Scotland to keep him from rousing any more anti-Catholic hate, and partly to obscure the fact that he alone was exempt from the Test Act. Before Christmas Charles reminded the Lord Mayor and Common Council of London that, by Act of Parliament, no one could be "placed, elected or chosen . . . that shall not within one year . . . have taken the Sacrament of the Lord's supper according to the rites of the Church of England." Also the Oaths of Allegiance and Supremacy, and against taking up arms—"and subscribe the Declaration concerning the illegality of imposing the oath commonly called the Solemn League and Covenant" . . .

Even among the Scots Council James' eager curiosity to watch torture—now illegal in England—cast a chill. John Churchill, later Duke of Marlborough—"The First Churchill"—was in attendance on the Duke, and his wife Sara, when an old woman, left her plain words on the times. "I saw it myself," wrote Duchess Sara, "and was much grieved at the trials of several people hang'd for no reason in the world, but because they would not disown what they had said, that

169

King Charles had broke his Covenant. I have cried at some of these trials, to see the cruelty that was done to these men, only for choosing to die, rather than tell a lie."

When Richard Cameron had reached Holland the year before, a reputation as a fire-eater had preceded him. Coming as he did from a conforming family, and with the over-enthusiasm of the convert, he naturally roused suspicions. "The common report of poor Mr. Cameron," wrote McWard, "was that not only did he preach nothing but "bable" against the Indulgence, but that he could do no other thing."

They soon heard otherwise. McWard wrote that he found him "a man of a savoury gospel-spirit, the bias of his heart lying towards the proposing of Christ" . . . . With Brown and the Dutch minister Koelman they ordained him in the Scots Kirk in Rotterdam. (This was not the church later built: bombed: and rebuilt; but St. Sebastion's Chapel originally and appropriately erected for a society of cross-bowmen, with an added gallery and special pews for the Scots mariners who contributed to it, and to the needy in its care).

"Richard, the public standard of the gospel is fallen in Scotland." said McWard: and told him he was called to "lift the fallen standard and display it publicly before the world." But first he should ask the other field-preachers to join with him "and if they will not go, go your lone, and the Lord will go with you."

At the laying-on of hands, his lingered: "Behold . . . here is the head of a faithful minister and servant of Jesus Christ, who shall lose the same for his Master's interest; and it shall be set up before the sun and moon in public view of the world."

Brown, who has been called the first Cameronian, died shortly after this. He believed, with the exiled Sir James Stewart of Goodtrees, author of *Naphtali* and *Jus Populum*, that no man is born with a crown on his head: that the people choose the government, and can alter it. Stewart pointed to the triumphant resistance of the Maccabees of Israel, the Waldensians of Italy, the Swiss cantons. Brown pointed out that peaceable living now meant peaceful acceptance of cruelty, tyranny, the suppression of the gospel. "I cannot see how such a liberty can without sin be accepted or bargained for." With this Cameron agreed.

Cameron was back in Scotland, by way of Newcastle, at the end of 1679. The country was still mourning its dead. Claverhouse and his troop were enforcing evictions and confiscations through the West, right down to Wigton. The tiny parish of Borgue suffered heavily, all the fluffy black Galloway cattle, now so famous, driven off: the widow and children of Lennox of Plumpton homeless for years. From Carsphairn to Parton they devastated, and across to Dumfries where Bell of Whiteside was forfeited, and later shot by Grierson of Lagg. Gibson the younger of Ingliston was shot by the dragoons. A fugitive from Bothwell Bridge escaped in his wife's clothes as the soldiers arrived, and to find where he had gone they tied matches between her fingers and lit them. They burned them down to char the bone, the whole hand gangrened and she died mad.

Cameron went round the outed ministers, as promised: but only Peden would listen, and only the fiery Thomas Douglas and old Cargill would join with him. Under the persecution the church had gone underground. Later, the Society People as they were called, had their own rules and General Correspondence—news-letter—but now there were simply small groups of people, ten or twelve at most, each one personally vouched for. They were those "known to make conscience of secret prayer" and of "prayer and spiritual conference in his family." The meetings for "godly matters" lasted four hours at a time, "every one to take his turn at prayer. Every member may impart any light that he hath gotten."

There was another side to it. No one could be a member who "took any of the bonds tendered by the government, who paid cess, locality or militia money to the civil authorities or stipends to the curates or indulged clergy . . . supplied the enemy . . . or in any form recognised the ministry of the . . . silent Presbyterians."

These then are the true Cameronians, guarding their own narrow frontier between the Two Kingdoms; clear of religious compromise on the one hand and of political commitment on the other.

"Those that cry down defensive arms, when they see it comes to this, you must do this or suffer, they will never suffer . . ." said Cameron in Carluke: "but they will suffer the gospel to go away—I wot well, say they, I did it against my will and so it was my affliction. The Lord will not thank you for it, it is not suffering, it is yielding."

It was a knife-edge business.

Next April, when the spring snows were past in the Lowlands, Cameron and Cargill held a great conference of the Lord's people in Darmead. They came fasting, these starveling folk, while they sought God's guidance for the remnant of his people. "I have been loyal, and do recommend it to all", the minister King had said on the scaffold. "We are to be submissive to the commands of superiors, not to imitate their practice," Fraser of Brea had written on the Bass. But passive resistance was no longer possible. Now they must either abandon all their witness and succumb: or continue on a path whose horrors rose dreadfully before them. It was all or nothing.

"Thus we offer Christ unto you in the parishes of Auchenleck, Douglas, Crawfordjohn and all ye that live thereabout!" cried Cameron, his head so soon to be stuck on a spike: "And what say ye? Will ye take him? Tell us what ye say, for we tak' instruments before these hills and mountains around us, that we have offered him unto you this day. Ye that are free of cess-paying, will ye take him? Ye that are free of the bond, now tendered by his enemies, will ye accept of him this day, when the old professors are taking offence at his way and cross? O will ye cast your eyes upon him? Angels are wondering at

171

this offer: they stand beholding with admiration, that our Lord is giving you such an offer this day . . ."

"Now what say yet to me? And what shall I say to him that sent me? Shall I say, Lord there are some yonder saying, I am content to give Christ my heart, hand, house, lands and all I have, for his cause. Now, if ye can make a better bargain, then do it. Look over to the Shaw-head and these hills, and take a look of them, for they are all witnesses now: and when you are dying, they shall all come before your face."

He had a word of hope for them too.

"If we saw the days that our Lord is to bestow upon us . . . if we had a sight of the ministers that shall be in Scotland . . . it would make us sing . . . if we saw the good days that are coming upon the back of these troubles, we would not get men and women keepit from singing and dancing for joy."

But in the way was "the Devil's Vice-regent:" Charles.

"I think there was never a generation of more worthy men about an evil deed than the bringing home of that abominable person from Breda in Holland to be set up again in Scotland." He was not enrolling men for an army, or even as agents or resistance: "Our help is in him who delivered our fathers from the subtilty and cruelty of that fox, James VI."

A month later Cargill and the elder, Henry Hall, met in Queensferry. They were discussing a draft paper to put the Cameronian principles of continued resistance to absolutism on a formal basis. It contained all the main points of the Rutherglen Declaration, with a proposal for a republican form of government to be considered as well. As they sat quietly talking in the inn they were recognised by the curate, who quickly called out a guard. Both Hall and Cargill fought for their lives and both were wounded. Hall was taken prisoner and died that night. Cargill got away on an officer's horse, was found unconscious by a woman who tied his wounds up with her headcloth and hid him until he could escape.

Within weeks he was preaching again "in his blood and wounds," On 22nd June, the first anniversary of Bothwell Bridge, Ritchie Cameron and twenty horse-men with drawn swords cantered up the crooked street of Sanquhar, hill-town of Dumfries (a street which so far survives). Round the town cross they drew up and sang a psalm: men's deep voices rising triumphantly above the shaggy ponies and the thatched cottages. A Declaration was read, loud and clear, and fixed to the Cross.

"It is not among the smallest of the Lord's mercies to this poor land," begins the Sanquhar Declaration: "that there have been always some . . . a remnant in whom he will be glorious . . . in their carrying on of our noble work of reformation . . ."

"Therefore, although we be for government and governors such as the word of the Lord and our covenant allows, yet we . . . do by thir presents disown Charles Stewart, that has been reigning (or rather tyrannising as we may say) on the throne of Britain these years bygone, as having any right, title to or interest in the said Crown of Scotland for government . . ."

"As also, we being under the standard of our Lord Jesus Christ, Captain of Salvation, do declare a war with such a tyrant and usurper, and all the men of his practices, as enemies to our Lord Jesus Christ, and his cause and covenants . . ."

"And by this we also homologate that testimony given at Rutherglen . . . disclaim that published at Hamilton . . . because it takes in the King's interest . . ." and they totally disowned the Duke of York.

Once more the psalm soared up; then these ragged fugitives who had just declared war on one of the richest Kings in Europe fled back into the hills.

Their war was at hand.

"We getting notice of a party out seeking us, sent two, on Wednesday night late," wrote Hackston of Rathillet, one of Cameron's band, in his account of Thursday, 22nd July: They "lay on a moor-side all night . . . and after we had gotten some meat, we came to a piece of grass, and lay down, and presently we were all alarmed that they were upon us, and so making ready, we saw them coming fast on . . ."

This was at Ayrsmoss, for they had been making up the river Ayr for the safer uplands. They had time at least for prayer.

"Come, Michael, let us fight it out to the last," said Ritchie to his young brother as they finished: " . . . This is the day we shall get the crown!" Perhaps he saw fear there for he prayed "very earnestly" several times over, "Lord, spare the green, and take the ripe!"

Both the Camerons were killed in the first onslaught and nine others. Hackston survived the first charge and was "pursued by severals, with whom I fought a good space; sometimes they following me and sometimes I following them. At length my horse bogged, and the foremost of theirs, which was David Ramsay, one of my acquaintance; we both being on foot, fought it with small swords without advantage . . ." But three troopers rode up behind and cut him down with three deep slashes on the head.

Richie Cameron's head and hands were then cut off—not for mere brutality, but in order to claim the bounty. They apparently made a mistake over Michael's, and took the wrong ones. The bodies were all tumbled into a hasty pit, which became, and in some ways still is, a place of pilgrimage. The story goes that the soldiers frightened a woman by playing football with Richie's head—a very possible reaction; but Hackston says twice over that they used him "civilly, and brought me drink out of an house . . . At Douglas, Janet Clellan was kind to me." Was she sister, or mother, to the young Covenanter soldier?

It was a different matter at the foot of the Canongate on Sunday morning with the blood-thirsty Town Magistrates "sitting me on an horse with my face backward, and the other three bound on a goad of iron, and Mr. Cameron's head carried on a halbert before me . . . and so . . . up the street to the Parliament Close . . ." The head and hands were shown with request for proof, to Richie's old father, once so respectable and now a prisoner in the Tolbooth, who kissed and tidied them and said:

"I know them! I know them! They are my son's, my dear son's . . . Good is the will of the Lord, who cannot wrong me nor mine."

When presented for payment to the Council, someone said: "There are the head and hands of a man who lived praying and preaching, and died praying and fighting." They were duly nailed up above the Bow; the hands, as the custom had become, in mock prayer. Hence Cameron's allusion, when washing the day before Ayrsmoss, that "there would be mony to see them."

One prisoner, Manuel, died in prison; the rest were hanged. But Hackston, who had been at Sharp's killing, was tenderly preserved, and his wounds carefully dressed; to preserve him for the English death for "traitors." He left a cool and steady account of all his interrogations: and in that apparent stoicism mounted the scaffold, where first one hand was hacked and hashed off; then the other, which he suggested should be done at the joint, to save time. Then he was hauled up on a pulley: half-choked: let down until his feet touched: his private parts and a piece of his bowels cut off and burned: and finally the executioner ripped him up and pulled out the heart with the traditional cry: "here is the heart of a traitor!" His assistant carried it round the scaffold "fluttering on the point of his dirk," said Patrick Walker, who was there.

The psalms in the hills had been silenced.

CHAPTER SIX

THE NEW WAR

The Sunday after Richie Cameron's death old Cargill preached at "Starry Shaw, near Benty Rigg," Shotts: home of brothers Marshall, Patrick Walker's "dear billies" who were later sold to Malloch and died in the Carolinas. His text was: "Know ye not there is a great man and a prince fallen this day in Israel?"

Did his hearers find this extravagant? Cameron's irregular ministry was of little more than a year: his active preaching about six months: and his end predictably swift.

Only the following centuries saw the Cameronian philosophy give birth to a great church, and to smaller ones; begetting schools and colleges and missions to the ends of the earth; and contributing through its thousands of members to the American way of life. The regiment that bore his name—though held by some an unworthy memorial—was one of the most famous in the British Army, its battle-honours world-wide. But his greatest legacy of all was his conception of warfare between the Two Kingdoms.

For when, at the head of twenty men, he declared war on one of the richest Kings in Europe, it was not just a bad joke. He never armed or drilled, or recruited followers, or collected money for arms. He did not even conduct the traditional guerilla war of cutting bridges, plundering transport, harassing the enemy. He drew no sword until his last stand, outnumbered four to one.

He declared a totally new kind of war; the non-aggressive war of positive protest and passive resistance. These men and women who followed him were the new weaponless Ironsides, with steel only in their spines. Their troops were the Societies: their disciplined lives and prayer-meetings their only training: the psalms their marching-songs.

The twentieth century, in face of possible extinction, gropes after the scope of Richie's vision. But only a little old Indian has ever gone "naked into the conference chamber": and beaten the British Raj. The main Cameronian witness shifted from national issues to social: but never lost force.

At the beginning of August Cargill preached at Craigmad, near Stirling, where a student called Alexander Shields was deeply moved to hear him. Cargill was now 70, and must have known his time was running out. He had it in mind to carry the warfare a step further. In September he convened a great meeting of "the people of God" at Torwood, between Stirling and Larbert.

175

"I as a minister of Jesus Christ and having authority and power from him, do in his name and by his spirit excommunicate and cast out of the church and deliver up to Satan"—he pronounced against Charles II, King of Scotland: James, Duke of York: John, Duke of Lauderdale: John, Duke of Rothes: Sir George Mackenzie, King's Advocate: Thomas Dalziel of the Binns . . .

In weeks a royal proclamation denounced him afresh, the price on his head hugely increased and anyone caught near his conventicles was hanged or shot on the sketchiest of evidence. In January '81 two girls, Isobel Allison, a quiet girl from Perth and Marion Harvie, a servant lass from Bo'ness, were hanged together in the Grassmarket: possibly in vengeance for the woman who had helped Cargill escape at Queensferry. Three men were hanged on March, another three that summer.

"Go on, valiant champion, you die not as a fool," he wrote to a condemned man in the Tolbooth: "Fear not, and the God of mercies grant you a full gale and fair entry into his Kingdom, which may carry you sweetly and swiftly over the bar, that you find not the rub of death."

A year after Cameron's death Cargill preached to his last conventicle, a huge gathering on Dunsyre Common, West of the Pentlands. "It came from the heart, and went to the heart," said a hearer. His text was from Isaiah 26.20: "Come, my people, enter into thy chambers . . . hide thyself as it were for a little while" . . . He spoke of safety: of differing sorts of security and protection: he spoke of hiding oneself in the wounds of Christ "and exhorted us all earnestly to dwell . . . under the shadow of his wings." . . .

That very night he was betrayed, and taken by Irvine of Bonshaw, a horse-coper turned bounty-hunter, at Covington Mill where he slept. There, it seems, they will still show you the room, the very bed, it is believed. With him were a young student called Boig and a young preacher, a brilliant student of theology from Utrecht University called Walter Smith. His signature is in the roll-book there for 1680—"britanno-scotus". Four names below is Alexander Shields—"scoto-britannus." Jamie the Saxt had invented a new nationality which holds precariously to this day.

Smith was not a rigid Cameronian. The rules of devotion he had drafted for the "Society People's" meetings and private use were prefaced with: "Beware of a spirit of bitterness." "If contentions or debates be like to arise . . . break off abruptly and go to prayer again." Again: "let everyone carefully shun being tedious" . . .

Yet though they disagreed in doctrinal points they all—some dozen were taken and condemned together—"agreed cheerfully," wrote Patrick Walker, "in hanging together". Smith's Professor in Utrecht is said to have wept for the loss of his most outstanding student.

Cargill was 71 when he went to the gallows, and it was said to have been Argyll's casting vote that condemned him. "The Lord knows," said the old man with the rope round his neck, "I go up this ladder with less fear and perturbation than ever I entered the pulpit to preach." With him as well as Smith and Boig, there was William Cuthill, seaman, of Bo'ness and William Thomson of Fife, all hanged together. Cargill died with his head on Smith's breast.

Gabriel Semple was also caught, but was only exiled to London. His son was later minister of Liberton. Even such stalwarts as Maclellan of Barscob accepted some kind of oath or bond, from war-weariness or despair as one by one all the outed preachers were silenced.

That same year of 1680 Mr. Blackadder, now 66, set out on his last circuit. He went first to his own folk at Troqueer: then to Irongray where, seeing by the mourning-band in his hat that Mr. Welsh had indeed gone home "they raised a heavy groan, and several cried out of sorrow . . . After sermon all the Irongray people came about him . . . he took them kindly by the hand, one by one . . . but his heart being over-charged with sorrow, he could offer them no comfort then."

He preached at Dalscairth, near Closeburn, to a "vast assembly" from Galloway, Annandale, Nithsdale and "almost the whole town of Dumfries." To rest, he spent some days at Fairgirth "ayont the Fell", near Soothaik. On his way home, at a conventicle at Dunscore, the snow lay so deep worshippers had to pull tufts of heather to sit on. He had one more preaching, at Whitekirk Hill opposite the Bass, for whose prisoners he specially prayed.

On 5th April a soft knock came to his door, between five and six in the morning. They thought it was the carrier: but it was Major Johnston, the Sheriff's Officer, with a guard: who gently parted the bed-curtains with his staff, as a warning to those within to rise and dress: and so he was taken under arrest up the High Street. After much waiting around, he was "examined" by the Council, including "Bluidy" Mackenzie, Dalziel and Bishop Paterson. Accused of field preaching, he said he saw no difference in conscience "between preaching in houses or in the fields, as may best serve . . . the convenience of hearers," nor any such restriction "from the word of God, where I have my commission, which reaches houses and fields, within and without doors."

He went to the Bass and survived four and a half years, writing his lucid, fair-minded memoirs. When crippled with rheumatism and clearly dying from a form of dysentry, a petition was granted to let him die on shore: but only if he promised not to preach.

"That is absolutely out of my power," he said, "being only instructed to follow my Lord and Master's call . . ."

So he died on the Bass: and his epitaph in North Berwick kirkyard likens him to John on Patmos. There were now no more preachers on the moors.

The last years of Charles II were singularly rich and happy, as chronicled by Pepys and Evelyn. He drew an annual pension from

Louis XIV that kept him in mutton and whores forever, and did away with all need of Parliaments. He had defeated the Whigs, the Popish Plot, and all attempts to prevent James succeeding him. He got rid of his last Parliament by a trick, and could then give all the time he could spare from his women to his other great interest, which has set such a seal on the English monarchy to the present day: horse-racing.

Even Scotland seemed subdued at last. The day after Cargill and the others went in shabby procession to the gallows in the Grassmarket a very grand one came up the Royal Mile from Holyrood. By summons of Lord Lyon all the members of the Scots Parliament "with their gowns, robes, horses and foot-mantles" rode in attendance on the King's Commissioner, James, Duke of York, to open Parliament. The King's letter was read out, full of his "Constant care of and affection to our ancient Kingdom;" pointing out that the "security and property of our people" are inseparable from his own: "And since some (corrupted with the rebellious principals of the last age, or the blind zeal of this) have at first raised schisms . . . and afterward frequent rebellions against us, we cannot but expect . . . effectual and adequate remedies for curing these violent distempers . . ." This being "so necessary to the securing of the Protestant religion." He then commended "our most dear, most entirely beloved brother James"—the Roman Catholic.

Parliament grovelled in reply to "your Majesty's sacred person" for "your Majesty's extraordinary kindness to such as have continued in their duty." It has to admit "inconveniences." But "though some rebellious and deluded people have disturbed your Majesty's government here, yet their principles are so extravagant, and so few persons of any note or quality are engaged . . ." that the Parliament "will cheerfully provide suitable and sufficient remedies."

The first of these was the Test Act, an acknowledgement of total royal supremacy forced on everyone: first on all officials, then on small burghs and throughout the parishes, combed by a special Porteous (portable) Roll: name by name. Except for the Cameronians, who were thus isolated, it was generally accepted one way or another. The bairns of Heriot's Hospital tried it, well-buttered, on their official watch-dog: and when it spat out the core, threatened it with prison for "treason and leasing-making;" that being the sentence just passed on Argyll for taking it "with reservations." He escaped from Edinburgh Castle dressed as a page, holding up Lady Sophia's train—no doubt her idea—and reached Holland safely, being helped by Veitch in Northumberland on the way.

But three Cameronians were caught in Glasgow, and when they refused the test, were hanged and handed, and their naked bodies hung in chains to decompose publicly. In Edinburgh the Tolbooth was always full, and three more were hanged in the Grassmarket, and five at the Gallowlee, in Leith Walk.

Claverhouse now had a seat on the Council, Lauderdale being dead, and when a member pleaded leniency for the West as being now "orderly and regular," he said there were "as many elephants and crocodiles in Galloway as loyal and regular persons." General Drummond described the independent bonnet-lairds of Lanark and Ayr—successors to William Wallace—as "a sort of mongrel curs, half heritor, half common, and whole brute." They planned a new campaign "without blood": of sheer devastation. "Their wyfes and schildring brocht to starving," as Claver's wrote it. Commissions to dragoons ordered them to dispossess "the pretended heritors"—that is, the owners—and take possession of all they needed.

They were assisted by a hard winter. When the laird of Baads, in the Calders, had to try two servant-lassies for stealing kail from his own garden he asked, reasonably, why they passed so many other kail-yards on the way? They answered, because they belonged to poor folk as hungry as themselves. He let them off.

"It was cast up to me, both at the Council and here," wrote Hackston of Rathillet in his last letter from the condemned cell: "that there were not 200 in the nation to own our cause. I answered both times that the Cause of Christ had been often owned by fewer . . ."

While the Council hoped that resistance had been finally extinguished, the hill-men believed there might be "7,000 who had not bowed the knee to Baal." They called their first A.G.M. at Logan House near Lesmahagow the December following Cargill's execution. From now on they kept quarterly meetings and records and issued newsletters. But they had no preacher to inspire and lead them, no voice to speak to them and for them: no shepherd for the sheep.

Among the outed men only old Peden was left to lift a lonely but still powerful voice. The two most notable elders with the hill-men were Alexander "Bull" Gordon of Earlston, on the run since Bothwell Brig, and his brother-in-law Sir Robert Hamilton of Preston who had commanded there. The Societies sent Gordon to Peden, to give him a call.

Peden was still pacifist. Preaching in Kyle on bloodshed, from the text: "The ploughers ploughed upon my back" he said "Would you know who first yoked this plough? It was cursed Cain, when he drew his furrows so long and so deep that he let out the heart's blood of his brother, Abel: and all his cursed seed has and will . . . follow his cursed example: and that plough has and will gang, summer and winter, frost and fresh-weather, till the world's end."

Peden had slipped back from Ireland to live in a cave. When pursued he "darned himself in a moss-hag," in Patrick Walker's wonderful phrase. He had wig and mask, grey cloak to mix with the mist and a stick "with a whistle at the hied o't"—the whaup's warning cry! Deliverance would not come by the sword, he insisted: and none should try to be martyrs. "Pray meikle, for it is praying folk that win through the storm."

"Where is the Church of Scotland at this day? It is not amongst the Government clergy. I will tell you where the church is. It is wherever a praying young man or young woman is at a dykeside in Scotland: that is where the church is."

"Well then, thou poor body that will resolve to follow him, pray fast: if there were but one of you, he will be the second: if there were but two of you, he will be the third. Ye need not fear that ye shall want company: our Lord will be your company Himself—he will condescend as low as you like to you that will resolve to follow him in this stormy blast . . . He is not worth his place in Scotland the day that prayeth not half of his time . . . O Sirs: ye must pray ploughing, harrowing and shearing, aye and at all your labour, aye when ye are eating and drinking, going in and out . . ."

When Gordon asked him to consider being preacher to the hill-men he "went some time his alone." Then he refused. Gordon pleaded that it was a call, but he was fixed. "I can get nothing to say to your people."

Peden was on terms with many of the indulged ministers, who saw themselves as keeping their flocks in true ways, even at cost of their integrity: and also with people who paid cess-tax to save their lives. The hill-men rejected both absolutely. (The tax was specifically to pay the soldiers).

Within weeks of their A.G.M. the Societies re-stated their position in a protest read at the Cross of Lanark, denouncing the Test and the Duke of York's succession. Sixty of them came, armed for defence. They hammered the Cross, stuck up their protest and burnt a copy of the Test. Those caught were savagely dealt with and the unfortunate magistrates fined. One Harvey was hanged there in March, and the son of the Town Clerk of Lanark, a young lawyer called John Wilson was sent for trial at Edinburgh. He had been at Bothwell, so had no hope: but conducted his own defence with professional coolness and summed up: "I have read of some single ones dying for opinion (not truth), yet could I never read of a track of men such as has been in Scotland these twenty-two years, laying down their lives for naked opinion, so calmly, so stolidly and composedly, with so much peace and serenity."

At their spring meeting at Priesthill on the Ayrshire moors the Societies resolved to send two commissioners to explain their position to the Scots congregations—some ten or twelve—in the Netherlands, and to the Dutch Kirk with which they were in full communion. Gordon, his man Aitken and Hamilton were chosen. They were particularly well-received in Friesland: where, before the Reformation, Duchess Anna had sheltered refugees. The Rev. Mr. Brakel of Leeuwarden there wrote deeply sympathetic letters.

By autumn they were back, and at the meeting held in Edinburgh it was decided to follow this up by sending four young men for that training in theology they could no longer get freely in Scotland. They were chosen by prayer, and casting of lots: and one of the names so chosen was that of James Renwick.

Renwick was a slightly-built fair-haired lad, always younger looking than his years. He was the "long-looked for, long prayed'for" child of poor parents in Moniaive: but he had an engaging confidence in his dealings with others, and a headlong eagerness in his own. With sacrifice he had been sent to Edinburgh University: but the year he finished there he saw the five men hanged and handed—some before death—at the Gallowlee in Leith Walk.

The executions had been moved there because the crowds in the Grassmarket, hearing the last testimonies through the drum-rolls and joining in the psalms, had been more moved to sympathy and support than by any armed victory. Lauderdale had coined the jeering phrase, "to glorify God in the Grassmarket:" but the Covenanters had redeemed it. However, there can have been few that cold and ghastly dawn at the Gallowlee: but Renwick was one. His reaction was typical. He gathered some friends and in the October dusk they stole the bodies and buried them in Greyfriars. They then took on the far more dangerous enterprise of stealing the heads and hands off the Netherbow Port. A woman, holding over a candle to light a friend, "marred them". They were chased, and had to go round by the Pleasance. As it grew light, they had to bury them in a market-garden in Lauriston Yards—about where the Fire Station is now. Rosebushes were planted on top, and the secret kept for seventy-five years, almost to the day, when they were dug up and the funeral completed with dignity. Renwick joined the hill-men and was with them at Lanark.

The Societies took a collection, and raised £25 for each of the four students, for their travel, clothes and board. Renwick went to Groningen University, and wrote faithfully afterwards to his Dutch friends there, particularly two maiden ladies, who showed him special kindness.

Hamilton of Preston seems to have settled meantime in Holland with his wife and children, and also Gordon of Earlston's. He had become almost like a father to young Renwick, whose own father was dead: and Renwick's letters to him always carry a message to the children. It was Hamilton who suggested that Renwick accept ordination, before even his year was up. His Dutch professors agreed. He was described as "one notable and learned young man of great hope." Rev. Mr. Brakel had written to attest his call, and Renwick read his discourse in Latin, "answered to all the heads of Christian doctrine, both doctrinally and controversially propounded, pertinently and learnedly in the original tongues, Hebrew and Greek . . ."

So he was ordained by the Classis (presbytery) of Groningen on May 10th, 1683. Three Scots elders including Hamilton and Gordon took part in the laying-on of hands.

N

Up till now Renwick's letters are mainly outpourings of evangelical fervour: but he must have been only too aware of what he was taking on. "I am at present in a confused, anxious and disconsolate condition," he wrote in his last letter from Holland: "Let us lay our all under the feet of all men, but quit a hoof of God's matters to no man. Let us be lions in God's cause and lambs in our own." Action was his usual outlet. He took "the mercat schuyt" to Rotterdam, but there was held up. "I cannot tell what may be before my hand, but my longings to be in Scotland I cannot express."

What held him up was the discovery of the Rye House Plot, an attempt to kidnap Charles and James on their way back from Newmarket Races, and to put Monmouth on the throne as a Protestant King. The Whig legend of Lucy Walters' marriage certificate in "a black box" lived on. Colonel Rumbold, owner of the Rye House and an old Cromwellian Anabaptist, fled to Holland, as did Monmouth. Lord Essex, a chief conspirator, committed suicide in the Tower, Lord Russel, Bedford's heir, and Colonel Henry Sidney were both executed. And "all these lands . . ." Renwick wrote: "being in an uproar by reason of challenging and suspecting all persons, and the transmitting of letters," he took a round trip by Dublin, under the name of James Bruce, before getting to Scotland.

Carstares was caught with secret writing in London, and he and old Baillie of Jerviswoode were sent to Edinburgh for trial. Fraser of Brea was arrested in a London market on suspicion—perhaps it was his accent—and sent to Newgate for six months. Earlston was caught trying to land at Newcastle and seen throwing a packet into the sea when challenged. It was fished out and dried and contained such statements as "After they have despatched the Old Cotin Stufe they will then think of what new commodetys will be best." Could "Cotin Stufe" mean Charles Stewart? "Bull" denied it: but was not perhaps a convincing cloth merchant. He too was taken to Edinburgh Tolbooth, along with his man Edward Aitken: who was condemned, then reprieved.

Earlston was examined, would tell nothing: was remanded, examined again and threatened with torture. Still he said nothing. So he was taken down to the Laigh Hall, that gloomy place, and the Boots produced. Then, like the Galloway bull, so placid until it takes off, he went berserk: tossing guards and macers around like straws till borne down by numbers. He was loaded with chains, and moved from dungeon to dungeon for six years, always fettered in heavy chains: but never tortured.

Long years after, when Patrick Walker was collecting material on these times, he found Gordon a wandered old man, who could remember very little, but one thing most vividly: how the young Patrick had taught him to manage his chains, and so survive.

Aitken, like a man Lapsley formerly reprieved, was now packed with twenty others, mostly condemned, in two small cells of the

Canongait Tolbooth. They had files, and set to work on the grating of the lower one, still on the third storey and opposite the lodging of the Earl of Linlithgow, Colonel of the Red Regiment, with a sentry at the door. By bad luck the first bar fell outwards into the silent street with a ringing clang. Perhaps its own noise cancelled suspicion. Next day a visitor smuggled it back in, to be propped in place as they worked on. Finally a square was cut, and a hole in the floor above, and two obliging friends held a knife to the sentry until all were out and clear.

One "Millar an Englishman" knowing not where to turn, knocked at a door where there was a light. It was the Bishop's house! But the servant-lass generously hid him just the same. Only one man, a theology student called John Dick, was ever caught. He had time to write a vivid testimony in the six months before he was seized and hanged.

By September Renwick at last reached the Clyde and was "cast out in the night-time at a hill-side, some few miles below Greenock." The Cloch perhaps? "In coming through the country we had two field meetings, which made me think that, if the Lord could be tied to any place, it is to the mosses and muirs of Scotland."

In October he presented himself to the Societies gathered at "that kenned place, Darmead." The Minute records that "after prayer Mr. James Renwick being come there, gave an account of his ordination and showed his certificate of the same, subscribed by several ministers, to the meeting, by whom he was called and received as their minister which he accepted and embraced."

His testimony was so outspoken, it caused some resentment which he afterwards regretted. But then he was only 21. By the end of the month the Laird of Dundas and the Trades House of Glasgow were both fined for conventicles on their land—Brownridge and Little Dumbreck—at which he "took upon him to preach, and baptise . . ." In the next six months he baptised between 500-600 children—he lost count of how many.

In the short dark day of November 23rd he preached for the first time officially to a great gathering of the hill-men at Darmead. He took as his text the one with which Cargill had ended, from Isaiah 20: "Come, my people" . . . Come all ye that labour and are heavy laden! . . . Come, ye that thirst! . . . Come, ye beloved of my Father! . . . "We must preach this word COME to you as long as you are here until you be transplanted out of this spiritual warfare into celestial triumph. O Sirs, Come! Come!"

His voice rang out like a trumpet, putting fresh heart and hope in the weary people. In the great wave of response that swept up to meet him he found himself and his life-work: and they found their preacher, their hero, their shepherd-king.

CHAPTER SEVEN

DRUMS AND TRUMPETS

A nest of gorgeous mistresses with powdered hair, bare bosoms, jewels and beauty-patches was described by Evelyn in Whitehall in 1685: Charles II in their midst: "a French boy singing love-songs out of that glorious gallery" and a ring of courtly gamblers with "at least £2,000 in gold before them."

Five days later "all was dust". Charles was dead, neither mournful nor repentant, but happily sanctified into the Church of Rome, by way of Father Huddlestone and the back stairs. The English accepted their new King James VII & II in spite of his devout Roman Catholicism: "distinguishing between his Popery and his Person." The Scots managers followed suit. Only Renwick and his remnant repudiated him.

Renwick had been preaching for a year on moonlit moors, or in torchlit barns: for conventicles were now by night. Men stole out to them like thieves. His first winter was savage: "a long and great frost from November to March: no labouring of the ground possible, the earth was iron." Yet from some heather-hole he wrote to Holland: "I cannot express what sweet times I have had, when the curtains of heaven have been drawn, when the quietness of all things, in the silent watches of the night, has brought to my mind the duty of admiring the deep, silent and inexpressible ocean of joy and wonder . . . each star leading me on to wonder what he must be who is the Star of Jacob, the bright and morning star . . . Indeed, . . . I am meikle obliged to enemies . . ."

His enemies the troopers were in no way obliged to him, as they searched constantly through hills and heather. Sometimes so close, he wrote, he could "hear their drums and trumpets." Yet in spite of increased numbers of hearers and ever-increasing persecution, he was not betrayed.

Persecution was stepped up savagely, because of the new King James' fear and insecurity. He knew that a Whig rebellion had been preparing in Holland; and possible support in Scotland must be crushed. So in the year 1684 nine men were hanged in Glasgow, and twenty-one in Edinburgh. This included old Captain Paton of Meadowhead, who was now close on seventy. Even Dalziel, once an old comrade-in-arms, was sorry to see this: but Paton said he was "weary of his life: being so hunted . . . and stricken in years . . . his hidings the more irksome . . . As for his interest in Christ, of that he

184

was sure." His descendants in Fenwick were for centuries notable radical reformers and missionaries.

His well-thumbed Bible and chipped sword—"a short shabble"—can be seen at Lochgoin to this day, in the Howie's farm-house.

In summer Bishop Paterson's thumbscrews became official, and were used on two Whig agents: Argyll's secretary and Carstares, son of the Manse, and future minister of St. Giles. He "for near an hour continued in the agony of torture, the screw being by space and space stretched and forced till he appeared near to faint."

At the end of that month of July, fifteen Galloway prisoners were sold to Malloch, the slave-dealer, to be shipped from Leith to the Carolina Plantations where they would fetch £10 per head. They were marched from Dumfries Castle, under escort of half a troop of horse, up the Enterkin Pass, that black cleavage in the mountains where farms look like toys in the bottom of a box. There a shot cracked, and Sergeant Kelt toppled down into "Kelt's Linn," killed by Black McMichael, fowler of Maxwelton. In the skirmish a prisoner, Robert Smith, was killed, Grierson carried off wounded and later shot: McKechnie re-captured wounded and later died: but the other twelve escaped. Patrick Walker, young fighter and old recorder of these days, dates the Killing Times—the frenzy of cruelty—from Enterkin.

Powers of "Fire and Sword" were given to the Council by London, and the right to execute all suspects on the spot, without formal trial. McMichael was shot, and Clavers rounded up seven more to be hanged in Edinburgh, only one making his escape. Two young lads, Patrick Walker and a journeyman tailor called, suitably, Tacket, were both taken for questioning.

Patrick was now 19. Three years before he had seen a drunken dragoon run amok, threatening prisoners, notably James Wilson, with death: and had put a tiny pocket-pistol to his head and shot him dead. He took a list of names from his pocket, replacing money and "popish pictures." Nor did he ever count this sin, as he did voluntary sabbath-breaking, for instance. But who, not so tempted, can judge?

Tacket was tortured with the thumbscrew, his legs being too thin for the boots. Then he was hanged for being at Bothwell Bridge and at Renwick's preachings. Malloch asked for Patrick un-maimed, as a likely slave, so he was not tortured but left in irons and questioned eighteen times in fourteen months before being sold to him.

At the end of summer came the first of five official edicts from the Government against Renwick by name, denouncing "that rebel aforesaid" and all who gave him "meat, drink, house, harbour, victual . . . or to have any intelligence by word, writ or message or any other manner . . ."

In Autumn the Societies brought forward an Apologetical Declaration that apologised for nothing, but breathed defiance and even hinted at retaliation. Renwick spoke against it in vain, and regretted its being spread abroad, on town crosses and kirk doors. He believed it gave a wrong viewpoint: and it still further increased persecution. Leading the Societies was one of his sorest struggles.

That same month three men were hanged, in the cold, early darkness of the Gallowlee, with few to see them go. One called Watt flung down his Bible "for my brother," and Miss Janet Fimister, that decent body who kisted the corpses, tried to catch it. But the Captain of the Guard got it first.

"Who owns this book?"

"I do," said Miss Fimister, "for his brother."

"Secure her!" And off she went to the Tolbooth prison, never to be free again.

Half a dozen more were hanged in the Grassmarket at the beginning of December, including James Graham of Crossmichael and that survivor of Pentland, John Nisbet of Hardhill, who was taunted before the Council of owning "No King but Mr. Renwick." He was taken wounded after a fight; but the man who had dug graves for his wife and daughter and lived as an outlaw for sixteen years welcomed death as a friend: "Naked came I into this world, and naked must I go out of it," he said: "The Lord is making my passage easy."

Old Baillie of Jerviswoode had been brought to trial that same month, tottering to the bar in his night-gown, his legs impossibly swollen. He defended himself ably all day: but the few facts dragged from Carstares under torture were used: and Bluidy Mackenzie himself had paid a friendly visit to the Tolbooth, when the old man had talked with unguarded garrulity: all now used against him.

"I find I am intended for a public sacrifice," he said at last. "My Lord Advocate . . . when you came to me in prison, you told me . . . you did not believe the charges."

"My thoughts then were as a private person, but what I say here is by special direction of the Privy Council!" cried Mackenzie, pointing to the Clerk: "*He* knows my orders!"

"Well, my Lord, if you keep one conscience for yourself and another for the Council, I pray God to forgive you. I do."

He was carried to the gallows on Christmas Eve, and his daughter-in-law Lady Graden, a daughter of Johnston of Warriston's who had nursed him in prison, stayed with him through the whole obscene execution of hanging, drawing and quartering: boiling the pieces in brine, soaking them in tar and oil: leaving her the butcher's bits to bury.

In January of that New Year of 1685 which saw Charles II snatched from all earthly joys in Whitehall there was minor incident in Gutter Lane, Cheapside, London. A congregation of dissenters met in the Embroiderers' Hall to hear a young Scot, Alexander Shields, graduate of Utrecht, preaching on his favourite text: "Naphtali is a hind let loose" and on his favourite subject: liberty. "A subject that I

186

was very unfit to speak on, and therefore the Lord saw it good to interrupt me and send me to school to learn it better since; . . .I have been made to prize it more by the want of it, and to understand by some experience the excellency of that more lovely liberty of the spirit."

The interruption was the City Marshal and soldiers; and the eventual upshot, after badgering and bullying and five months in a foul hole in Newgate Prison, was being shipped back to Scotland and almost certain death. Alexander was now 25, and both he and his brother Michael, who was already with Renwick, were outstandingly intelligent. For seven months he fought verbally for his life, but in the end he was too clever: and slid into a compromise " . . . nibbling at equivocations and ensnaring shifts . . . a shameful thing in a resolved sufferer."

"After I had done it"—taken a form of oath—"one that sat next said to me, I had done like a gentleman, which words gave my heart a knell . . ."

He now had better conditions, with some semi-indulged ministers: and finally signed an equivocal form of words. " . . . there was such a noise that nothing could be heard, the advocates came about me and buzzed in my ear, and said subscribe, subscribe, for it is admitted: . . . and so I did subscribe it."

He had won his life but not his freedom. He was sent to the Bass Rock.

Because of fear, the cruelties of 1685, in both England and Scotland, surpassed all others. The ever-increasing tension was due to the Whig Rebellion against James, now almost ready to sail from Holland. The late King's most beautiful bastard, Monmouth, whom Dryden had described in his poetry, had been persuaded to stand again as Protestant heir to the throne, and to lead the landing in the South: while Argyll landed in Lorne, and marched on his own capital of Inverary. Young Cleland left Utrecht to join him.

The Societies were asked to support the rising, and having fully debated it at their A.G.M. at Blackgannoch, turned it down. This was not the Kingdom they sought, nor the men they could trust.

Peden went further than this. At a meeting near Wigton of men ready to rise, where they "gat meat" he gave every one of his own parishioners who were there a piece out of his own hand, advising them against any support of Argyll. "For you that are my bairns, I discharge you to go your foot-length, for before you can travel that length he will be broke."

In readiness for new prisoners from the rebellion the Council emptied the Tolbooth of the 224 prisoners there, and marched them all to Leith. As well as Patrick Walker still in his 'teens, and Miss Fimister in her 'fifties, there were three ministers, some "dames of good family," some "auld decrepit creatures," some paralysed, and several women great with child: also "Nicholas McKnight, a dying woman." Forty were weeded out, the rest ferried across to Burntisland, then force-marched up the bleak coast to far Dunottar, a castle on sea-battered crags, separated from the mainland by great chasms. Here they were crushed into the "Whig vaults;" the main one was 54½ft. x 15½ft. x 12ft. high, with a chute down into a small wet chamber of 15ft. x 8ft. x 9ft. Light and ventilation came through a small drain at floor level and prisoners lay down to suck in air in turns. Forsyth of Annandale was followed by his pregnant wife, who was shut in with him. Her baby was born there and both died.

At one point twenty-four escaped: but they were too weak with hunger to get far. Their emaciated bodies were flogged, and several died.

The survivors were all marched back to Leith, to be sold as slaves. Patrick Walker contrived to escape from Leith Tolbooth, and made his way to "the never-to-be-forgotten Mr. Renwick" on the moors: where he found him, in a miserable and bloody world, "in the same calm, sweet gospel-air."

Poor Miss Fimister, that unlikely slave, who had so valued decent burial, prophesied truly "the waves shall be my winding-sheet." Adding, "The purchased and promised blessings of the Lord—and mine—be multiplied upon the poor suffering Remnant, the excellent ones: in whom I have had all my delight and pleasures on earth."

They were embarked in grim November for America. It was a terrible voyage. Twenty-nine died, including Miss Fimister, the ship's owner and most of his family, and two ministers.

But those who reached the New World found far more kindness than they had known in the Old. They settled at Woodbridge, New Jersey. McLellan of Barmagechan bought land, and a minister, Frazer from Alness married a fellow-prisoner, Jean Moffat of Netherbarns Farm on the Tweed. All three eventually won home, after incredible adventures. So did Riddel, minister of Kippen, after two years in a French prison.

Another returned slave was only recognised, like Ulysses, by his aged collie dog. Mathieson of Closeburn won home at hairst, was given food with the rest by his harassed wife who, seeing him linger in the harvest-field, cried: "The gangrel body wants another dinner!"

Both Renwick and Peden had written to encourage the prisoners in Dunnottar: but it is Peden's letter that is outstanding.

"I long to hear how you spend your time and how the Grace of God grows in your hearts. I know ye and others of the Lord's people, by reason of the present trial, have got up a fashion of complaining upon Christ, but I defy you to speak an ill word of Him, unless you wrong Him. Speak as you can, and spare not; only I request you, let your expressions of Christ be suitable to your experience of Him. If ye think Christ's house be bare and illprovided, harder than ye looked for, assure yourselves Christ minds only to diet you, and not to

hunger you, our steward kens when to spend and when to spare . . .
Grace and glory comes out of Christ's lucky hand . . .

He is the easiest merchant ever the people of God yoked with. If ye
be pleased with his wares, what of His graces makes best for you, He
and you will soon sort on the price. He'll sell goods cheap, that ye may
speir for His shop again, and He draws all the sale to Himself . . .
blest is the man that gives Christ all his money . . .

. . .it seems God has a mind to search Jerusalem with lighted
candles, and to visit all your chambers . . . He will not want a hair of
His people's head, He knows them all by head-mark . . . I defy the
world to steal a lamb out of Christ's flock unmist."

"Put on courage in thir sad times," Welwood, "minister of the
Gospel at Tundergarth in Annandale" had written before he died in the
hills, after Drumclog: "brave times for the chosen soldiers of Jesus
Christ to show their courage into . . . brave times, offering brave
opportunities . . ."

They needed all their courage. In that same sweet month of May
1685, came two executions that the Scots have never forgotten. Both
were perfectly legal. John Brown—"the Christian carrier"—had
known all the Covenanting preachers and would have been a
preacher himself but for some slight stammer. It was sheer luck for
Claver's that a chance swoop on his distant cottage, Priesthill on the
Ayrshire moors, should have found him at home, cutting the peats for
winter.

"Now, Isabel, the day is come that I told you of," he said to his
young second wife; and she repeated her promise "willingly to part
with him." "That is all I desire. I have no more to do but to die."

She stood firm, his child in her arms and another by her side: her
own unborn. Claver's cut short his prayers—the soldiers may have
grown restless—and the heavy balls struck him full on the head,
scattering his brains on his doorstep. One—ricochet or deliberate
miss?—cracked a wooden coggie on the window-sill: and the New
College keep this homely memorial still. One tradition says the
soldiers were unwilling to fire, and Claverhouse used his own pistol at
point-blank range. His own official report to Edinburgh could be
read either way. He wrote that, after finding "treasonable papers,"
(sermons or notes, or a Bible possibly), "I caused shoot him dead,
which he suffered unconcernedly."

"What dost thou think of thy husband now, woman?" he asked the
widow, as they reloaded.

"I aye thocht meikle, and never mair than now."

"It were but justice to lay thee beside him." She answered that she
did not doubt his cruelty would go that length: "But how will ye make
answer for this morning's work?"

"To man I can be answerable," he said: and Patrick Walker wrote
down her own account: "and as for God, I will take Him in my own
hand."

When they had moved off she set down the children, gathered together the broken skull and straightened the limbs and covered them with a plaid: and then and only then did she cast herself down to weep. "It being a very desert place, where never victual grew, and far from neighbours."

A second piece of frightfulness came through the Council's decree that all females convicted as traitors were to be drowned. (In England they were to be burned alive: and after the Rebellion an elderly gentlewoman had a narrow escape, going to the block instead, by James' special dispensation.)

Margaret McLaughlan was an old widow of about 70, whose husband had been a joiner and carpenter in the parish of Kirkinner, near Wigton. She was not an ignorant woman, but "of more than ordinary knowledge, discretion and prudence." Her house, and her company, must have been known to all friends and supporters of the hill-men. Two girls, Margaret and Agnes Wilson, aged 18 and 13, daughters of a farmer at Penninghame, near Dumfries, were among those who made their way to visit her. On one visit they found she had been arrested: they were informed against, and put with her in the town jail, along with another young woman, Margaret Maxwell, a serving lass, aged 20.

The "court" to try them consisted of that savage persecutor, Sir Robert Grierson of Lag: Claverhouse's brother, David Graham: David Strachan: Major Winram: and the Provost of Wigton. The Abjuration Oath was tendered: and all refused. Margaret Maxwell was sentenced to be flogged by the hangman on three successive days, and to stand an hour in the jougs. The others were to die by drowning in the Solway. This sentence had the presumably desired effect of sending shock and horror through the country.

Gilbert Wilson, the father, raised every farthing he could and raced for Edinburgh. With £100 he bought the life of Agnes. But Grierson and the others were determined to make an example of the other two. "It is now known", wrote Dr. Hector Macpherson, student of those times, "that the Privy Council actually granted a reprieve . . . discharging the magistrates from executing the sentence." Grierson, with the reputation of a sadist, is given the blame for seeing that notwithstanding the sentences were carried out in full.

Perhaps at first it was not believed that the girl, quiet and well-educated, would hold out. Her mother had begged and prayed, then raged and cursed. Why would she not at least hear the curate? What harm could it do? It could make the hill-men in the wrong, she said. (Had she a secret love among them? Did she, unknown, die for Renwick?) She wept sorely, but said: "If father and mother forsake me, the Lord will take me up."

On 11th May the stakes, driven into the Solway at the Blednoch Burn, had the old woman tied far out, the girl near the shore: and the whole town out to watch. Ahead of the enormous tide comes the bore: a long level ripple of light, with a lisping sound: and behind it the great weight of water, all at once. The old woman struggled, briefly. "It is Christ wrestling there," said the girl, and began to sing Psalm 25: "To thee I lift my soul . . ."

> "My sins and faults of youth,
> Do thou O Lord forget:
> After thy mercy think on me,
> And for thy goodness great."

The crowd screamed, and begged her to give in: "Dear Margaret, say God Save the King! Say God save the King!"

"God save him if He will," she said, the water lapping her face. "I desire salvation to all, damnation to none."

"She has said it! She has said it!" they shouted: and she was dragged out and revived. The Oath was tendered again; and again she refused. "I am one of Christ's children . . . Let me go!"

So they dragged her back, and by tradition one of the guard thrust her head under with his halberd, and the cry: "Tak' another drink, hinny! Clep wi' the partans!"

Episcopalians for some reason have always bitterly resented this execution in particular. Whole books have been written to prove that it never took place at all. Biographers intent on making Claver's a stainless cavalier began it—to the believer all is possible. But the men who carried it out had in truth no devout religious convictions as such: they were simply Scots who, in the classic phrase, knew on which side their bread was buttered. Where Grierson and Clavers got rich estates Gilbert Wilson, the girls' father, died destitute.

Yet there was a touch of mercy. Patrick Walker, years after, sought out Margaret Maxwell, the serving maid, by then an old woman, and she told him she had never doubted but she would share the same fate. As it was, she was brought out tied by her bound hands to the tail of the cart, stripped to the waist for the hangman's lash. But the instant they appeared Wigton's street emptied, every door shut, every window shuttered. The hangman used her "very gently," and wanted to release her from the jougs before the hour was up. But she told him she was "neither wearied nor ashamed. Let the nock go on."

At the very end of that month of judicial murder Renwick led 200 horsemen into Sanquhar and read and nailed up the Second Sanquhar Declaration, totally disowning James VII and II, his person as well as his popery, as a claimant who had not himself taken the oaths he enforced on his subjects.

In June Monmouth landed in Devon, shaking hands, kissing housemaids, and charming all he met. Dissenting parsons flocked to him; but his ablest general was a Scots Republican home from Hungarian wars, Fletcher of Saltoun: and his wealthiest supporter a merchant's son with fine horses, one of which Fletcher needed. They quarrelled, he slashed Fletcher with his riding-crop and he in rage shot him dead. Then he had to fly overseas, leaving them leaderless. Defeat came shortly after among the deep ditches of Sedgemoor. Monmouth, betraying everyone he could, went to the Tower.

Argyll landed the same month, but got nowhere near Inveraray. He was finally defeated at Kilpatrick, managed to cross the Clyde but was captured at Inchinnan and taken back prisoner to Edinburgh Castle again. King Monmouth had no appeal for Scots. The Rebellion was over. Cleland was lucky to escape back to Holland.

Old Rumbold of the Rye House Plot was caught at the same time and sent to Edinburgh to be hanged, drawn and quartered.

"What shall I say in this great day of the Lord," wrote Argyll in a last letter to his gallant step-daughter, Lady Sophia: "wherein in the midst of a cloud, I have found a fair sunshine." His composure was genuine. He was found sleeping in his cell "within an hour of eternity, as sweetly as ever man did."

He went to the scaffold in Edinburgh High Street on 30th June: and as the blade of the Maiden snicked his head off his body shot to its—his?—feet "fountaining blood", and had to be held down.

Monmouth was beheaded in London, in spite of all his betrayals and grovellings. He had no luck with Jack Ketch, who took five chops at that beautiful head, and had to finish the job with his gully, amid boos and hisses.

The appalling cruelties of Judge Jeffreys and the Bloody Assizes in England which followed the defeat at Sedgemoor were unequalled since the reign of Bloody Mary Tudor. Some 330 prisoners had to be hanged, drawn and quartered—a ghastly industry.

Thousands more were flogged not once, but on successive market-days, and then sold as slaves. In Scotland slaves were also branded.

The wave of bloodshed subsided, and weary peace set in. Even in Scotland there were only two killings in as many years: a boy Wood, aged 16, was shot mainly on suspicion: and young Hislop only son of a widow who had taken in a wounded Covenanter and nursed and finally buried him, was condemned and shot. Holyrood Chapel was now done up for Masses with nearly £8,000 worth of bon-dieuserie, paid for by James and organised by one of the Drummond brothers who was now Earl of Perth. Both Drummond brothers were devout converts to Rome, and to peerages. This one, Lord Perth, obligingly rocked a cradle in Holyrood Chapel on Christmas Day.

On the Continent too Rome was re-building her empire. The Huguenots were again attacked: the Waldensians were soon to be massacred in Piedmont. England seemed re-possessed. James and his Queen went faithfully to Mass in chapels wreathed with the dark beauty of Grinling Gibbons' carving. They knelt humbly to a visiting Papal Nuncio. Even Pepys was flattered to have a Vatican castrato sing for his supper-party.

James now needed only two final seals to his security. One was the death of Renwick, that inspiration of the rebel remnant in Scotland. The other was a son and heir by his young Italian Queen: for his two daughters by the late Ann Hyde who were at present his heirs—Mary, wife of William of Orange in Holland and Ann wife of Prince George of Denmark—were both stoutly Protestant. Presently, his prayers were answered. He got both.

CHAPTER EIGHT

THE VICTORY

Early in the new year of 1685 old Peden, last of his generation, knew that he had reached the end of the road.

"Lord, thou hast been both good and kind to auld Sandy through a long tract of time, and given him many years in thy service which have been as so many months: but now he is tired of the world, and has done the good in it that he will do: let him win awa' with the honesty he has, for he will gather no more."

He had one piece of unfinished business. He and Renwick had never met, for he disapproved of the Societies' exclusiveness and militancy, and had disliked reports of Renwick himself. But now there was no one else, so he sent for him. By secret paths through the January mirk James Wilson and young Nisbet brought Renwick to a bend in the river Lugar in Ayrshire, above a deep pool. Fifteen feet up, a sauchen bush was swept aside, and he stood at the entrance to a cave. As he paused a voice said, perhaps incredulously, "Are ye the Mr. Renwick there is so much noise about?"

"Father, my name is James Renwick, but I have given the world no ground to make any noise about me; for I have espoused no new principle or practice, but what our Reformers and Covenanters maintained."

"Well, Sir, turn your back!" And then: "I think your legs are too small and your shoulders too narrow to take on the whole Church of Scotland. Sit down, Sir, and give me an account of your conversion and of your call to the ministry, and the grounds of your taking such singular courses in withdrawing from all other ministers."

As Renwick willingly did so he saw before him an old, sick man, presumably on a heather bed, "lying in very low circumstances, overgrown with hair, and few to take care of him, as he never took much care of his body, and seldom unclothed himself or went to bed."

When he had finished Peden said: "You have answered to my soul's satisfaction, and I am very sorry that I should have believed any such ill reports of you . . . But Sir, ere ye go ye must pray for me, for I am old and going to leave the world."

Renwick prayed "with more than ordinary enlargement." Then the old man took his hand, drew him close and kissed him, saying: "Sir, I find you a faithful servant to your Master: go on in a single dependence upon the Lord, and ye will win honestly through and cleanly off the stage . . ."

Peden contrived to die under his ancestral roof in January 1686, and was buried discreetly. But six months later the dragoons dug up his corpse and carried it to Cumnock, where it was hung on a gallows. And the people of Cumnock counted the place holy ground, and buried their own dead round him.

He left words that still dirl on the heart-strings. Blackadder was an intellectual shepherd: Welsh, Cargill and Cameron all famous preachers. It is far harder to understand the power and authority of Renwick. To begin with, he had no appearance at all: which was one reason he escaped detection so long. One thin, ragged, barefoot lad was much like another. There are tales of him walking up to troops searching for him—which was always safer than running away: and even of him talking to the officer in charge.

Still more surprisingly, there is nothing in his few writings—sermons, letters, speeches—to suggest any power of oratory or original thought. They are purely evangelical. Why then should a great Government issue one Proclamation after another, promising large rewards and fearful retribution: sending soldiers to ransack the country and tear apart houses: and all to destroy a youth whose words ran entirely in praise of Jesus Christ?

Yet perhaps that is the answer. In a world as black with treachery and violence as our own, he walked in his own shaft of sunlight. He created his own climate, as some people do: clear daylight and unstinted warmth. Here was refuge for the desperate, riches to the needy: and to an unjust Government an implacable menace.

As for his baffling writings, they are like the network of birdsong that covers a hillside in spring, blackbird to blackbird, unconcerned for groundlings. He breathed his gospel-air, spoke a lyrical language to those who could hear—fellow-citizens of the other Kingdom. "Grace is young glory," Peden had said.

"Heaven and earth publish and preach forth the knowledge of God: sun, moon and stars are all written over in legible characters, teaching us the knowledge of God: the earth, trees, mountains, hills and valleys, yea and the piles of grass are all written over backside and foreside with legible characters of the knowledge of God."

So he preached, his neck in the noose. "I have turned every stone," a spy reported at this time, intent on the bounty.

That year of 1686, which began with Peden's ending, ended with a new beginning. Alexander Shields was brought from the Bass to the Tolbooth with other prisoners, all offered liberty for swearing full Oaths of Allegiance. But Shields had been studying the meaning of freedom in that crammer's course, the Bass. There he had seen Blackadder die, refusing a conditional release. He too refused the oaths; and escaped from the Tolbooth in women's clothes.

It caused a sensation. His mother's relatives—Fishers the glovers—were brought in for questioning: but nothing could be proved. The authorities could only dismiss the two chief jailors.

After lying low for six weeks Shields, with his brother Michael, had a moving meeting with Renwick at a preaching "in the wood of Earlston" in Galloway on December 5th. (Gordon had made a hiding-place there). Renwick trusted him completely, and presented him to the Societies at a meeting at Wanlockhead on December 22nd. To this meeting Shields made a full and free confession of his sin and cowardice in saving his neck by compromise; and of his bitter regret for it: and was as freely accepted. From now on he took much of the burden from Renwick's back.

Renwick had been increasingly troubled, both by the widespread propaganda against him, and by his huge responsibility: what he calls "the right carrying of the Ark of God through this howling wilderness . . . I see it so difficult a thing to move one step rightly forward with it, I am in continual fear anent what I do . . . If I shall give the ark a wrong touch . . . it will be through blindness and not through biasness."

He had written a letter that spring of gentle reproach to "the famous, learned and godly" Koelman in Holland, who had believed tales against him: and he was trying to put together an *Informatory Vindication* of the hillmen's position. With Shield's help it was completed in time to put before the Societies' A.G.M. at Blackgannoch on April 6th. There it was agreed to accept it, and to send both Shields brothers over to Holland to get it printed as quickly as possible. They went to Utrecht, where Alexander had been a student: and had the work published by July. It sold freely in Scotland at 8d—"7d unstitched"—the cheapest rate possible.

The *Vindication* gives a clear history of the Hillmen's position and principles: and defends the need for defensive arms under tyranny. It denied that they were revolutionaries, separatists or a new church; claiming that they were in fact the survivors, the "remnant," of the true historic Church of Scotland. Reading it is "an enlightening experience," says Sinclair Horne: for "there is only one basis . . . the Word of God."

"I bless the Lord who hath given you zeal for himself, and hath helped you to stand with a poor despised party in making stours for his interest," Renwick had written to the Society of Strangers at Leeuwarden in Friesland. But he had no boast in being a minority, and had written the year before that "union in the Lord would be a most rejoicing, pleasant and desirable thing: I say *that* union that is bottomed upon the truth and cemented with love, for *any* kind of union would be but a conspiracy and not union . . . I think that would be the Church of Scotland's restoration."

There is nothing revolutionary in all this: but revolution clings to Christ's teaching like the shadow to his heels. Before Shields, who also believed in Church union, left Utrecht he left with the printer his own great work of freedom under the law, which he had begun on the Bass, called *A Hind Let Loose*. In it he not only quotes Buchanan and

196

the "mutual compact" between king and subjects: but goes further and claims not only man's birthright to the best government he can get, but his inescapable duty to work, fight and take on its burdens if need be, to secure it. "Kings and tyrants are for the most part reciprocal terms," he says, 100 years before the French Revolution: and "Every man created according to God's image is a sacred thing."

These publications could hardly have been worse timed. 1687 was the year of King James' olive-branch: his Proclamation of Indulgence for Tender Consciences. The Toleration was primarily to encourage those of his own faith, the Roman Catholics: but extended to cover even Quakers, and any indulged dissenters or presbyterians who had taken the Oath: to all, in short, except the Hillmen. It was welcomed by all weary of blood and glad of peace; and brought in several veteran resisters in Scotland, such as Veitch, who was preaching at Beverly near Hull; Erskine, who became minister of Whitsome: who by his second wife, Margaret Halcro of Orkney lineage, had two famous sons, Ralph and Ebenezer: and Kirkton the church historian and son-in-law of Robert Blair—the enemy of Sharp—into whose writings creeps already that bitterness of the indulged to those who, by holding out, were a reproach to them. Known Whig and Royalist supporters too took advantage of this Toleration to come home from Holland and from Ireland, to claim their own again.

So Renwick was more and more isolated. Even Galloway was stirred up to disown him. Gordon of Earlston, still lying in his heavy chains in prison, had heard the tales and begun to doubt him, and Renwick writes frankly. He had met with organised opposition from "all those between Cree and Dee" as a paper claimed, and even in Irongray: but those of the Glenkens are still "as bows of steel in the Lord's hands."

Of the men who occasionally preached with Renwick, Boyd had gone off to think over the Toleration: and Barclay, once a fireater, had quitted the "watery mosses and bogs," as Patrick Walker puts it, "for the witty lown-warm air of Edinburgh with all its comforts" and though promising to return "suffered them to shift for themselves." They jeered at the Remnant round their firesides: and Renwick knew.

So he was alone, and his health was breaking. He had fevers and fainting-fits: which helped him to survive, he wrote cheerfully, by making him often change plans at the last minute. The way he continued to survive was thought to be uncanny. His enemies put it round that he was secretly a Jesuit, wiling people out to their deaths: and they gave him a new name which ran through Scotland: the White Devil.

With unshaken confidence he took his life in his hands that November and went into Edinburgh to lodge a protest in the hands of the Moderator against his Indulged Assembly then taking place, as being no true court of the Kirk.

"I have been in Peebles this week and . . . wonderfully escaped," he wrote next month. His meeting was timed for 9 p.m. But as darkness fell the hue-and-cry was raised for a thief, and when the Town Clerk and guard turned out they were amazed to find all the population of Peebles, who should have been snug at their own firesides, thronging the streets and melting into the dark countryside. At once the thief was forgotten and the cry raised for a very different hunt, for a far greater prize: Renwick! "I came within speaking and hearing of the Clerk," writes the quarry calmly. He heard their excited plans—to ransack suspect houses, to arrest four men—and "with great difficulty" got his horse and rode once more into the black December night.

"Being now near the end of his course, he ran very fast and wrocht very hard," wrote Howie of Lochgoin long after. He crossed into Fife, where he preached on Isaiah 53.1. then back to Bo'ness, that Covenanting stronghold. At the end of December he was preaching in the Braidhills, on the outskirts of Edinburgh. Then he went down to stay with friends—a dealer in "uncustomed goods" as Howie puts it (a smuggler), on the Castlehill: in the very shadow of Edinburgh Castle and its garrison. He took no special precautions, finding this, he once wrote, "not the worst way." But here at last, through a door, he was recognised: by his voice, clear and confident, in family prayers.

Soldiers burst in, Renwick drew his pistol and fought his way out. But in the scuffle he got a heavy blow, with a cudgel or musket-butt, and as he ran down the Castle-wynd towards the head of the Cowgait he fell twice: and the second time he was caught. When Graham, Captain of the Guard, saw the slight figure brought before him he said, "What, is this boy Mr. Renwick, that the whole nation hath been so much troubled with?" "which he answered with smiling and great meekness," wrote Shields in his "Life". With apparent regret Graham said later, "I have handed Renwick over to the Presbyterians . . ."

He had long faced death, but had a horror of torture: that assault on the inner citadel. Under threat, he gave the names of those whose initials stood in his note-book, along with his sermon notes: but only when he was sure it could bring them no more harm. He was indicted on three charges: disowning the King's lawful authority: preaching against the cess-tax to pay the army: and supporting the carrying of defensive arms. On these points he spoke boldly and clearly, pointing out that by law no Roman Catholic could inherit the throne: and that the other "crimes" were simply commonsense. One member of the Council was heard to say that "he was of old Knox's principles, . . . now made treason." But there could be no reprieve. He was sentenced to die on February 8th.

But Edinburgh, and even the Council, would have been glad to let him off. It had been a shock to find that "that dog, Renwick", the White Devil, was in fact more of a boy David: "ruddy and of a beautiful countenance." He had a stream of visitors begging him to moderate his views and save his neck: including the Lord Advocate, University professors and Bishop Paterson of the thumbscrews, who came often and found his resolution "a great loss" . . . for he was a pretty lad." Renwick himself says he was told "if I would but let a drop of ink fall on a bit of paper, it would satisfy," Life was his for the taking: but he would not.

Although he writes that "pen, ink and paper are kept from me" he smuggled out a short farewell letter to Robert Hamilton in Holland. Hamilton was neither an attractive nor popular character, but Renwick was loyal to him to the end. He asks him to destroy his first testimony, as being "too tart" in expression. "If I had lived, and been qualified for writing a book," he goes on; and it were dedicated to anyone—"you would have been that man." He sends remembrances to all, including the old ladies in Leeuwarden: and underlines: "DEATH TO ME IS AS A BED TO THE WEARY."

His execution was put off for a week, a traumatic delay. His widowed mother and sisters came up from Moniaive to plead with him: and he passed his 26th birthday. He seems to have had his black hour of doubt: but he found certainty again. "I am persuaded that my death will do more good than my life for many years has done." Somehow he got a last testimony written and smuggled out: "I have had many a joyful hour and not a fearful thought since I came to prison. He hath strengthened me to outbrave men and outface death . . . and there is nothing in the world I am sorry to leave but you." So he writes to his flock, which covered all Scotland. "Farewell, Christian and comfortable mother and sisters; farewell, sweet Societies: farewell desirable General Meetings: farewell, night wanderings, cold and weariness for Christ . . ."

In the cold dawn of February 17th St. Giles' bell began to toll: and his mother to weep. "It is for my wedding-day," he cheered her: "I am ready, I am ready!" He praised God he had done with "The King of Terrors:" "I have many times counted the cost of following Christ, but never thought it would be so easy."

Round the scaffold in the Grassmarket and crowding all the high tenement windows was a huge crowd. They could not hear the psalms and prayers for the dreary rolling of the drums, which continued without pause. Through them Renwick shouted to the crowd: "I am this day to lay down my life for three things: for disowning the usurpation and tyranny of James Duke of York: for preaching that it was unlawful to pay the cess, expressly exacted for bearing down the gospel: for teaching that it was lawful for people to carry arms for defending themselves in their meetings for the persecuted gospel ordinances. I think a testimony for these is worth many lives."

Here he was ordered to have done. He answered "I have near done;" and then said: "Ye that are the people of God, do not weary . . ."

Going up the ladder: "Lord, I die in the faith that thou wilt not leave Scotland . . ." As they tied the napkin round his face, he said to the friend beside him: " . . .as to the remnant I leave, I have committed them to God: tell them from me not to weary, nor to be discouraged in maintaining the testimony. Let them not quit or forego one of these despised truths . . . Lord, into thy hands I commend my spirit . . ."

His body jerked into space, aged 26 and 3 days. It was 22 years since Hugh McKail had died the same death at the same age: but now defeat seemed final.

King James saw his prayers finally answered that spring. His son and heir was born on 10th June, securing the Catholic Succession. To him it was a crowning triumph: to the English the last straw.

Seven Bishops, who had refused to proclaim his Edict of Toleration from their pulpits, had been charged with sedition. On 30th June they were cleared and cheered. One of them with six of the landed nobles—including a Russell and a Sydney, as at the Rye House Plot—went over to Holland to offer the throne of England to the House of Orange. To William of Orange a Protestant England was a bulwark for his beloved Netherlands against France: and the time seemed ripe. The Whig lilt, "Lillibulero," was whistled and sung louder and louder through England—the overture to the last Act: with curtain-up in November.

Dr. William Blackadder was busy in Edinburgh. He had been caught in Orkney at the time of Argyll's rising in June 1685 but his family had rallied round. Sister Elizabeth had slid between the files of soldiers marching up from Leith to learn his prison; brother Adam had sat patiently at the slit of a turnpike stair till he came to his cell window, when he demonstrated the false bottom of a metal Swedish box. "Next day I sent with the maid the open box full of salad in the one hand and shoulder of roasted mutton in the other" . . . Out came the empty box with a letter to the Grand Pensioner of Holland in the secret drawer to go in the first ship: and in no time William was released as "a naturalised Hollander."

In August 1688 he was arrested again, while attending Captain Mackay in the Castle: either as medical man or agent, or both. Papers were found on him, and he was imprisoned, "vexed and harried" until November, when news of William's landing in Devon broke, and he was released.

"No sooner was my brother at liberty," continues Adam: "a committee of the then confused Council sitting in Hugh Blair's, a vintner at the Pillars, entering the Parliament Close he sits down with some of his comrades in another room next to that where the committee were met, and writes a general petition in favour of all those yet in prison . . . some in Blackness, some elsewhere."

"Sir William," says my brother to the Clerk, "Here's a petition which you are to deliver to the Committee."

"I 'faith, Doctor, I dare not give this in."

"Will you not?" says my brother: "then I charge you in the Prince of Orange's name, and as you shall answer to him . . ."

"Then Doctor, in conscience, I'll venture."

He returned with a scrawl on the back of the paper, granting everything.

"Now," says my brother, "Sir William, I warrand you'll be expecting your fee"—(ordinarily, 5 dollars):- "Not one farthing!" says he, "and besides you must sit down here with us and call for a quart of wine to the company."

Which he did: "and they were very merry, and drank to the Prince of Orange, his health."

When William landed near Torbay in Devon that November 5th there was another Scot, William Carstares, at his side as Royal Chaplain. It was Carstares who called for a psalm on landing, and William agreed. The Army halted while they sang psalm 118, and Carstares put up a prayer.

> "This is the day God made, in it
> We'll joy triumphantly.
> Save now, I pray thee, lord. I pray
> Send now prosperity."

There was no resistance. General Churchill joined William: his wife Sara escorted Princess Ann out of Whitehall. James and his new family fled. "The Virgin Mary's to do all," commented Jeffreys of the Bloody Assizes as he too fled. He was caught, and died in the Tower.

In Scotland the scene-shifters rushed into action once more. Down came the heads and hands from the Netherbow Port—("for fear lest these monuments of their cruelty left standing might occasion the question—by whom and for what were they set up?") Out went the bon-dieuserie from Holyrood chapel: (though probably not wasted.) Out too went Chancellor Drummond, Earl of Perth, and into prison for four years. The mob drank his Holyrood cellars dry. Out went hundreds of curates from manses, particularly in the west, "rabbled" by resentful congregations, compelled to hear them for all those years. Patrick Walker attended fifteen, and much regretted that the Bishops were not brought to trial and hanged. ("How they would tremble and sweat going up the ladder!") But not one life was taken.

The bishops had become overnight "the Church Invisible." Their last letter to James—"the darling of heaven"—vowed their allegiance to him as an essential part of their religion. Where had it gone?

Early in January the hillmen met at the Cross in Douglas and totally disowned the rabbling of curates. Shields, stepping into Renwick's place, preached to them. In March they met in Lesmahagow church, and all marched up Borland Hill, where they read both Covenants, (with "civil magistrate" instead of "king") and swore them with uplifted hands. They would own the new monarchy if it recognised them. But William disclosed nothing.

In February Queen Mary arrived in Whitehall "laughing and jolly," wrote Evelyn: turning up the beds and poking into cupboards, "as if at an inn". The "double-bottomed monarchy" was established, with Dutch orderliness, and the blue-and-white delft that became a craze.

In March a committee of the Scots Estates met to find a way out of their dilemma: was the throne of Scotland vacant or not? They were still confused: and now divided into Williamites and Jacobites. In early April they reported back with lawyer Patrick Home of Polwarth's solution as to the throne: since James was a devout Roman Catholic, he had never sworn the mandatory oaths; and therefore "the Duke of York had never a legal right to it, nor legal Parliament." Struck by something uneasily familiar (it was indeed the very core of the Sanquhar Declaration) someone protested: "If ye mention that, ye will be as wild as ever Renwick was!" The Laird of Blair brushed this aside: (was there a drunken hiccup?) "Wild! We have been hanging and shooting honest men for wildness, and now we are all turned wild together!" So, just over a year after hanging Renwick, they all subscribed much the same articles.

Hamilton was back from Holland, Earlston out of the living death of chains. Both wanted a hard line from the hillmen. Shields pleaded strongly for a healing of the wounds. "The want of peaceableness as much as the want of truth can cause our salt to lose its savour."

William still withheld his decision on the church. Most of all he wanted a peaceful union of the two national churches under episcopal rule. He dreaded strife: and dreaded still more an implacable minority on the moors, incorruptible martyrs in the Grassmarket. With Carstares prompting him, he came down for a Presbyterian Church of Scotland, with a strong plea for moderation.

But had there been no Hillmen, he would hardly even have hesitated. Had Renwick given in at the last, there could have been no real opposition to episcopacy. Had Renwick chosen life, the Church of Scotland would have died.

EPILOGUE: JERUSALEM, JERUSALEM

Patrick Walker, in one of his accounts which leap to life, tells how Peden was sitting one day where he often went for counsel: on the bog-turf which covered Ritchie Cameron and his companions. His friend James Wilson, carried away with his vision, had been holding forth on the glory of the Great Day of Victory, for which they had waited so long:

> "That day in whose clear shining light
> All wrong shall stand revealed:
> When Justice shall be throned with Might
> And every hurt be healed."

When, above all, the Covenants would be exalted and the outlaws take their seats with acclamation in the General Assembly: and the last Testimonies and the sacrificial blood of the martyrs be revered and glorified . . .

Peden, "sitting upon the grass gave James a clap on the shoulder with his heavy hand and said: "James, I am going to tell you a strange tale."

James said: "I am willing to hear't!"

"And who but you and your bits of paper, and drops of blood!" Peden's voice comes alive in the telling . . . "when that day comes, there will be a byke of Indulged, luke-warm ministers come out of Holland, England and Ireland, together with a byke of them at home . . . and they will all hive together in a General Assembly . . . and your bits of paper and your drops of blood will be shot to the door, and never a word more of them . . . and ye and the like of you will get their backside!" He gave him another sore clap upon the shoulder, saying: "Keep mind!"

By William's Act of Settlement for Scotland Episcopacy was abolished: and also the Lords of the Articles who had ruled the Estates. The Church of Scotland and its General Assembly were established as Presbyterian with the *Westminster Confession of Faith* as their "subordinate standard." But it was the Indulged ministers who were supreme. The Act Rescissory was not repealed: the Covenants were not even mentioned. They and the Covenanters were shot to the door and never a word more of them. They got their backside forever.

Hamilton, logically, denounced King William as an un-Covenanted King. He refused estates, even went to prison, rather than take the Oath to him. He and most of the Hillmen stayed out of the Kirk. Most of the curates re-conformed and stayed in, though without voting powers. Even so, the Kirk was desperately short of ordained men.

One man who saw that the supreme need of the times was reconciliation was Alexander Shields. "And this reconciliation cannot be obtained any other way, there must be mutual forgiveness: not judicatory ... that is God's prerogative; but charitative ..." "Cleave to the best," he also advised: "for it was not only dreadfully dangerous to separate from all, but utterly unwarrantable."

He had the personal humility and courage to seek acceptance by the Church at the Assembly of 16th October, 1690: the first free Assembly since Cromwell's Lt. General Cotterel had ordered them all out of St. Giles. With him were two other Hillmen preachers, Boyd and Lining, and they presented a paper of their full position and scruples: but it was trampled underfoot. "That is a fell sort of paper," observed one old Indulged minister: "it deals the beetle amang the bairns, and gies me a cuff in the by-going."

They were grudgingly received. Boyd became minister of St. John's Town of Dalry, where the Pentland Rising began, and Lining of Lesmahagow, in the conventicle country. Shields refused parishes, for fear of rousing ill-feeling. He was first ordained as Chaplain to the Cameronian Regiment: then taught briefly at the University of St. Andrews: then went as Chaplain with the Darien Expedition and died, aged barely forty, of fever in the Indies: as did his brother Michael. But he had kept the Covenanting strand in the Church of Scotland, and with it that breadth of toleration that is its saving grace today.

"If there were more love, there would be more union and communion notwithstanding differences," he had written.

The Cameronian Regiment—called "Angus's" at first—had been raised, at the Societies' instigation, to combat a last Jacobite threat under Claver's. It is said that twelve hundred men came forward to volunteer in one day in Douglas kirkyard. It was raised specifically to combat "Popery, Prelacy and Tyranny:" and though eventually, as Patrick Walker put it, they "now cry as much for damnation as they did then for salvation," they did keep through a long and most distinguished battle-history their own traditions: issuing Bibles to recruits, carrying arms and posting piquets to report "All Clear" before services: and these services, in the absence of a Chaplain, were often conducted by the commanding officer. The English Government disbanded it where it was raised a few years ago: a shabby end to a story not without glory. It was an attempt to dignify, even dedicate, the necessary use of force.

James' last gesture before flight had been to make Clavers Viscount Dundee, an honour that only lasted a few weeks: but at least Clavers was loyal. He raised the clans the spring after William landed, 1689, and was joined by a force of Irish. When Mackay from Edinburgh Castle was sent North with a scratch force by the Scots Council, Clavers led him on through the gorge of Killiecrankie: then swung round and held him trapped. Clavers waited all day until the setting sun shone directly in the troops eyes before attacking and defeating them: but he was shot and killed as he rode over the battle-field.

The newly-formed Cameronians were sent rushing North under Colonel Cleland, the one-time divinity student now aged 28, with orders to hold Dunkeld at all cost. Outnumbered six to one, they were driven back on the Cathedral by the river, which they held. They fought so brilliantly and bravely the clansmen said they were "devils, not men," and retreated. But Cleland too was killed by a stray shot in the hour of victory, and lies in Dunkeld churchyard. He left a few poems published posthumously.

The leaderless clans were finally routed on the Haughs of Cromdale in a battle of which the pipe-tune is the only memory. Mackay gradually subdued the Highlands, and built Fort William: but for a few weeks it had been touch-and-go.

William's own victory at the Boyne secured the English Revolution Settlement, the continued existence of the Northern Irish Protestants, and his own lasting fame there. But "King Billy" was a patriot only for his own beloved Netherlands. He neither knew nor cared for Scotland. Two of the blackest episodes of all Scottish history, the Massacre of Glencoe and the Darien Disaster, took place in his reign. There is no evidence that he cared in the slightest. At one point he wished to enforce an Oath of Allegiance on the Kirk: but Carstares opened the packet and destroyed it, then roused William from his four-poster in the middle of the night—"to beg for my life, Sire!" And to get the dispatch re-written.

Carstares, Royal Chaplain, then Principal of Edinburgh University, minister of Greyfriars and later St. Giles, and twice Moderator, was nick-named Cardinal Carstares. He believed he could secure the Kirk on the basis of the State. He let the 1707 Act of Union between Scots and English Parliaments go through without protest, believing the Kirk secure for ever by the statutory Coronation Oath of each succeeding Sovereign (down to the present day) to "uphold the Church of Scotland in its Presbyterian doctrine and discipline."

But five years after, in 1712, the Act of Patronage gave the lairds the right—ultimately—to appoint the ministers, instead of the people calling them, as Knox had laid down. This neatly deprived the Kirk of its independence, and its dangerously free voice. In the centuries of exploitation that followed, it was muzzled. Scotland had now become, as Fletcher of Saltoun had furiously defined it: "a farm managed by servants, and far from the master's eye." Promises made for the Kirk were worthless: and, to this hour, all protests lost in the loss of sovereignty.

Patrick Walker was one of many who found the Settlement ended in disillusion, and a Kirk without salt or savour. It was full of "backslidden, upsitten, lukewarm ministers and elders . . . wizened, wersh, cauldrife, formal sermons;" divinity professors a mere "hotch-potch or bagful of Aryan, Arminian, Socinian, Pelagian old condemned damnable errors . . . wasting the Assembly's time and pratting like parrots in a cage . . . on the foul monyplies of 'as's' and 'which's' . . .; The Church of Scotland was now "a strange building, that wants both foundation and chief part:" and in both Church and Nation he found "the Scots blood gone out of our veins, honesty out of our hearts, and zeal off our spirits: and the English abominations drunk in as sweet wine."

So forty years after, he set forth to find out what had happened to that Kirk of his youth, with the glory in its eyes and the heroism in its heart; whose members had lived as outlaws and died as criminals, their mouths singing praises.

No weary soldier from the wars returning will be surprised to learn that he found "some dead, some rusted and did not want to remember: the edge of their zeal as blunt as coulters. Some promised to write and did not: some attacked from both sides . . . ." But he was unmoved by them being, "weather-beaten . . . between left-hand defections and right-hand extremes, upward of forty years." He travelled "upwards of 1,000 miles" getting "information and confirmation far beyond my expectation, especially in Ireland; which so refreshed and revived my old drooping spirit that it made my body some way light like my purse."

The next battle was to get his account published: and here the Edinburgh Establishment opened up all their batteries.

"A great deal of pains were taken to dissuade him from printing it," wrote Lord Grange. "At least until it should be revised by men of sound judgement: but all in vain."

Patrick was thrawn as granite. His book was printed unrevised, uncensored, undiminished by literary graces: unique as a standing-stone. It became Robert Louis Stevenson's passionately-admired model.

Stones defy the scene-shifters. It was one of the stated aims of the Societies to maintain the Covenanters' memorials: and from Old Mortality to this day it has been done. They mark the battle-sites: not simply between "Christ's Kingdom the Kirk" and that of King James: much less between episcopalians and presbyterians: but rather of a ragged army claiming a New World as wide as all men's liberty.

If Ritchie Cameron was wrong, then so was Dietrich Bonhoeffer in

Nazi Germany: so is Solzhenitsyn of Russia: they too being men of faith.

However much politicians compromise, however often would-be Bishops betray, the stones still mark the boundaries of the other Kingdom: where some of those climbing the dark cleuch were surprised by joy.

"None knows the marrow and sweetness that is to be had in suffering and contending for Christ, but them that has felt," wrote John Mathieson of Closeburn after returning from slavery in the Plantations.

"The pleasantest time that ever I had," wrote John Wilson, (hanged in the Grassmarket) "was when I was joined with that suffering Remnant, while hunted as partridges upon the mountains in following the persecuted gospel."

"Oh, who can remember the glory of that day without a melting heart?" wrote Alexander Shields of Cargills' conventicles. "I have not language to lay out the inexpressible glory of that day."

"When the storm blew hardest, the smiles of my Lord were at the sweetest," said Cochran, a cobbler from Lesmahagow: "It is a matter of rejoicing unto me to think how my Lord hath passed by many a tall cedar, and hath laid His love upon a poor bramblebush, the like of me." He left his wife and six children "with much confidence" on the Lord, and was hanged, with two others, on 30th November 1683: having confessed "he was at Drumclog and Bothwell Brig, and had a "fork."

"What means all this ado?" cried an Indulged minister: "we will get to heaven, and they will get no more!"

"Yes, we shall get more," said old Cargill: "We shall get God glorified on earth, which is more."

After the mass escape from the Canongate Tolbooth only one young lawyer, John Dick, was re-captured: and sentenced to be hanged next day. As dawn broke he wrote to his father, adding: "Let none see this till I be in my grave."

"This hath been one of the pleasantest nights I have had in my lifetime; the competition is only betwixt it and that I got eleven years ago, in Nesbit in Northumberland, where and when in a barley-ridge upon the Saturdays' night and Sabbath morning, before the last communion I did partake of in Ford Church"—the Lord so filled him over and over with an overwhelming sense of free grace and love that "I was forced to cry, 'Hold, Lord, for the sherd is like to burst!"

"I am a free-will offering!" he called to the crowd round the scaffold.

"I got a smile from him," said his friend at the ladder-foot.

If these men were crazy then so were all the saints who ever tried to redeem this lost world, whether accredited by Popes or known only to God; and so is Christ's gospel that God is not on the side of the big battalions but on the run: with hunted men in the heather, or in the death-cell.

The earth-ball sways continuously to sunlight, as ships to moon-tides: these men steered by different stars, homed on a different wave-length. Radio-active dust, they neither bury nor quench. What primal energy possessed them, from their different sun? What way, what truth, what on-going life?

INDEX

Anne of Denmark, Queen of Scotland: 15, 17, 19, 39, 50.
Anne, Princess: 193, 201.
Andrewes, Bishop Lancelot: 45, 50.
Argyll, Archibald Campbell, eighth Earl and first Marquis of: 64, 65, 68, 73, 75, 89, 90, 98, 99, 103, 104, 109, 110, 120, 122, 127, 128.
—Lady Sophia (daughter-in-law): 156, 157, 178, 192.
—ninth Earl (son): 104, 120, 176, 178, 187, 192.
Armstrong, Archie, the King's Fool: 52, 53, 59, 65.
Arran, Capt. James Stewart of Ochiltree, first Earl of: 6-11, 13, 22.

Baillie, Robert: 64, 66, 67, 68, 72, 74, 80-84, 86, 87, 89, 92, 93, 98, 101, 102, 107, 114, 116, 117, 119, 121, 131, 132, 133.
Baillie of Jerviswoode: 140, 182, 186.
Baillie, Grizzel: 125.
Balcanqual, Walter, 9, 10.
—Mrs: 11.
Balfour of Burleigh: 160, 164, 167.
Bannatyne, Sir William: 153.
Beza, Theodore: 31, 34.
Black, James: 24, 25.
Blackadder, John: 137, 141, 142, 147, 150, 151, 155, 156, 159, 162, 163, 164, 166, 168, 177, 195.
—Family: 142, 156, 157, 162, 200, 201.
Blair, Robert: 77, 78, 100, 113, 116, 120, 122, 139.
Brakel, Willem of Leeuwarden: 180, 181.
Bothwell, Francis Hepburn, Earl of: 13, 19, 21, 22.
Bowes, Sir Robert, English Ambassador: 6.
Brown, John, of Priesthill: 189.
Brown, John, of Wamphray: 138, 140, 152, 154, 170.
Bruce, Robert: 14, 15, 21, 28-32, 36, 37, 38, 56, 58.
Buchanan, George: 2, 3, 11, 12, 22, 53, 196.
Buckingham, George Villiers, first Duke of: 50, 51, 53.
Bunyan, John: 79, 84, 87, 112, 152.

Burnet, Archbishop Alexander: 130, 154.
Burnet, Bishop Gilbert, historian: 119, 130, 138, 140.

Calderwood, David: 52.
Cameron, Richard: 160, 162, 170-175, 195, 203, 206.
—Michael: 173.
Cargill, Donald: 131, 160, 164, 166, 167, 171, 172, 175, 176, 177, 178, 183, 195, 207.
Carr, Robert, first Earl of Somerset: 49.
Carstares, John: 107.
—William (son): 161, 182, 185, 186, 201, 202, 205.
Cecil, Robert, Earl of Salisbury: 31, 42, 43, 45.
Charles I: 49, 53, 54, 58, 59, 63, 65, 67, 68, 72-76, 80, 83, 86, 88-94, 96-101.
Charles II: 101-104, 106-112, 118-121, 123, 126, 129, 132, 139, 148, 153, 160, 161, 169, 176, 177, 182, 184, 186.
Churchill, John, Duke of Marlborough: 169, 201.
—Sara, Duchess of Marlborough: 169, 201.
Clarendon: Edward Hyde, first Earl of: 76, 118, 119, 120, 128.
Claverhouse, John Graham of: 163, 164, 165, 170, 179, 185, 189, 191, 205.
Cleland, William: 165, 166, 167, 187, 192, 205.
Cromwell, Oliver: 79, 81, 83, 84, 85, 89, 90, 95-100, 102, 103, 105, 106, 107, 108, 111-116, 118, 120, 126.

Dalziel, General Tam, of the Binns: 144, 145, 146, 148, 163, 184.
Davidson, John: 7, 13, 23, 24, 25, 36, 39, 176, 177.
Dick, John: 183, 207.
Dickson, David: 54, 56, 61, 68, 78, 114, 131.
Dickson, John: 158.
Douglas, Robert: 81, 107, 110, 114, 120, 130, 131, 132, 148, 154.
Douglas, Thomas: 160, 164, 171.
Durie, John: 6, 7, 9.

209

Lilburne, John: 100.
Livingstone, John: 5, 7, 104, 115, 139.
Lowsone, James: 1, 5, 6, 9, 10.
—Mrs: 11.

MacDonald, Colkitto: 88, 90, 93.
McKail, Hugh: 131, 145, 148, 200.
—Dr Matthew: 148, 162.
Mackenzie, Sir George: 127, 128, 176, 177, 186.
Maclaughlan, Margaret: 190.
McLellan of Barscob: 143, 146, 155, 177.
McWard, Robert: 139, 140, 170.
Malloch: 175, 185.
Mar, Countess of: 2, 19.
—"Jockie": 2.
Mary, Queen of Scots: 1, 3, 5, 12, 13, 19, 44, 52.
Mary, Princess of Orange: 76.
Mary, Princess of Orange and Queen of Britain: 161, 193, 202.
Melville, Andrew: 2, 4, 6, 7, 8, 10, 11, 15, 22-26, 36, 46.
—James: 2, 10, 11, 46.
Milton, John: 3, 82, 84, 85, 86.
Middleton, Sir John: 111, 122, 123, 128, 129, 132, 133, 153.
Monk, General: 112, 116, 118, 119, 120, 126, 128, 161.
Monmouth, Jamie, Duke of: 103, 166, 167, 169, 182, 187, 191, 192.
Montrose, James Graham, Marquis of: 61, 68, 73, 75, 86, 87, Book II, Chapter III: 102, 103, 104, 123, 128.
Moray, James Stewart, Earl of: 19, 20.
Morton, Douglas, Earl of: 3, 4, 5, 6.
Muggeridge, Malcolm: 71, 72.
Mure of Rowallan: 83.

Neilson of Corsock: 138, 143, 148.
Nisbet, John, of Hardhill: 147, 186.
—James (son): 147, 194.

Parker of Busby: 147.
Paterson, Bishop: 163, 168, 177, 185, 199.
Paton, Captain John of Meadowhead: 146, 166, 167, 184.
Peden, Alexander: 71, 141, 144, 155, 159, 167, 171, 179, 187, 188, 194, 195, 203.
Pepys, Samuel: 112, 120, 145, 149, 177, 192.
Pym, John: 72, 76.

Raleigh, Sir Walter: 46, 49, 51.
Renwick, James: 181, 183, 184, 187, 188, 191, 193, 194, 195-199, 202.
Rizzio, Signor Davie: 11, 32, 33, 44.
Rothes, John Leslie, sixth Earl of: 61.
—seventh Earl and Duke of: 119, 148, 153, 176.
Rous, Francis: 84.
Rumbold, Colonel: 182, 192.
Rupert of the Rhine, Prince: 76, 83, 90, 91.
Rutherford, Samuel: 3, 54, 55, 56, 78, 81, 84, 85, 111, 116, 122, 133, 139, 160.

Semple, Gabriel: 137, 141, 145, 150, 160, 177.
Semple, John of Carsphairn: 77, 121.
Sharp, Archbishop: 112, 115, 119-122, 128, 130, 132, 135, 138, 139, 141, 147, 153, 158, 159, 163, 164.
Shields, Alexander: 159, 175, 176, 186, 187, 195, 196, 198, 201, 202, 204, 207.
—Michael: 187, 196, 204.
Smith, Robert of Coen: 139.
Smith, Walter: 176, 177.
Spang, minister of Campvere: 80, 82, 83, 87, 117.
Spottiswoode, Archbishop: 48, 58, 65, 67, 130.
Spreul, "Bass": 159, 164.
Stevenson, Robert Louis: 18, 150, 155, 206.
Stewart, Sir James, of Goodtrees, Lord Provost of Edinburgh: 93, 121, 154, 170.
Stafford, "Black Tom", Wentworth, Earl of: 72-76.
Strang, Christopher, of Kilbride: 148.

Traquair, John Stewart, Earl of: 67, 116.
Torphichen, Sandilands, Lord: 150.
Turner, General: 93, 137, 141, 143, 144, 145, 148, 151, 153.

Ure of Shargarten: 166, 167, 168.
Usher, Archbishop, of Ireland: 55.

Veitch, William: 146, 168, 178, 197.
Verney, Sir Edmund: 53, 65, 66, 67, 72, 76, 77.
—Ralph (son): 65, 66, 67, 72, 73, 75, 76, 77.
—Peter: 65.